QUIETLY COURAGEOUS

QUIETLY COURAGEOUS

Leading the Church in a Changing World

Gil Rendle

An Alban Institute Book

ROWMAN & LITTLEFIELD
Lanham • Boulder • New York • London

Published by Rowman & Littlefield
An imprint of The Rowman & Littlefield Publishing Group, Inc.
4501 Forbes Boulevard, Suite 200, Lanham, Maryland 20706
https://rowman.com

Unit A, Whitacre Mews, 26-34 Stannary Street, London SE11 4AB,
United Kingdom

British Library Cataloguing in Publication Information Available

Library of Congress Cataloging-in-Publication Data
Names: Rendle, Gilbert R., author.
Title: Quietly courageous : leading the church in a changing world / Gil Ren-
    dle.
Description: Lanham, Maryland : Rowman & Littlefield, an imprint of The
    Rowman & Littlefield Publishing Group, Inc., [2018] | "An Alban Institute
    Book." | Includes bibliographical references and index.
Identifiers: LCCN 2018029089 (print) | LCCN 2018042852 (ebook) | ISBN
    9781538112915 (ebook) | ISBN 9781538112892 (hardcover : alk. paper) |
    ISBN 9781538112908 (pbk. : alk. paper)
Subjects: LCSH: Christian leadership. | Leadership—Religious aspects—
    Christianity. | Change—Religious aspects—Christianity. | Courage—Relig-
    ious aspects—Christianity.
Classification: LCC BV652.1 (ebook) | LCC BV652.1 .R46 2018 (print) | DDC
    253—dc23
LC record available at https://lccn.loc.gov/2018029089

Printed in the United States of America

CONTENTS

PART I: GOOD LEADERSHIP IS NOT ENOUGH

1 Nashon's Quiet Courage   3

2 The Change That Demands Quiet Courage   19

PART II: THE ASSUMPTIONS

3 A Word about How: Assumptions about Change   57

4 A Word about Enough: Assumptions about Resources   75

5 A Word about Structure and Process: Assumptions about Fear, Organization, and Democracy   93

6 A Word about Learning: Assumptions about How Leadership Is Formed   125

PART III: THE TEMPTATIONS

7 The Temptation of Playing It Safe: Nostalgia   155

8 The Temptation of Christian Empathy   173

9 The Temptation of Tiredness   193

PART IV: WHERE DO WE START?

10 Telling the Story That Will Get Us through the Wilderness   215

11 Lessons in Style   239

CONTENTS

Notes	269
Bibliography	283
Index	289
About the Author	293

Part I

Good Leadership Is Not Enough

For the past two decades, organizations have been grasping for ways to deal with the alarming rate of change they are experiencing, both internally and in the marketplace. We have developed countless methods for managing change and, despite a completely abysmal record of results, we continue to see that the issue is not one of method but of mindset.

—Alpesh Bhatt, *The Triple-Soy Decaf-Latte Era: How Businesses and Organizations Are Fundamentally Transforming*

At this juncture in our common life, the chance of the preacher is crucial—as it has not been in a long time—precisely because the dominant texts are failing. . . . It is a task of the church—with synagogue and mosque—to offer this countertext of generosity, fidelity, and neighborliness. It is the chance of the preacher to permit people to give up old, failed textual construals and to reimagine and redescribe using this countertext. It is our human work to switch texts, and we do not do that easily.

—Walter Brueggemann, *The Word That Redescribes the World: The Bible and Discipleship*

The work of leadership must do more than improve. It must change.

1

NASHON'S QUIET COURAGE

Nashon, son of Amminidab, was a prince of the tribe of Judah and was with Moses and the fleeing Israelites during the escape from Egypt that led them to the banks of the Red Sea. This is the heady story of the Exodus, when the captive Israelites, as the chosen people of God, were freed from slavery by Moses, who challenged Pharaoh and led the people into the wilderness. The Hebrew Midrash provides detail that isn't in the Hebrew biblical text—detail that leads to rabbinic explanations and wonderful storytelling. Lawrence Kushner describes the Midrash as the stories and reflections of the rabbi scholars that rest before and after, above and below, the biblical text.[1] Where the stories in the biblical text were a bit sparse, the rabbi scholars filled in the empty spaces with challenging ideas and tantalizing stories. In this case, the story from the Midrash about the Exodus from Egypt tells that when the Israelites got to the shore of the Red Sea the waters lay before them unparted, and there was much anxiety.[2] To lead the people into the water would be to drown, but to wait without action would be to give themselves to the capture and punishment of the Egyptians. They were trapped. Someone needed to be the first to go into the water to test the promise of God for deliverance.

The Midrash tells that the leaders of the tribes of Israel all gathered at the water's edge, sat down, and argued with one another about who would go into the water first. I have often joked that I have been to that church meeting so many times myself! Action was needed, but the leaders did what they knew how to do and had a committee meeting instead. Apparently no decision was forthcoming and anxiety and fear grew and grew. Waiting for a decision no longer, Nashon, son of Amminidab, simply remembered why they were there and the promise that brought them there, so he stood up and began to walk into the water.

As the story is told, he walked into the water up to his ankles and the waters did not part. He walked into the water up to his waist and the waters did not part. Up to his shoulders, up to his chin, and the waters did not part. He continued. As he took the step that would have put his nose under water, the waters parted. It is fitting that his name in Hebrew means "stormy sea waves."

Quiet courage. No memorable words to be included in the biblical text, no persuasive arguments—not even the hero's assurance that he knew what he was doing. Simply remembering the purpose of fleeing the Egyptians, remembering the promise given to Moses, he quietly got up and did what was required. Quiet courage. Above all, purposeful but also poised and risky. While others argued about the right way to do things, quiet courage stepped up to fulfill the intended purpose of the moment.

I will argue that such quiet courage is needed because the depth of change that the church now faces makes it exceedingly difficult for long-established institutions (the "organized religion" of congregations and denominations reported in the media) to thrive. Later, in chapter 2, I will argue that long-established institutions, such as congregations and denominations, are now countercultural. These well-established institutions no longer fit comfortably into the current cultural value system that focuses heavily on individuals. That later chapter is critically important to my argument about quiet courage because until leaders recognize the depth and permanence of the change that they face, they will always be tempted to revert to learned behaviors—to sit by the Red Sea's shore and have conferences, make public statements, pass organizational legislation, and continue their practices as usual when a much more radical quiet courage is needed. Central to my argument in this book is my conviction that the established institutional church cannot now thrive on the good leadership it currently has.

Don't gloss over that sentence. *The established institutional church cannot now thrive on the good leadership it currently has.*

Having worked with a vast number of congregational and denominational leaders (lay and clergy) over a period of many years, I am convinced of the goodness of these people and the good leadership that they work diligently to provide. Each year and every decade give me an increase in evidence of how our leaders are working differently and more efficiently. Nonetheless, the established institutional church will not grow or thrive with its current good leadership even though they are good people with hearts, minds, and hands in the right places. Different and efficient are not enough. It remains continually and increasingly clear that this good leadership is not making the leap to the new changed mission field. Trends of increasing generational disinterest and trends of cultural irrelevancy of organized religion continue unabated. Something more is needed. Leaders must change from good leadership to quiet, courageous, purposeful leadership.

To claim that the established institutional church cannot now thrive on the good leadership it currently has does not seek to disparage the people who are presently leading. The claim, however, is based on my experience of hearing leaders describe the new and creative things that they are doing while simultaneously observing how closely the new and creative things are actually defined by and constrained by current approved institutional practices. It is the difference between what we say we do (or what we think we are doing) and what we are actually putting our hands to. Leaders commonly talk about making significant changes and cutting new territory but in fact are simply making incremental improvements to what no longer works well. This is the essential adaptive challenge that Ron Heifetz identifies in his classic book on leadership—the "gap between aspirations and reality."[3] Not addressing this gap confines both the leaders and the church to a tiredness from running harder in place without actually going anywhere. This difference between aspirations and reality is as old as Saint Paul's wrestling with the law. Paul wrote, "The desire to do good is inside of me, but I can't do it. I don't do the good that I want to do, but do the evil that I don't want to do" (Romans 7:18–19). Perhaps not the difference between good and evil, the adaptive gap that leaders face is the difference between the leadership that they understand is needed for a new future and the leadership that they practice that continues a more comfortable demise.

THE TWO MISSIONS OF ESTABLISHED INSTITUTIONS

How can this be? How can our brightest and best (which I contend are getting brighter and better as we learn more about our changed context for ministry) continue to work with increasing diligence and energy at what isn't helping the institution fulfill its purpose in its changed cultural surroundings? One answer—one big answer—lies in the very natural and normative development of the mission of any long-established institution, corporation, military, or government. Over time purpose shifts internally and produces a dissonance between what the institution says it does and what it actually gives its attention and resources to. Let's walk into this more carefully.

Robert Quinn, professor of organizational behavior and human resource management at the University of Michigan, describes an organization as a coalition of coalitions.[4] As institutions and organizations grow and mature over time, they are composed of an increasingly complex network of coalitions, subgroups of people with different interests and needs based on their parts of the work of the institution and based on their statuses and access to resources within the institution. For example, in a public school there is a network of interlinked coalitions made up of students, teachers, staff, administrators, school board, parents, government agencies, local taxpayers, and other groups. All of these coalitions share in the concern for the critical mission of educating children. However, each of the coalitions has its own particular interests and needs in relationship to the school—interests and needs that don't necessarily fit well together.

This leads Quinn to identify a confounding reality that, over time, an institution such as a public school develops and operates with two separate and competing missions. One is the *public* mission, what the institution publicly says that it does, which in this case is to educate students. The public mission may go on with greater aspiration to say that the school prepares the students for leadership or for citizenship that will be undergirded by the education provided. But alongside this public mission is a *private* mission—operative goals, as Quinn would say— that is hidden from the public but that overrides the public mission. The private mission is to satisfy the interests of the strongest coalition or coalitions within the institution. If the public mission is to educate children, the private mission to satisfy strong internal coalitions redirects attention and resources to teachers, administrators, parents, or taxpayers as these internal constituencies pursue their interests within the system. In fact, students can actually fall fairly low on the list of priorities. Over time the leaders in a school will talk about how they are stretching to meet the educational needs of their students, yet their actions and resources will more likely be controlled and constrained by the interests of the strongest coalitions within. The leaders talk about change. However, any change will be within the constraints and guided by the preferences of the internal coalitions related to the private mission.

Religious institutions also have a public mission, such as that of the United Methodists, which states the denomination's purpose is "to make disciples of Jesus Christ for the transformation of the world." The church claims a public mission to change people and to change the world in which those people live. However, there are strong internal coalitions within a denomination, chief among them the coalition of clergy, the coalition of local congregations, the coalition of the agencies and service providers whose livelihoods depend on their relationships with the denomination, and coalitions of caucus groups. Leaders of the denomination may publicly speak about reaching out with boldness to providing radical hospitality to new groups of people or about experimenting with new, less congregational forms of faith communities in order to connect with new generations, but the private mission of satisfying the internal interests of the already established internal coalitions will constrain the actual actions of the leaders to conform to the rules and standards already set and with which the competing coalitions know how to contend. Similarly at the congregational level, leaders may speak about their public mission of reaching out to welcome and include new people and the surrounding community, but the private mission of satisfying the members already involved in the church will override attempts to redirect attention or resources in any way that might diminish the satisfaction of the people already present and involved.

The two missions of established institutions make it possible for leaders to talk about the change they are leading while simultaneously constraining any change to fit within the practices and rules by which the current coalitions already know how to live. As we will discover repeatedly, a leader cannot do truly new things by following the rules of old ways. It is the public mission that stirs the heart and moves the blood, but it is the private mission that gets rewarded.

So it takes quiet courage, Nashonian purposefulness and risk, for a leader to step out into waters where others may not follow and in which there is no guarantee of a better future. More than increasingly good leadership, the church now needs radically quiet, courageous leadership.

Dealing with Assumptions and Temptations

Quiet leadership, the kind of leadership that will address deep change that moves beyond constituent self-interest, requires leaders to behave in quite different ways that will be contrary to the established norms of the institution or organization. Quinn notes that "deep change differs from incremental change in that it *requires new ways of thinking and behaving*. It is change that is major in scope, discontinuous with the past and generally irreversible."[5] In his own work Heifetz is clear that making progress on truly adaptive work requires *"changes in people's values, attitudes, or habits of behavior."*[6]

New ways of thinking and behaving. Changes in people's values, attitudes, or habits of behavior. It is increasingly clear that the way ahead will not be mastered by cleverness with which some leader or leaders will see something that is hidden to others. The way ahead will not be mastered by improvements on what we already know and what we already know how to do. The quiet courage of leadership comes from the much deeper work of being determinately purposeful while challenging the constraining assumptions and temptations that undergird the present ways of being in which our institutions have learned to live in the world.

So this will be a book about *assumptions*. Organized religion currently rests on assumptions developed in an earlier time in which those assumptions served well. However, to move ahead there are a number of assumptions that will need to be challenged and changed or else the practice of leadership will be constrained and the changed cultural context will overwhelm any effort at a public mission. Established assumptions need to be met with new ways of thinking. Without challenging and changing the underlying assumptions, the behavior will not change.

This will also be a book about *temptations*. The temptations that currently constrain our institutional leaders are the product of the current reward system. A friend continues to remind me that people don't do what you ask them to do. People do what you pay them to do (even when it is different from what is asked). We need to understand clearly that while the public mission of institutional religion can excite people's minds, it is the private mission that gets rewarded as constituent interests are satisfied. In order for temptations to be avoided, they must be brought to light.

Assumptions and temptations are difficult to deal with because they are tacit. We can identify them if we intentionally search them out, but they commonly operate below our daily awareness. Because they operate with common agreement, they are hidden. It is hard to challenge what we are not aware of. That is why courageous leadership begins with a focus on ideas, assumptions, and temptations rather than with a focus on action or on what to do. Until we see things in new ways we will be constrained to act in old ways, despite our efforts to change.

Seeing things in old ways and being constrained to act in known ways keeps the role of leader tightly tethered to problem solving—to fixing what seems to have gone wrong. What if the questions we now face are not the product of things gone wrong but rather of the world grown different? A primary goal of this book is to offer the argument that seeks to shift the primary orientation of leaders from problem solving to exploration—from working better and harder to exploring new ways based on new learning. Such a shift requires quietly courageous leadership—a purposeful willingness to walk into unparted waters.

COUNTING OUR MORE COMPLICATED BLESSINGS

Saint Augustine was to have said that hope has two beautiful daughters—anger and courage. Hope depends on anger over what could be but is not and on courage to make it different.

In 2010 I ended one of my earlier books, *Journey in the Wilderness*, with that same idea from Augustine. That book was subtitled *New Life for Mainline Churches*. I have since been given clear feedback that what I described there pertained to more than the mainline church.

People from far wider traditions of faith, within and beyond the Christian church, resonated with the book. Moreover, in the intervening years conversation partners from nonprofits, businesses, and institutions beyond the church have helped to further extrapolate and enrich the conversation begun there. For me, it has been an ongoing conversation about and driven by hope. It is clear that hope continues to draw us forward because of the way that so many leaders go to their daily tasks not just trying to get through the day but willingly entering into a search for a way to unleash meaning and purpose in their fast-changing world. If we are worried about our institutions of faith, worried about the relevancy of faith, or worried about our culture that is uncomfortable with those who practice a disciplined faith, it is clear that our faith itself, and the hope that it carries, remains vibrant.

I have argued that hope is not passive. It is not the blithe "I hope you have a nice day," in which I may wish you a nice day but don't extend myself in any way to actually help to make it so. Hope is much more active and demanding than that. And as I will argue in this book, it is quietly so. I will argue as well that hope arises from our doubts, dilemmas, quandaries, and failures. Hope does not prevent or escape them but is built on what we learn from them. As Saint Paul wrote, "We take pride in our problems, because we know that trouble produces endurance, endurance produces character, and character produces hope" (Romans 5:3–4).

Hence the notion of "our more complicated blessings," a phrase that comes from a prayer written by Bill Coffin while he was at Riverside Church in New York City. It has long traveled with me. I invite you to read it slowly, paying close attention to the wording of each sentence.

A Prayer for the Church in These Times

O God, whose mercy is ever faithful and ever sure, who art our refuge and our strength in time of trouble, visit us, we beseech thee— for we are a people in trouble.

We need a hope that is made wise by experience and is undaunted by disappointment. We need an anxiety about the future that shows us new ways to look at new things but does not unnerve us. As a people, we need to remember that our influence was greatest when our power was weakest. Most of all, we need to turn to thee, O God, and our crucified Lord, for only his humility and his strength can heal and free us.

O God, be thou our sole strength in time of trouble. In the midst of anxiety, grant us the grace to count our blessings—the simple ones: health, food, sleep, one another, a spring that is bursting out all over, a nation which, despite all, has so much to offer so many.

And, grant us to count our more complicated blessings: our failures, which teach us so much more than success; our lack of money, which points to the only truly renewable resources, the resources of our spirit; our lack of health, yea, even the knowledge of death, for until we learn that life is limitation, we are surely as formless and as shallow as a stream without its banks.

Send us forth into a new week with a gladsome mind, free and joyful in the spirit of Jesus Christ. Amen.

—William Sloan Coffin, Riverside Church[7]

Coffin's words gave clear shape to the hope that I witnessed, muddy as it may have been at the beginning, so his prayer went with me over the years in a variety of forms. I began my consulting work prior to the explosion of the Internet, prior to email, and prior to laptop computers that could travel with me as I moved about. So at first Bill's prayer went with me on a piece of paper tucked into my briefcase. Later, as time and technology matured, the prayer was always with me, moving from laptop to laptop, through cities and farmlands, over the years as I moved about as a consultant, teacher, and colleague to leaders. For almost thirty-five years it provided me one of my dependable spiritual anchors that consistently invited me to see God's hand in the dilemmas and disappointments, in the chaos and conflicts that are a staple of a consultant's life as he or she stands with leaders in their all-too-real situations. Hope *does* come from our mistakes and failures, from our limited resources that force us to see and think differently as those resources shrink, and from letting go—a form of death that acknowledges real boundaries. Such hope demands courage. Sometimes it is the simple courage of seeing what is in front of us.

For example, recently I was part of a team that planned a gathering of senior leaders of Jewish, Christian, and Unitarian Universalist denominations that met in Austin, Texas. The gathering was cohosted by the Fetzer Institute, the Texas Methodist Foundation (TMF), and Harvard Divinity School.[8] The purpose of the gathering was to help these denominational leaders think differently about the futures of their institutions—futures that would require changes from within. These leaders were all in a shared but difficult position of being simultaneously expected to maintain their institutions and to change them. But the full two days of conversation were held in the context of hope. There was hope because we had evidence to share of so many new forms of faith and meaning-based communities that were newly dotting the landscape all around them, even if these new communities did not take on the standard shape of congregations that they were so familiar with.[9] Further, there was hope that came as one of the participants shared his research demonstrating that a high percentage of the entrepreneurial leaders who were birthing these new experiments and new communities of meaning and purpose were, in fact, the young people who came from, and were formed in, the very congregations that these denominational leaders represented.[10] The new cultural context that so baffled them was actually the product of their good work with the children of the congregations of their systems. Something new was actually happening, but these leaders found it difficult to see because the new didn't fit within the constraints of old assumptions. Our planning team was very actively hoping that we could help these leaders face their frustrations, disappointments, and the difficulty of their institutional situations and find courage in one another to make their reality different.

So this is a book about a thoughtful and purposeful courage, not the blustery heroics of those who think they have the "answer." But because it is about a thoughtful and purposeful courage, it is also, as noted, necessarily a book about the assumptions and temptations that keep us from courageous leadership. One of the realities that I will explore is that in times of great turmoil, leaders are always asked to produce change—to make things different in their systems so that others will find a better future. But *if asked for* change, leaders will *not be rewarded for* the change produced, only for how well they keep things the same—following the known ways and the established rules so that they don't make people uncomfortable. It is the difference between management and leadership, following the old adage that management asks the question of whether we are doing things right, while leadership asks the question of whether we are doing right things. Doing things right is comforting because it is a known and familiar path, even if it doesn't lead to a viable future. Being asked if we are doing right things is, by contrast, deeply disturbing. Because now the people must stop to figure out, again, who they are, what their purpose is, and how they will live out that purpose in the context that has changed around them. It is, I suppose, as natural as it is disconcerting that we ask our leaders for change that will prepare our way into the future but then reward them for the comfort of continuing to do things in the old, known ways that make us feel secure but lock us into the limits of the present.

It takes courage to make people purposefully uncomfortable. There are temptations aplenty for leaders to avoid this difficult but faithful work. I am convinced that the temptations need to be exposed in order to be avoided. If our leaders are regularly asked for leadership (which, by definition, discomforts) but are as regularly rewarded for management (which, through familiarity, comforts), then leaders need to know the temptations that provide comfort but don't address purpose, and leaders need to know which rewards to avoid. Our more complicated blessings, indeed.

WHERE THIS BOOK COMES FROM

The reflections in this book come from having more than forty-five years with "feet on the ground," first as a pastor in urban settings and then for more than thirty years as a consultant to congregations and denominations, during which I stood with leaders as they addressed their own settings. My background and training through a PhD in psychoeducational processes (a multidisciplinary degree in education, psychology, and business) is heavily influenced by the discipline of "action research" in which one stands with a leader in his or her own setting in order to learn and then use the learning toward intended change. It is not dispassionate research in which the researcher assumes not to influence the outcomes. Action research does not pretend to be "objective" by the norms of research science. Action research recognizes that the researcher—the consultant—by virtue of standing in the field with others, also contributes to the results of whatever action or intervention takes place. In fact, the repeated cycle of observing, diagnosing, planning action, and reviewing results provides the learning that can move us into the future. So I have always understood that as I do my work I too have the old, proverbial "skin in the game." My work has always involved my understanding of faith communities, my own sense of faith, and my ongoing conviction of God's movement in our lives. I believe that congregations and faith communities do have, and will always have, the potential to reflect God's purpose in our lives if we continue to be open to discernment, discovery, and surprise. And if we keep our courage, for courage is needed in the wilderness.

In that earlier book, *Journey in the Wilderness,* I noted that ours is a time of confusion much like the various wilderness times in which God transformed the people in the past—the Exodus, the Exile, and the multitude of times in which the prophets, the disciples, and Jesus himself wandered off into the midst of the unknown and into places of danger in order to find strength and renewed purpose. As people of faith, we have a history of having been in the wilderness before, which should assure us of our own future in the wilderness of the current moment. I wrote,

> We have learned to sing the Lord's song in a foreign land before. Despite our best efforts to escape hard and, at times, distasteful work, we have been delivered up on the shores of Nineveh before and been given new directions. And through it all, we today have received an inheritance from those earlier people who faced the wilderness and who responded with deepened theology, richer hymnody, and more authentic community. It has been messy, but we've done it before. [11]

I still believe that the wilderness changes people for God's purpose. If we have been in the wilderness in the past, we are in the wilderness once again. If we knew how to manage in the wilderness in the past, we are learning how to do it again. But the wilderness is a curious place for leaders to lead. By definition, one must lead without being sure where one is going. Again, if to be called to lead is a blessing, it is a complicated one.

This current book is an amalgam of theory and experience gained over the many years of standing with leaders in congregational settings and with leaders at middle judicatory, national, and global denominational levels. Particularly for my former readers I want to acknowledge that what will be found here is

- a recapturing of the significant insights from a series of leadership monographs I wrote as a senior staff member of the Texas Methodist Foundation. For twelve years I have facilitated regular multi-day gatherings with bishops and with district superintendents of the South Central Jurisdiction (SCJ) of the United Methodist Church. It has been the longest ongoing, structured effort of practitioner-based leadership learning with such leaders within that denomination. The monographs were written for this audience in order to capture what the leaders were learning as well as to facilitate conversations for further learning. While written for this audience of SCJ bishops and district superintendents, through the generosity of the Texas Methodist Foundation these monographs have also had free and wide distribution to support leadership conversations across many denominations, both within and beyond the United States.

- a recounting and rehearsing of a number of the key ideas/constructs/theories that I cling to, now more than ever. I am a true believer in Victor Hugo's oft-quoted observation that "nothing is more powerful than an idea whose time has come." Readers familiar with my previous writing will find critical ideas from earlier books recaptured here again because of their proven importance. Some might also notice ideas not here because they were less helpful or transitional to deeper truths and clearer perspectives. I have been instructed in the value of theories and ideas by the leaders who stand in the field and work with the ideas directly.

- some reconsiderations. My friends all know that on greeting me with the standard question of "How are you?" I am more likely than not to reply, "Not bad for a man my age." The response started for me as a joke when I was in my thirties and soon became a habitual reply. It is a bit ironic after all these years that this, now standard, unthinking reply to my friends has become a truth. The reality is that, as a man of my age, I can't have practiced action research and stood with so many leaders for so long without also learning where I was wrong or needed to reconsider. To that end, this book will also rehearse a few of the more significant corrections I now hold to. In particular:

  - I no longer believe in linear change as the dominant model by which leaders need to understand their setting. Linear change remains the appropriate way to address problems when, in fact, the situation is authentically a "problem." However, the linear problem solving that is still so heavily taught in our culture is not up to the task of understanding the complexity and fluidity of the situations our leaders currently face today. There are other, less linear ways in which we need to learn to look at our world.

- I no longer believe in "expertise." Nor do I believe in the necessity for leaders to "get it right." In fact, it is harder to learn new things when one is an expert or when an expert is in the room. And the courage and capacity to get things a bit "off right" may well be more instructive than having the right answer the first time out. Today's leadership rests more firmly on *being* and *learning* rather than on correctly *doing*. I now caution people to be wary of the one who arrives with all the answers, because learning is about to be sacrificed.

- I no longer believe in myself (or others) as the primary agent of the future. Like so many others, I have worked long and hard to figure out how things work and how to lead. But to proceed as if I have the answers has often brought me up short as a functional atheist—as one who speaks of God but believes that what really counts is all up to me, to my wisdom, and to my action. I continue to learn that it isn't until I make room for God (and the surprises that come from God's hand) that the future begins to find shape.

This book will argue for a quiet courage, often a spiritual courage, amid the temptations that make us ask for security, familiarity, and the assurance of the louder bombast that comes from those claiming to be in charge and having the right answers.

I will, of course, admit to having gotten things wrong all on my own. And I am very clearly aware of the debt I owe to those who helped me get things right. I am deeply in debt, first, to the thousands of leaders who over decades have allowed me to stand with them, allowed me to learn with them, and have worked with quiet courage to make things different. I am particularly in debt to the commitment of several multiyear, ongoing learning groups of United Methodist bishops and district superintendents, a group of Presbyterian Executive Presbyters, and two cohorts of gifted laypeople who have regularly "stepped onto the balcony" with me and away from their leadership tasks in order to reflect on their purpose and practice. I am deeply indebted to the Texas Methodist Foundation that has provided a platform for my work. Theirs too was an act of courage when over fifteen years ago they took the risk of stepping beyond their original role of providing financial services to the United Methodist churches of Texas in order to address the importance of leadership as a resource critical to the purpose of the church.

Still in the wilderness, we are making progress. There are, of course, assumptions that blind us when seeking to move ahead and temptations to return to Egypt—many to be explored in this book. But increasingly there are pillars of fire to follow that give us confidence for the next day's journey. To be a leader at a time when God is so actively changing the church in order to sustain its purpose in a fast-changing mission field is a blessing. A very complicated blessing.

2

THE CHANGE THAT DEMANDS
QUIET COURAGE

There is no going back. This may be the most difficult lesson for the aging leaders of established organizations and institutions, including congregations and denominations. Nonetheless, the first task of leadership is to paint an honest picture of the current reality. The current reality is so deeply changed that it challenges old ways of leadership and asks for quiet, purposeful courage.

The average age of clergy is fifty-three years old in mainline congregations as of 2015; the single age most represented (the mode) is sixty.[1] That means that the bulk of the leaders in these denominations were born in the period of the mid-1950s through the mid-1960s. They are baby boomers, and like baby boomers, they like to look back, often with rose-colored glasses. Their music, its roots in Woodstock and rock and roll, remains the soundtrack for their generation's living, and the fiftieth anniversary of The Beatles' *Sgt. Pepper* album just nudged the volume a bit louder. There is nothing wrong or unusual about all that. The parents and grandparents of every generation have been equally nostalgic about their own good old days. The critical issue for the present cohort of leaders is that those fond baby boomer memories that continue to provide the backdrop for their present leadership include a period of massive growth among congregations in the United States. *New York Times* columnist Ross Douthat wrote, "The strength of Christianity in this era rested on a foundation of swift demographic growth, as the steady, linear increase to which most American churches were accustomed gave way to a surge in membership and attendance that left denominations and parishes struggling to match supply to the new-found demand."[2] Church membership grew faster than population growth. "Enrollments in seminaries and Sunday schools increased steadily, and there was a great surge in church construction: Americans spent $26 million on sacred architecture in 1945, $409 million in 1950, and a *billion* dollars in 1960."[3] The memory that still captures baby boomer church leaders is growth and strength and having to run to catch up with the wave of people ready to join and be active participants in the life of congregations.

That memory shifted by 1965 when mainline denominations began their continuous trend of posting losses of members. Those buildings are now much less used, a growing percentage of them suffering from deferred maintenance that the dwindling number of parishioners can no longer manage. Yet clergy and lay leaders continue to look out the doors and windows wondering why more people aren't coming in. Within the past year I was at a meeting of church leaders in one midsize church in which a baby boomer–aged (and frustrated) chairperson suggested that the church newsletter carry a description of each of the church's committees so that others could see what was going on and begin attending. The assumption seemed to be that the natural way of things was for people to attend worship, and if they just had a bit more information, even about committees, they would surely turn up. In fact, this statement had so many unhelpful assumptions that it was clearly an effort to reach back to remembered days in which men, women, and children sought out local congregations. A surprising number of leaders still wonder why it isn't so anymore. Rose-colored glasses can hide some pretty dim realities.

There are, of course, other non–baby boomer voices in our congregations and denominations that are not constantly reaching back to this same period of remembered growth. Younger voices among our leaders often reflect a realism that comes from their own experiences, allowing them to accommodate current facts and statistics. Hope rides heavily on these younger voices. Nonetheless, tenure tends to provide a powerful platform from which one can be heard and, with such a large percentage of clergy and lay leaders in their sixties and older, the wish to recapture old days remains strong. For many, not being able to recapture old memories produces confusion and guilt.

However, there is no going back. This is the essential reality for leaders with long memories. Until leaders can accept that ours is not a turnaround situation, it cannot be addressed as a move-ahead situation. It takes courage to face a reality that is difficult and can't be turned around to reclaim an earlier day that is remembered as strong and was certainly easier from a leadership perspective.

This is why it is critical to understand the context that requires quiet courage that goes beyond the current practice of good leadership. It takes steadfastness to the purpose as faith communities (not the preferences of those already in those faith communities) to provide a steady path in the current wilderness. Steadfastness is not bombast. It is not the loud leadership of the one who has the answer for everyone else. It is the much quieter, steady pursuit of the "why" that lies at the center of our communities of faith. If the secret of real estate is location, location, location, then the current secret of courageous institutional leadership is purpose, purpose, purpose. There are many who remain anxious about the future of the institution of the church and who seek institutional corrections. It takes quiet courage to face anxiety and remain purposeful without being unnerved. Again, the words of Bill Coffin's prayer echo, offering reason once more why this prayer was continually with me in my travels: *We need a hope that is made wise by experience and is undaunted by disappointment. We need an anxiety about the future that shows us new ways to look at new things but does not unnerve us.*

THE ABERRANT TIME

Quiet courage is needed when there is no going back because the "back" that is remembered doesn't exist anymore.

Our current reality is that we are not in a turnaround situation. Leaders cannot take us back to a more comfortable time when the church (especially the mainline church) was established at the heart of the culture as a bedrock, trusted institution. We have steadily lost members and participants since 1965—for more than fifty years. Our members have steadily gotten older, not being replaced by younger generations in numbers sufficient to keep us as young as our communities. As demographics and geography change, a large number of our long-established congregations are now located away from easy access to the people they wish to attract. We hold an immense investment in property that is often dramatically underused and poorly maintained but serves as an albatrossian anchor, restricting movement. Organized religion attracts a continuously shrinking percentage of each successive generation since World War II. Ours is not a turnaround situation, and we have little that we can return to.

Importantly, we need to understand that the losses we have incurred and the challenges that we face are shared by other membership-based organizations that have had similar experiences of loss and aging since the 1960s. The story of loss and age can also be told by organizations and activities from Kiwanis, Rotary, Masons, Elks, Eastern Star, bowling teams, and bridge parties. Concern over the lack of institutional trust that plagues organized religion is also shared, deservedly, by the whole host of large organizations within government, business, education, the military, and the church.

Faced with the data about their institutional decline, the mainline church began a deep investment in the 1970s and 1980s in ways to renew, redevelop, or transform congregations with the assumption that if congregations got stronger and more effective at what they knew how to do, they could reclaim the strength of their remembered past. The current work of strengthening congregations through denominational and local efforts of "making vital congregations" is still critically important—*when focused on congregations that actually have the potential to be vital*. But it will not reclaim the past. Such current work on vitality will only provide a new base from which vital congregations will learn how they need to continue to change in order to live in the culture that now is and not how to recapture a culture that once was.

There are times—epochs, ages, cultural moments—when a convergence of unique conditions creates an environment that births and sustains flourishing growth that is uniquely tied to that moment but that cannot continue beyond the moment that created it. Consider that in the mid-tenth century to the mid-eleventh century a Chacoan Indian culture suddenly flourished in remarkable ways in what is now New Mexico territory. The Anasazi Indians lived together in populous great houses, developed elaborate irrigation systems that nourished their farming, built razor-straight highways, established "lighthouses" on distant mesas to send messages in signal fires, developed a powerful priesthood, and were able to follow the movements of stars and planets in ways sophisticated well beyond their time. All of this was unprecedented in the history of this prairie/desert land. They were a people well ahead of their time.

Important for our consideration here is that this advanced Chacoan culture did not last and it was not repeated. As historian Hampton Sides tells the story of the Anasazi, after about one hundred years, "just as quickly as they had burst upon the scene, the Chacoan culture ebbed. The agent of their demise seems to have been an environmental collapse brought on by two devastating droughts in 1085 in 1095, and in part by the impact of a dense population living on a marginal desert landscape. Their expansion had been predicated on a kind of meteorological accident; they had been living in a hundred-year cycle of *aberrant* wetness."[4] The Anasazi were a strong and vibrant people who could not sustain their present or reclaim their past because the time in which they thrived was an aberration; it was not the norm. Sides's use of the word "aberration" is important here because it notes a departure from the normal state of affairs. Strength and success can be a departure from the norm.

The Anasazi experience is noteworthy for us in our own moment because it can help us to see the impact of our own recent past, which was also an aberration—a confluence of conditions that prompted growth and strength that later could not be sustained or repeated, not only by the church but by myriad other organizations and institutions.

In a helpful way of understanding our own aberrant time, Yuval Levin offers a masterful description of the larger twentieth century in his recent study *The Fractured Republic*, subtitled *Renewing America's Social Contract in the Age of Individualism*.[5] He describes the first half of the twentieth century as an age of growing *consolidation* and *cohesion*. It was a time of massive growth of economic industrialization and centralization of government. A fifteen-year period of challenge and sacrifice through the Great Depression and World War II bonded the American people into a cohesive force built on a consensual national and global agenda. It was a time in which people "agreed to agree" and sublimated their differences in order to work together on a greater common agenda. It was particularly in this time of consensus and cohesion that the American culture pushed people toward membership in congregations and a legion of other membership organizations. The

United States exited World War II as the only global economy not devastated by the war, and for a period it held its remarkable position of producing a full half of all global manufacturing and production. We were a unified people with resources at hand. The widely shared story among many organizations was strength and growth.

Levin then goes on to describe the second half of the twentieth century as an age of growing *deconsolidation* and *decentralization* in which our economy diversified and deregulated in energizing ways. This second half of the century produced a sustained pushback against the uniformity and cohesion that marked the first half (consider Salinger's *The Catcher in the Rye* [1945], Riesman's *The Lonely Crowd* [1950], and Whyte's *The Organization Man* [1956]). An upsurge of individualism and the need for personal identity began to rise, supported by newfound interest in psychology and tied to the economy through advertising and technology. It was an energizing and vibrant age as people and institutions rode a heady wave of progressivism.

Levin captures the aberrant moment, saying, "Keeping one foot in each of these two distinguishable eras, midcentury America combined cohesion and dynamism to an exceptional degree."[6] It was in this mid-twentieth-century time that the mainline church, like so many other institutions and organizations, aggressively pursued growth, bureaucratic structure and strength, and resource and property development. We became large, strong, and institutional in a cultural moment that favored large, strong, and institutional.

The age of large and consolidated strength, however, has waned, and "micropowers," decentralized organizations, and small expressions of community are now taking the global stage.[7] Ours is not a turnaround situation in which we can recapture the size and strength of a large institutional system once sustained and nourished by a culturally aberrant time. It is encouraging to recall that the church has gone through other aberrant times such as the several Great Awakenings and the Western expansion of the United States—and we found ways to thrive in the aftermath of each. It is, however, challenging to note that we are now living in this current aftermath that is defined by micropowers and small communities but are still dependent on our memories of size and strength and still constrained by the polity, policies, and practices once effective in large institutions.

A Time of Confusion

The ending of an aberrant time is a moment of confusion. This was a lesson learned among the congregations at the time that apartheid ended in South Africa. Apartheid, as a national policy in South Africa, was an institutionalized system of racial segregation between 1948 and 1991 in which the national form of minority rule socially enforced separation of black South Africans from other races. While colonial racial stratification began as early as the late eighteenth century under the Dutch, apartheid was a less than fifty-year aberrant period in which South African government policy, social convention, and economic policy all converged to favor the white race and white institutions. One of the white institutions that benefited directly from this aberrant time was the Dutch Reformed Church that took on an identity as an established institution of the culture. As an established institution it became one of the means by which individuals could "identify" as connected to the ruling party. To be part of the Dutch Reformed Church during that time was, in the minds of many, to be connected to the ruling, privileged order. As an institution, alignment with minority rule placed the Dutch Reformed Church in the privileged position of a church that people sought out—a place that, simply by being, attracted people to membership.

When apartheid ended, the internal confusion began. By 1997 I was contacted at the Alban Institute, where I was director of consulting, by congregational consultants working with the Stellenbosch University in South Africa. They were seeking conversation and resources for helping congregations develop visions and plans for ministry. Our conversations quickly revealed that these consultants were finding it difficult to get traction for visioning and planning work in congregations because such efforts were without precedent—the leaders they were working with did not have an easy vocabulary for vision, mission, purpose, or outcomes. For several generations, in their aberrant apartheid environment, leaders became acclimated to a condition in which the culture would push people toward their churches seeking membership. The leaders didn't need to articulate their mission, purpose, or identity. So, if you will, they learned how to live without any articulated mission, purpose, or identity. As a culturally established church, it was sufficient to simply be. When the aberrant conditions changed, the confusion began. Unseated from their established place, along with so many other institutions, simply being was not enough, and leaders were adrift as conversations about purpose and their new place in the culture were needed.

At times of disorientation people need to go back to identity, purpose, and context. Walter Brueggemann's biblical work and writing about the Exodus and Exile have been central both to my work and to my spirit for many years. His work has helped me to understand the need for lament when facing a deep loss. He has also helped me to understand that each time the Israelites went into the wilderness they needed to answer, again, two questions: How will we now be with God? How will we now be with one another? In the Exodus the responses to these questions can be found in the Ten Commandments and in the organization of the tribes. In the Exile the responses to these questions can be found, in part, in the Levitical Code. If the Israelites needed to ask such questions in their wildernesses, so do we in our own.

Because it pointed to the need to go back to essential questions in wilderness times, this insight was central to the work that Alice Mann and I did in strategic planning with congregations. Our book on *Holy Conversations* was subtitled *Strategic Planning as a Spiritual Practice for Congregations*.[8] In our own way we were seeking to help congregations have necessary conversations as they emerged from their American aberrant time in which growth was a cultural standard produced by an American culture that pushed people toward mainline Christian congregations. We, like so many other consultants, had been trained in linear models of strategic planning: draw the picture of what the congregation is currently doing, then draw the picture of what the congregation wants to do next, then connect the two pictures with action steps. However, as we examined our practice with the congregations we worked with, we had to admit that something was missing and that fewer and fewer congregations were being effective by following such a linear path. In fact, it appeared that as congregations became increasingly efficient at what they were currently doing (at what they knew how to do), they became increasingly ineffective at the growth that they sought. Fifteen years ago we could not have put our finger on the change in the aberrant culture that was driving this incongruity. Nonetheless, it was clear that the landscape was shifting and that a different conversation was needed. So we began to work with the "three questions of congregational formation" that formed the Holy Conversation work we did with leaders:

"Who are we?"—the question of identity.

"What has God called us to do?"—the question of purpose.

"Who is our neighbor?"—the question of context.

What was important in our work was that we had discovered helpful questions, not answers. It was a step toward learning about quiet courage, remaining focused on purpose and promise when easy answers were not to be found.

By 1994 Ron Heifetz, who directed the Leadership Education Project at Harvard's John F. Kennedy School of Government, published his book *Leadership without Easy Answers*, a book that continues to be central to a shift in understanding the dynamics of leadership.[9] By 1996 our full consulting staff at the Alban Institute was studying Heifetz's work, asking how his vision of leadership informed our experience with congregations. "Instead of looking for saviors, we should be calling for leadership that will challenge us to face problems for which there are no simple painless solutions—problems that require us to learn new ways," wrote Heifetz.[10]

The critical distinction made by Heifetz between technical work and adaptive work set the stage. Technical work is the application of known solutions to known problems. Technical work leads directly to action. If there is a known solution to a known problem, then the responsible act of leadership is to get on with it—act! In the aberrant time of growth of the 1940s, 1950s, and 1960s, created by a culture that pushed people toward churches, the responsible activity of leadership was to act—to train more volunteers, develop effective committees, add additional programs, add staff, and build more buildings. The work to be done was well understood and solutions were readily at hand for the problems faced. Congregational leaders learned to do this organizational work as their congregations grew in size and became more complex. Technical work is the application of known solutions to known problems, and because the problems are known the solutions can make a difference.

But what if the problems are not known? What if the aberrant time is over? What if the discoveries made and the leadership practiced in that aberrant time no longer fit? Noting a bias from biology, Heifetz introduced the idea of adaptive leadership framed by the normative shifts in biological systems that need to continually adapt to the changing circumstances of their environment. If technical work is the application of solutions to problems, then adaptive work is needed when one is faced with a situation that is not a problem but is instead a changed environment. The critical insight for me was that, by definition, something cannot be a problem if it does not have a solution. Perhaps it's a bit of a reach, but I can argue that if you can't fix your situation, then it's not broken—it's simply different. Instead you need to change your perspective and learn how to live with it.

If technical work leads directly to action, then adaptive work requires learning. Along with being the director of Harvard's leadership project, Heifetz was also a physician familiar with medical examples that helped to define the distinction between technical and adaptive situations. If the medical issue is a clear problem—perhaps a broken bone for which there is a clear solution—then the appropriate technical response is the action of fixing the problem by resetting the bone and immobilizing it with a cast. Both the problem and the solution are equally clear. But there are medical issues that are without solutions, such as chronic illness or terminal disease. By definition, that which is chronic or terminal cannot be fixed. Importantly, Heifetz points out that rather than being a problem, such an unsolvable situation is a "condition." A condition is something one needs to learn how to live with. The operative word is "learn." Problems lead directly to action. It is technical work. A condition, however, is not changeable by known actions and requires new learning. "In those situations," writes Heifetz, "the authority can induce learning by asking hard questions and by recasting people's expectations to develop their response ability."[11]

Leadership, when the aberrant time is over and the conditions have changed, is better framed by the questions asked rather than by the answers offered. In the wilderness leaders need to ask, again, how will we now be with God? How will we now be with one another? Who are we now? What does God call us to do now? Who is our neighbor now?

Do not miss the earlier point made in chapter 1 that questions from a leader are unsettling. What people want from leaders is comfort. Comfort is provided by easy answers from a leader who knows what to do and asks us to do things right. Comfort gets rewarded. Leadership that insists on questions is unsettling. (Management asks if things are being done right. Leadership asks if we are doing right things.) Consider that Heifetz's follow-up book was about sabotage and the risk to leadership when people are discomforted by questions that require learning.[12] Leadership when the aberrant time is over is indeed a complicated blessing, and quiet courage is required.

The Healthy Admission of Ignorance

In his recent book *Sapiens*, Yuval Harari offers a stunning big picture, 50,000-foot overview of history told from three revolutions: the cognitive revolution, the agricultural revolution, and the scientific revolution. Importantly, when he describes the scientific revolution beginning around the sixteenth century, the first critical step required was an admission of ignorance. "Modern science is based on the Latin injunction *ignoramus*—'we do not know.'"[13] Columbus's discovery of America in 1492 and Magellan's voyage that became the first circumnavigation of the globe in 1522 proved to be formative shifts in thinking because they provided both observation and the supporting mathematics that changed what people thought they knew about the world in which they lived. For the first time in the fifteenth and sixteenth centuries, mapmakers began to draw maps with intentional empty spaces. It was the first admission that they did not know what was out there, prompted by what they were learning through expeditions of discovery about what really was out there. Prior to this time, maps simply left unfamiliar areas out or filled them with imaginary monsters. Their acceptance of their own ignorance allowed them to begin to include intentionally empty spaces, which provided the questions that would support further efforts of discovery. It unleashed the power of "we do not know"—the power of ignorance to lead to inquiry.

In the period of the 1970s, 1980s, and 1990s the landscape of congregations and denominations was infused with maps of the future with no empty spaces. We were still infused with the hubris of knowing. In fact, where empty spaces were needed, competing answers were being provided in rich abundance. Visioning and strategic planning at both congregational and denominational levels were pursued with great energy. I often joked that it was a time in which no congregation was allowed to wake up in the morning without a mission statement in place. Consultants and consultations proliferated in efforts of renewal, revitalization, and transformation within congregations. Among those who were working to help congregations there was considerable debate about the language to be applied to the efforts. In particular the debate centered on the use of the preface "re-" and the meaning of transformation. If the work was about *re*newal or *re*vitalization, it meant that the congregation under question was once new and once vital and the work was seeking to take the congregation back to a time when it could be so again. If the work was about transformation, then it sought to take the congregation from one form to some other form, but no one was quite clear about the difference between the two. The debate over language did note some uncertainty of the direction of the work, but there was little question about the rightfulness of the work itself. Training, consulting, planning, and program development went on unabated. The tools of marketing along with the data of demographics and psychographics were developed for congregations, which added information that carried the certainty of numbers to the conversations. Continuing education of clergy became increasingly technical in its teaching about the religious marketplace.

I do not want to diminish the work done during those decades. After all, my own hands were deep in the mix and I did my fair share of consulting, teaching, and writing that contributed to all of this. I also do not want to diminish the various programs and models of planning that were birthed during that period and that continue today. Indeed, working in this area of leadership has been highly instructive in my own life and work and highly valuable in enabling a great many leaders, congregations, and other organizations to enter into conversations of purpose and change. I offered a more comprehensive description of this time and its impact in my earlier book *Journey in the Wilderness*.[14] It may sound somewhat glib, but I have often said that I never met a program of renewal, change, or transformation that didn't work . . . somewhere. Each of these efforts and each program offered found fertile ground somewhere among some group of leaders because they all offered a means of having structured conversations focused on purpose, intent, and effectiveness. Over time, however, each effort or program seemed to reach its limit of creating the renewal, revitalization, or transformation it sought among the unending number of congregations needing help. So consultants and leaders continued to modify and improve their models and techniques, and new demographic and trend data were brought to the table in the hope of creating larger change.

In review, however, the reality is that the anxiety-producing trends of shrinking membership and the growing number of congregational closings has continued unabated over the decades since the 1960s. While the largest 0.5 percent of congregations in most of our denominations still carry around 10 percent of the members of the denomination (indicating the vitality of this small number of very large churches and their ability to live effectively in our changed landscape), at the same time most denominations are posting fewer numbers of large churches on their rosters as increasing numbers of large churches slip into midsize categories, and increasing numbers of midsize churches slip into small-size categories. Despite all the good and necessary work, religious organizations continue to shrink in size in the changed American landscape.

Consider as well the shift in the cultural attractiveness of congregations as a form of organized religion. It is not news that people are increasingly reporting being spiritual but not religious. People continue to seek meaning that can be found in the life of the spirit. They increasingly, however, do not do their seeking in congregations and denominations or in organized, institutionalized forms. The growth in the percentage of individuals reporting being unaffiliated with any religion has gone through a progressive shift across generational cohorts (see table 2.1). One of the most telling descriptors of the level of the change that congregations and denominations now face is the decades-long trend of generational disconnection with organized religion—the percentage of generational cohorts that are unaffiliated with institutional religion.[15]

This is a trend that is both progressive and dramatic. Importantly, the progression and strength of the trend provides evidence to argue that we are not experiencing a temporary cultural preference that will self-correct to once again favor congregations and denominations in ways we once knew. Here is additional evidence that there is no going

Table 2.1.   Generational Cohorts of the Religious Unaffiliated

Generational Cohort	% of Unaffiliated
Silents (before 1946)	9
Baby Boomers (1946–64)	15
Gen X (1965–80)	21
Millennials (after 1980)	33

back to an earlier aberrant time. Becoming more efficient, even more effective, at what congregations and denominations already know how to do will not reverse these trends that make us the most anxious.

Congregational and denominational leaders increasingly must face the reality that they no longer have a problem because problems, by definition, have a known solution. This is truly an adaptive situation that requires not the loud assurance that comes with leaders with known solutions but the quiet, courageous resolve of leaders willing to enter the wilderness and look at deeper questions of purpose and context. In order to continue we need leaders courageous enough to lead from ignorance—from "we do not know."

Drawing the New Map with Empty Spaces

The argument so far is that we have now left an aberrant time that preferred institutions and organized religion and have entered a new time that is more complex and less understood. This new environment is not a problem to be solved because it is clear that we do not have ready solutions. Technical expertise will not turn the tide. What most congregations and denominations know best how to do has proven to be less than effective in attracting new and younger people to the truth that they hold and to the meaning in which they find hope and purpose. It seems clear at this point that established congregations and denominations have a much greater capacity to improve what they already know how to do rather than create new forms and vehicles for their purpose to thrive in a changed landscape.[16] Leaders must accept that the new landscape, the changed mission field of their ministry, is actually the condition under which organized religion will now live. And conditions require new learning before action is effective.

Real learning depends on ignorance—the acceptance of a "we do not know" that can release the power of inquiry rather than a defensiveness or protectiveness of what we do know from our earlier time of strength. Again, a reflection of Bill Coffin's prayer: *We need an anxiety about the future that shows us new ways to look at new things but does not unnerve us.*

Perhaps a good beginning place is the continual drawing of new maps that have the courage to include empty spaces. The more that we can draw the picture of what we now see and don't see, the more the new environment will take shape. Perhaps analogous to the sixteenth-century sailing explorers, we are currently at the stage of locating the continents and identifying the inlets and bays but are not at all sure of what lies inland or even how far the new land will stretch. So despite the unknown empty space that lies ahead and beyond, we can at least sketch the outline of what is apparent so far. And what we can see has profound implications for institutions and for efforts of organized religion.

Consider at least these four sightings, or cultural soundings, of the new land that lies ahead: the shift from a convergent to a divergent culture, the reversal of institutional trust, the changing social contract, and the counting of losses.

The Shift from a Convergent to a Divergent Culture

As early as twenty years ago Charles Handy gave language to a fundamental shift that made organizational life more difficult and complex than it had been earlier. Handy was an oil executive, an economist, a professor at the London School of Business, and a consultant to organizations. Reflective of what has been said earlier about the mid-twentieth century, he noted that as he was growing up, the central message of education was that every problem encountered had already been solved by someone, the answer was in the back of the teacher's book, and the student's job was to find out what it was and remember it. In other words, all problems were known and all had answers that could be found somewhere. In contrast, he reflected that most of the problems that he was facing in his work were new in one way or another. He wrote,

> I had come up against the difference between convergent and divergent problems. Convergent problems: "What is the shortest route to Bath?" have only one correct answer. Divergent problems: "Why do you want to go to Bath?" or even "Where do you want to go?" have answers that depend on the particular circumstances and that are, in a way, neither right nor wrong. Most business problems are divergent.[17]

The difference between a convergent culture and a divergent culture is fundamental to the current dilemma of leadership in institutions. This is an especially important shift to understand because the large baby boomer cohort of institutional leaders that most enjoy today's platform of tenure grew up and learned their leadership in a convergent culture only to be called to provide their leadership at a divergent time.

Perhaps the place to begin exploring that difference is by noting that certainty stands with convergence, with the perceived question or problem on which people agree there is only one right answer. Convergence and certainty exist when there is a perceived right answer and the people and the situation bend themselves to that common answer. Convergence is when the question and the answer are the same for everyone. In most congregations and denominations in the 1950s the question of what a vital service of worship looked like was a convergent question. Worship began and ended at the same time each week following a standardized, denominationally determined form in which only the hymns, collect, and sermon title would vary from week to week. It is not an overstatement to suggest that a person could tell what time it was on Sunday morning by how far the worship service had progressed. Vital worship was a convergent question in which the question and the answer were the same for everyone.

In divergence, the question might be the same, but the answers are multiple and defined by the particular circumstances and needs of the individual asking the question. Over the past several decades the once convergent question of vital worship has become increasingly divergent. Individual congregations within a shared denominational family now use liturgies that might reflect some common historic origins, but even those liturgies vary from congregation to congregation and from week to week to reflect the culture of the congregation or the personality and preferences of the clergy. Generational differences weigh in heavily on the form of vital worship, with a broad array of musical forms and the multiple uses of technology. Divergence not only takes certainty away, it also requires a willingness to acknowledge that there can be multiple answers to a question for which one is convinced he or she has a right answer to serve his or her own purpose.

The earlier aberrant time of growth and strength in the mid-twentieth century was a time of convergence. As noted, the fifteen-year period of the Great Depression and World War II leading up to the mid-twentieth century bonded the American people into a cohesive national group with a shared national and global agenda. People lived with shared identity, shared questions, shared convictions, shared expectations, and shared answers. It was a convergent time in which people felt that they were "all in this together." Assuredly there was an undercurrent of deep racial, ethnic, and socioeconomic differences. Nonetheless, for the most part the observable veneer of the culture was mostly monochromatic, and people with differences bent themselves to accommodate the cultural sameness to the best of their ability. In the great immigration waves from Italy, Ireland, and China, the new arrivals worked to be seen as American as quickly as possible before wanting to be identified as Italian, Irish, or Chinese—American first, and only then Italian, Irish, or Chinese. Not just with immigrant, ethnic, or racial differences, the pressure to conform impacted other fundamental areas of people's lives such as human sexuality. Looking back at my high school graduating class in the mid-1960s I marvel that I had no gay classmates. In a convergent culture the individual who is different knows to hide his or her difference and to live publicly out of what most looks the same to everyone else. It was only in later decades, when the culture shifted from convergent to divergent, that Americans who came from Italy proudly took up their identity as Italian Americans, and others identified as Chinese Americans or African Americans. It has only been in the most recent decades that I could go back to my high school class reunions and greet my gay classmates who, in that earlier convergent time, survived by appearing like everyone else, but who now in a divergent time find strength in aligning with their difference. In a convergent culture you lead with your sameness. In a divergent culture you lead with your difference.

Mainline American congregations thrived and grew in the convergent culture of the mid-twentieth century, and, in fact, religion was a source of the convergence of the culture. Researcher Charles Murray points out that in a Gallup poll taken in October 1963 two background questions were asked of responders: one of religious preference and one of church attendance ("church attendance," not "church or synagogue" or "worship service"). "Only 1 percent of respondents said they did not have a religious preference, and half said they had attended a worship service in the last seven days."[18] There was no variation in responses across classes. Religion was a formidable component to the glue that held a convergent culture together and, like the Dutch Reformed Church in South Africa during apartheid, the American mainline church was the "established" church in a country that famously disallowed an established church. White Protestantism was the default religion in a culture that pushed people toward joining because membership was a means of locating oneself in a community. When *Look*, the now defunct general interest magazine, ran its annual photo series of the top ten preachers in America, nine of the ten were white male preachers of mainline congregations. There was a close alignment between government and religion in that convergent time. When at the heart of the time of convergence in 1954 President Dwight D. Eisenhower signed the bill to include the words "under God" in the pledge to the flag, he said, "From this day forward, the millions of our school children will daily proclaim in every city and town, every village and rural school house, the dedication of our nation and our people to the Almighty. To anyone who truly loves America, nothing could be more inspiring than to contemplate this rededication of our youth, on each school morning, to our country's true meaning." To be American was to live under God—a convergence that disallowed differences and made leadership considerably easier. It isn't difficult to lead people in the direction they are already going.

For example, consider that when I was growing up I attended a Methodist Church that on highly attended holiday Sundays would have a worship attendance in excess of five hundred people—a large church for that time. The full staff for that congregation in those years included one full-time ordained clergy, one part-time music director/organist, one part-time secretary, and one-part time custodian. It was a large church with a large program and large facility with a very small staff, all possible because it was a convergent time. When people moved into the community they were expected to find a congregation like mine on their own initiative, and there were no evangelism committees. When people joined as members they knew that they were expected to be part of a committee and easily self-organized into patterns that were remarkably similar both across congregations and across denominations. Sunday School classes and adult groups proliferated as people subgrouped within congregations according to the similarities in their ages or marital status, providing their own leadership. Clergy worked hard in those convergent days, but it was work more tightly constrained around an agenda of visitation, pastoral care, membership, weddings/baptisms/funerals, and sermon preparation. It was a time of more technical pastoral work, providing answers to problems well understood. Organizational leadership, setting vision, and the negotiation of decisions was less of a pastoral responsibility because in a convergent time people knew what to do; it is what they already did in the past, and leadership did not have to cut new paths into divergent territory.

In contrast, by the 1980s consulting groups working with congregations were using rules of thumb to suggest that a congregation required at least one full-time professional program staff person for every 100 to 150 persons in average attendance (rules of thumb varied among consultants). After the 1980s a congregation of similar size to the one in which I grew up would more likely have a full-time senior pastor with two to four additional full-time clergy and/or lay professional staff, each with support staff assigned to them, as well as multiple music staff to manage a much wider array of music across traditional and contemporary worship services, one or more full-time custodians, and perhaps a part-time business manager to replace work once done by committees or individual laypeople. All of these staff were addressing the subgroup differences and increased diversity of needs and preferences that were blooming within the congregation. Divergence has a high institutional cost beyond the complexity of leading people who might have the same question but who all hold different answers.

Much of the shift to a divergent organizational culture came through the marriage of advertising and technology. With an ever-growing capacity to track and blend data about income, generation, marital status, and gender, and an ever-growing list of even more subtle variables, advertisers and media personnel began breaking up a convergent culture into smaller and smaller lifestyle groups. Joseph Turow of the Annenberg School for Communication at the University of Pennsylvania argues convincingly that "the U.S. is experiencing a major shift in balance between society-making media and segment-making media. Segment-making media are those that encourage small slices of society to talk to themselves, while society-making media are those that have the potential to get all those segments to talk to each other."[19] Before the 1970s, in a convergent era, most people participated in society-making media viewing, without charge, one of three commercial broadcast stations that were highly uniform in their programming. In his analysis of the impact of changes in media on the church, Rex Miller points out that in a broadcast era, individuals all shared the same experience, even if sitting alone with their TV.[20] Everyone knew who won the

World Series, who won the Miss America Pageant, and what happened on the TV show *Dallas* because these were the primary, among few, choices on TV. After the mid-1990s independent broadcast stations, cable and satellite systems, videocassette and DVDs, home computer programming, and a growing number of content providers such as Netflix and Amazon began to provide entertainment and information to increasingly smaller and more diverse subsets of viewers. We have moved into multiple and increasingly diverse and specific "primary media communities" (segment-making media)—each with their own preferred communication channels—that are much more easily targeted by media firms to help advertisers tailor a message with specific answers to the questions and concerns of each separate divergent subgroup.

The maturing of this marriage of technology and media is enjoyed by many and fascinating to all as the capacity of this divergent targeting moves closer and closer to the granular, individual level. The Waze GPS app on my iPhone now, in the midst of giving me directions for my travel, also tells me that a donut shop is just ahead on the left in case I want to stop for a snack. If I don't respond right away, the message just disappears, almost apologetically, in case it interrupted my travel plans. I can now download an app for stores that will, in real time, track which aisle I am standing in and know when I pause in front of a product that I have purchased there in the past, then offer me a special discount for that item that is available only to me because of who I am, where I am standing, and what I am looking at. In 1960 my grandfather was stopped by a policeman once for traveling five miles an hour *under the minimum* speed limit on an interstate highway because he thought the world moved too fast. I can't imagine what he might think now.

But there is a downside, a "darkside of the unrelenting slicing and dicing of America that advertisers are already beginning to orchestrate through all major media,"[21] as Turow uncovers in his research, which, far from being dystopian, simply describes the cultural impact of shifts that have already taken place. Nonetheless, we have been delivered to a divergent world in which any one question has multiple "right" answers—each dependent on the circumstances and preferences of the individual involved. To any one political action or situation, Fox News, MSNBC, CNN, and—at an increasingly granular level—an unending cadre of bloggers, all have their own answers and explanations that compete with one another. Each also has its own faithful audience of which few venture beyond their preferred reality or truth to try to understand how things might be seen differently. Convergent no more, we are no longer all in this together. We now live in the "electronic equivalent of gated communities,"[22] in which personal preferences can easily outweigh purpose and in which divergent answers easily move to become oppositional answers. We have moved from the convergence of shared large cultural identities to the divergence of individual preferences. At the end of his telling of the history of humankind in *Sapiens*, Harari takes up the question of happiness, asking whether in the many millennia of progression, from being hunter/gatherers to farmers and villagers to progressive technologists, people are actually happier. He acknowledges that the research methodology to understand happiness is less than mature at this point and that it relies heavily on subjective feeling—the self-reporting of either pleasure or meaning. To this he concludes, "To many of us, that seems logical because the dominant religion of our age is liberalism. Liberalism sanctifies the subjective feelings of individuals. It views these feelings as the supreme source of authority."[23]

The current elevation of the individual as the fundamental unit of meaning in the liberalism Harari describes takes us to a place where leadership is increasingly difficult and less rewarded as it seeks direction and purpose in a context of increasingly competing truths. There is an old joke that even a stopped clock is right at least two times each day. It is a joke that reflects on the difficulty of having only one right answer when things are constantly changing. Decades ago congregations experienced their strength at a time when they practiced their one-right-answer approaches to worship and liturgy, to structure and practice, and to theological explanation in a convergent culture. Religious organizations are tradition-based and highly sensitive to and highly reflective of their history and origins, making them easily less malleable than the cultural expressions around them. They are, if you will, much more convergent institutions by design—now living in a divergent landscape—seeking a way to be faithful to an unchanging truth, without betraying those who have found meaning in their faith, while also not dismissing those who seek meaning in ways less comfortable to their established theological convictions and religious practices. Leadership grounded in the comfort of convergence is not well prepared to enter into this new territory. Quiet courage is needed to step into these waters that do not easily part.

The Reversal of Institutional Trust

I grew up in a banking family. My father began as a teller in a local bank when he came out of World War II, and he steadily advanced until he was president of the local bank in our town by the time I graduated from high school in 1965. I trusted banks because I trusted my father, and I had ample evidence all around me as people, businesses, local officials, and my church leaders all sought out my father and his bank for advice and involvement in their plans. Banks were trusted institutions in my high school years, as were churches, schools, hospitals, the police . . . and the list could go on.

By 1972 I was part of a three-day urban experience in which a small group of seminarians met with a small group of men who were part of a black radical resistance group in Boston. Tensions ran high in Boston in those days, and it was necessary to check all participants in the group for weapons before we sat down together. By the evening of the first day, the conversation turned to the practice of red-lining, in which banks refused to make loans to people and businesses in certain communities because of the predominant race of people living there. I knew that couldn't be true because I knew my father, his bank, and the respect that everyone had for my father and his bank—so I said so. It was a long, scary evening in which there was both verbal and physical confrontation, my trust was uncovered as naïve, and I was shaken.

If the shift to a divergent culture has been difficult, one of the other markers that we can place on our new cultural map with empty spaces is the shape of the basic distrust that now accompanies most historic institutions in our communities—religious institutions included. In his critical and important assessment of institutions, Hugh Heclo writes about our modern impasse in which "we are disposed to distrust institutions . . . [yet] we are compelled to live in a thick tangle of institutions while believing that they do not have our best interests at heart."[24]

Institutions are meant to serve the common good, to manage the affairs of the larger community in ways that benefit both present and future needs. Heclo calls them the "well-worn handles" by which people manage their public affairs. As such, they depend on trust—trust in their purpose, governance and management, and equity in dealing with others. In the earlier period of convergence that was at its height in mid-century, post–World War II America, trust in our institutions was high. In particular, the institutions of religion were highly trusted. A quick Internet search of the ranking of trusted institutions in the United States shows that as late as 1973, 65 percent of the American public maintained a high level of trust in churches. However, by 2017 that level of trust in congregations shrunk to 41 percent. This precipitous drop in institutional trust over those same years was mirrored for a wide range of other institutions beyond churches as well.

Heclo helps to fill in the picture of that growing mistrust. The first of the explanations that he offers is that "today's institutions have gained our distrust the old fashioned way—they earned it."[25] This is *performance-based distrust*. To support his argument, Heclo offers a "Baby Boomer's Primer for Political Distrust," which is a cataloguing of forty-three political examples that stretch over five pages in his book and give proof to reasons not to trust the institution of government and its leaders. The list begins in 1958 with the resignation of President Eisenhower's chief of staff, Sherman Adams, for accepting a vicuna coat and other gifts from a business under investigation by the FTC. I don't personally remember that event, but I was struck by the fact that, as an early baby boomer, there were very, very few other examples in the primer that I did not easily recall. The list was all too familiar. Consider just a few:

- The Bay of Pigs and Washington's false denials (1961)
- The conspiracy theories surrounding the assassination of President Kennedy (1963)
- President Nixon's secret bombing of Cambodia (1970)
- The Pentagon Papers (1971–72)
- Watergate and President Nixon's resignation (1974)
- The Abscam scandal (1980)
- The Iran-Contra affair and the illegal sale of weapons to Iran (1986)
- The Keating Five Scandal (1989)

This is only a very tip-of-the-iceberg listing that covers just the time between 1958 and 1990, and it still has more than a quarter century's worth of examples occurring after 1990 before catching up to the present moment. People do not currently have a high level of trust in government and its leaders because of the evidence available demonstrating that they are not trustworthy. Congregations and denominations have their own lists of examples of racial discrimination and bigotry, televangelist scandals, mismanaged and stolen funds, and sexual misconduct, especially the Roman Catholic priests' sexual abuse of children. The new landscape that needs to be mapped includes an institutional distrust that is deeply grounded in experience.

There have certainly been efforts to manage the untrustworthiness of institutions. Public apologies have been offered, investigations have been mounted, criminal charges have been levied, CEOs have been fired, politicians have been turned out of office, clergy have been defrocked, and regulations have been put into place. This has not stemmed the tide of untrustworthy institutional and individual behavior. Nonetheless, at least performance-based distrust operates at a conscious level. We are aware of it and we know it when we see it.

Much less visible is the *culture-based distrust* of institutions that Heclo goes on to describe in his work. The culture-based distrust is closely connected to the changing social contract that we will continue to explore in the third of the new map soundings below. For the moment it is sufficient to acknowledge that we have gone through a deep cultural shift from the centrality of the group to the centrality of the individual. In a culture of convergence, identity is carried by the larger group (nation, community, church) and the individual bends his or her identity and behavior to conform to the group. Bending oneself to be more like others in the nation, community, or church is how one knows and is known to belong. In a culture of divergence, the individual ascends to the place of importance and the group must seek to accommodate an ever-widening range of differences in new definitions of identity and new accommodations of behavior.

This leads to Heclo's identification of the new "moral polestar." In this new landscape of individualism, Heclo argues that "our moral polestar amounts to this central idea: the correct way to get on with life is to recognize that each of us has the right to live as he or she pleases so long as we do not interfere with the right of other people to do likewise."[26] This is certainly not the way in which America and its leaders publicly talk about our values. Our public language talks more about the public good and the centrality of community. However, our public language also insists that we are not racist or sexist when we are denouncing moments of racial or sexual violence, despite the history of racism and sexism that set the stage for the violence that offends us. All cultures wrestle with the gap between espoused values and lived values. One reason that we continue to speak of ourselves as living out values better or different from those that we actually practice is to continually challenge ourselves to live a better story than the one we should honestly be telling. The shift toward divergence and the supporting segment-based media have, however, moved us decidedly toward an individualism that reflects the moral polestar that Heclo describes.

To the point of understanding our distrust of institutions, the centrality of individualism flies in the face of the purpose of institutions that are much more aligned with the common good. At the heart of the operative moral polestar is the *freedom of the individual*. In contrast, embedded in our institutions are *constraints on the individual.* Institutions, in order to address their own purposes, commonly carry with them disciplines that are recognized as good both for the individual and for the larger community. However, these disciplines infringe on the right of the individual to live his or her life in any way he or she chooses. The individual may want to be healthy and enjoy a long life, but when that individual becomes involved with the institution of the YMCA, which has physical health as part of its mission, or when the individual becomes involved with institutions committed to preventative medicine, he or she will immediately be introduced to disciplines of exercise and diet that infringe on the freedom to do or eat whatever the individual prefers and what the marketplace offers. An individual may want to send children to college and have a worry-free retirement, but as soon as that individual consults the financial advisor that is connected to the institutions that can help, the individual encounters disciplines of saving and investing that impinge on the freedoms of consumerism that are offered in the marketplace. An individual may want to have a clear sense of connection with God and a sense of meaning to his or her living, but as soon as that individual turns to the institution of the church he or she will be introduced to disciplines of personal sacrifice and personal disciplines of devotion that curtail personal desires in favor of greater purpose. Do unto others as you would have them do unto you is significantly different from let everyone do what they want as long as they don't stop others from doing the same.

In this tension between the desires of the individuals and the disciplines of our institutions we need to understand that "whatever else might be said about them, all institutions present themselves as authoritative rules for behavior. To say that some structure, process or precedent has become institutionalized means, at a minimum, that there is now a way of doing things to which people are expected to conform."[27] Quiet courage is needed in this new landscape as religious leaders hold the traditions and the disciplines of their historic faiths while often engaged with individuals who have learned to come with cultural dispositions to have their personal preferences affirmed rather than challenged. Quiet courage is needed in this new landscape as religious subgroups, both across and within their denominational differences, organize against one another to champion the interpretation of their faith tradition that they individually favor. The map of our new landscape is not fully clear, but there is no question that it is less favorable to institutions and that religious leaders cannot operate with an assumption of trust that once undergirded their work.

The Changing Social Contract

In drawing this new map of the changed environment in which organized religion now lives, it is necessary to go deeper into the nature of the changing social contract of which Heclo's moral polestar is a piece. History can be told from many different perspectives, but one view can be told from the perspective of an intentionally constructed "more." From the earliest Pilgrims and settlers in America, Western European immigrants understood that land or a marketable trade, along with family, were the essentials of a secure future. From those earliest settlements and communities where people huddled together to the isolation of the plains and the mountains where individuals took on so much more on their own, land was the greatest asset of security. If one did not have land, then a marketable/barterable trade or service in support of landowners was needed. Above all, family was the single unit that provided the workforce, the nurture, and the support needed. A secure future with these few assets in hand could be told from a fairly individual point of view.

However, also from the beginning, there were wise people who understood that having land, a trade, and a family could be too limited, providing only for the small circle of "me and mine." People understood that there were issues of the common good that lay beyond the bounds of personal security. They understood that there were issues of meaning and purpose that extended beyond a day's labor. So while working their land and their trades, people joined together to develop an intentionally constructed "more" that would be undergirded by institutions of government, finance, education, and religion. Institution building in those early years was a necessary companion to land or trade for a secure future that would go beyond the individual and family. As just one example, Bishop John Emory (1789–1835), while working at his own trade as a bishop in the Methodist Episcopal Church, was also prominent in founding New York University and Wesleyan University, was a principal organizer of Dickinson College, and was a namesake along with Patrick Henry of Emory and Henry College. Building institutions of the common good was not seen as a distraction from the pursuit of a secure future but as a necessary building block.

Institutions, as noted earlier, were needed to manage the common good as part of a national social contract, and the eighteenth and nineteenth centuries were infused with such institution building. The intentionally constructed "more" was a social contract in which people understood that they were responsible for more than their own security, that the pursuit of happiness defined by the national founders was meant to add to the larger community in ways quite different from an individual pursuit of pleasure. It was a day in which happiness was not confused with pleasure.

Social contracts are agreements on how we will live together and what we can expect and depend on from one another. The argument in this chapter is that we have left behind an aberrant age that we cannot work to regain. The aberrant time in the twentieth century saw the growth and strength of the institutions that enjoyed the inheritance of an earlier social contract. This aberrant time was at its zenith in the mid-twentieth-century post–World War II time and it had its own social contract, one that was reflective of and comfortable with the "golden rules" of life in which individuals were to be as concerned about others as they were concerned about themselves. Daniel Yankelovich called this twentieth-century social contract a "giving/getting compact" in which sacrificial behavior was expected to be rewarded with security. He described the giving/getting compact in this way:

I give hard work, loyalty and steadfastness. I swallow my frustrations
and suppress my impulse to do what I would enjoy and do what is
expected of me instead. I do not put myself first; I put the needs of
others ahead of my own. I give a lot, but what I get in return is worth
it. I receive an ever-growing standard of living, and a family life with
a devoted spouse and decent kids. Our children will take care of us in
our old age if we really need it, which thank goodness we will not. I
have a nice home, a good job, the respect of my family and neigh-
bors; a sense of accomplishment at having made something of my
life. Last but not least, as an American I am proud to be a citizen of
the finest country in the world.[28]

It was a contract in which one was required to give in order to get.

Using the tools and the data of a marketer, Daniel Yankelovich has
long been both recognized and honored for his work in tracking not just
the changes in behaviors of the marketplace but also the changes of the
underlying values as well. Like the large tectonic plates that rest below
the surface of the earth but that create surface disruptions when they
shift, Yankelovich was able to demonstrate that when cultural values
shift, surface behavior is disrupted as well. By 1981, when Yankelovich
was doing his research on the link between values and behavior, it was
becoming increasingly clear that the social contract that allowed for the
common good was being deeply changed by shifts in American values.
By 2008, twenty-seven years later, Heclo, as noted earlier, was able to
describe a very different social contract, his moral polestar: "the correct
way to get on with life is to recognize that each of us has the right to live
as he or she pleases, so long as we do not interfere with the right of
other people to do likewise." Consider the shift from a contract in
which by giving you receive to an understanding that I should claim
what I want as long as I don't impede others from doing the same. A
shift from a search for communal happiness to a search for personal
pleasure. A shift from the values of shared security to the values of
personal fulfillment.

Again, this puts many of our institutions, our churches in particular,
culturally out of step as they continue to ask of us more than the social
contract of the day. For institutions are based on membership, and
membership has its obligations. If I belong, I am responsible for my
part, defined by the vows or contracts of membership that I agree to. If
I skip membership and seek only participation, I am responsible only

for myself. In the new land for which we are still trying to draw the map, we seem ambivalent about membership and about how much of a social contract we willingly sign on to. Loyalty to any given workplace is suspect at the same time that people give an increasingly large percentage of their lives and time to work. Long-term memberships in institutions focused on health wane while short-term, expensive fees for intensive boot camps and stationary cycle exercising seem to thrive. Ongoing, active engagement in religious congregations is shrinking ("regular attendance" is now defined as less than two times per month), while Internet-advertised, intimate, one-time, faith-based community meals are attracting increased attention in urban areas. In our ambivalence it seems that the wavering social contract of the day is less comfortable with a deep commitment to a lifestyle than it is with paying for an experience. All of this leaves institutions unsure of how to live in the new landscape.

The Counting of Losses

The final feature that needs to be placed on the new map of the changing landscape is the "land of losses." For our present institutions and their leaders, one of the dominant features is the haze of ennui that comes from the sense of all that has been lost over the decades of change. Reflective of that sense of loss, Robert Jones, founding CEO of the Public Religion Research Institute, has written about the end of white, Christian America. This is predominantly a loss of identity. Jones uses the term "White Christian America" to describe the domain of white Protestants in America that developed in the twentieth century along two main branches: "a more liberal mainline Protestant America headquartered in New England and the upper Midwest/Great Lakes region and a more conservative evangelical Protestant America anchored in the South and lower Midwest/Ozark Mountains region."[29] Jones introduces his thesis using three buildings that he suggests are monuments to what was once White Christian America's power, one of which is the United Methodist building, completed in 1923, across the street from the U.S. Capitol in Washington, DC. The building was a monument to the optimism of the time, "conceived by the nation's largest and most prominent Christian denomination as a 'sentinel' for Protestant Christian witness and social reform in the nation's capital."[30] It was a symbol of the effort to meld Christian social values with the ideals of American government. Nearly one hundred years later the purpose and the identity of this building have changed. "Rather than sticking to the original mission—to be a 'Protestant presence' on Capitol Hill—they have rented office space to a wide array of faith-based organizations, including the Islamic Society of North America, Catholic Relief Services, and the General Conference of Seventh-Day Adventists."[31] The purpose of the building is now to house an inclusive voice for justice and in the transition represents a loss of what was once a clear identity of Protestantism as the dominant moral voice in America. "More than anything else," Jones concludes, "the death of White Christian America has robbed its descendants of their security and their place."[32]

Jones's argument is not that Protestantism should try to recapture or be given back its central role as the established religious voice in the culture. He has, however, done the hard academic work to clarify the shift that has happened and that is perceived as a loss by those who remember standing within the sphere of the former influence of a Protestant convergent culture. Where once religious institutions operated out of a sense of power, they now contend with a sense of loss. It is part of a series of losses that are generalized in a number of ways.

Along with a loss of identity, consider the cultural loss of social capital to which religious organizations were considerable contributors. A wide array of membership organizations and institutions are contending with the loss of social capital that they once depended on to cement the loyalty of persons with their organizations and purpose. Robert Putnam defines social capital as the "connections among individuals— social networks and the norms of reciprocity and trustworthiness that arise from them."[33] Social networks provide the infrastructure for a convergent culture. They bind people together through membership and shared activities that help people know how and where they belong in their communities and help people find their common interest and convictions that provide connection to one another. The title of his book *Bowling Alone* reflects one telling example of his research in which he demonstrates that while the bowling industry is doing well, and the annual number of individual games bowled by people remains strong, the idea of a bowling league has floundered as people no longer commit to being on a team that must meet regularly. Belonging to a team, a group, an organization, or an institution has a greatly diminished appeal as a convergent culture that once preferred belonging to groups has given way to a divergent culture that prefers individual experiences. The diminished social capital and the shrinking social networks that brought people together in shared identities are felt as a loss to membership-based organizations like congregations that were, within recent baby boomer memories, organizations sought out by people who wanted to be connected.

If there is a loss of connection through diminished social capital, there is also a loss of opportunity. Putnam is a professor of public policy at Harvard University and has taken on a role as a dominant academic voice in the changes of American culture. Along with social capital, he has also researched opportunity and social mobility, asking if youth today who come from different social and economic backgrounds have equal life chances for successful, happy lives—one of the basic tenets of the American Dream. What he describes is how "graphically, the ups and downs of inequality in America during the twentieth century trace a gigantic U, beginning and ending in two Gilded Ages, but with a long period of relative equality around mid-century."[34] The up and down of inequality is a description beginning in the late nineteenth-century period of conspicuous wealth that was held by a small percentage of the population, which is now being mirrored by another, contemporary period of a small percentage of people holding conspicuous wealth. In between these "gilded ages" was a time of greater egalitarianism in which the middle class held sway and opportunity was much more widely shared. The twentieth century was the middle period of egalitarian opportunity, and mid-century was its zenith as GIs returned from the war and education became the primary tool of social and economic advancement. The U shape of opportunity again marks the mid-twentieth-century period as an aberrant time, once assumed but now permanently reshaped. It is another of the losses felt by religious institutions that, along with institutions of education, were seen as the vehicles of opportunity giving people reasons to align with those institutions.

And so we get to the loss of the middle class, one of the most significant losses felt by mainline Protestant religious institutions that heavily depended on the middle class in the twentieth century. With an impressive use of data, Charles Murray describes a "coming apart" of American culture in which there is a new upper class of elite and a new lower class—and a new missing middle.[35] *New York Times* op-ed columnist David Brooks identified Murray's 2012 book *Coming Apart* as the most significant book of that year and said, "The word 'class' doesn't even capture the divide Murray describes. You might say the country has bifurcated into different social tribes, with a tenuous common culture linking them."[36] Murray describes the new elite as highly educated and highly remunerated, which gives this small portion of the population many advantages, one of which is the freedom of choice of where to live. They choose to live together in "SuperZips," which are a new formulation of residential segregation as this subset of people moved to live together in and around urban centers such as Boston; New York City; Philadelphia; Washington, DC; Chicago; Los Angeles; and San Francisco.[37] Significantly, we have now moved to a time in which the people who make most of the decisions now live together and apart from the people who necessarily live with their decisions. Because the new elite and the new lower class do not live together, they are unaware of one another's contexts for living, which means that the new elite who make decisions that influence other people's lives do not understand the people over whom they hold sway. The frustration generated by this new coming apart, unmediated by what is now a missing middle class, propelled J. D. Vance's book *Hillbilly Elegy* to the top of the *New York Times* bestseller list, as Vance provided a voice to Murray's new lower class, the unheard and unlistened-to part of the new divergent culture.[38] More than the loss of the middle class, what many leaders have been feeling is a deep loss of understanding.

Losses of identity, of social capital, of opportunity, and of understanding. Leaders of religious institutions are confronted with a new cultural landscape that no longer provides a number of powerful advantages that once gave incentives for people to align themselves through membership. Much of the recent argument related to the weakening of religious institutions has focused on an ill-described creeping secularization of the culture. Indeed, it is accurate to say that there is a growing consumerist individualism that has reshaped values, making individuals more central than communities or the common good. However, to frame the situation as merely a growing secularization invites religious institutions to address a false "enemy" and invites leaders to see "more religion" as the solution to the "problem" of a secular culture. Religious leaders and institutions can easily exhaust themselves shouting with more and more energy about what is wrong with the secular culture and how people must turn to religion. Indeed, if secularization was the clear problem, religious institutions do have a viable solution, and they would feel stronger in a situation they could understand. However, rather than a secular challenge or problem against which one might mount forces, the more accurate description is that leaders now face a landscape of losses—a condition depleted of advantages once provided to them by the culture. This is not a problem to be solved or a battle to be mounted with the answers and resources at hand. This is now the new land-scape—the new condition under which the institutions of the Spirit must now live.

Disruptions Already Appear

This new landscape is far from fully formed. It is, however, certain that the newer forms for the search for purpose, faith, and meaning that people will continue to pursue will vary widely from the congregational forms we are most familiar and comfortable with. One glimpse into this new landscape is provided by Angie Thurston and Casper ter Kuile, who in 2015 were students at Harvard Divinity School. Both came to the seminary with nontraditional, non-Christian backgrounds but with an awareness of the importance of meaning-making communities. Their unique backgrounds and their sensitivity to millennial values provided them with a lens to see what easily escapes the vision of baby boomer institutional leaders. As they looked about they found significant evidence of spiritual community among millennials, despite the increasing religious disaffiliation that most worries institutional leaders.

Instead of asking how many millennials are participating in already established religious congregations, they asked what millennials were seeking in the communities in which they were involving themselves. From this different question they identified seven themes:[39]

- community: valuing and fostering deep relationships that center on service to others;
- personal transformation: making a conscious and dedicated effort to develop one's own body, mind, and spirit;
- social transformation: pursuing justice and beauty in the world through the creation of networks for good;

- purpose finding: clarifying, articulating, and acting on one's personal mission in life;
- creativity: allowing time and space to activate the imagination and engage in play;
- accountability: holding oneself and others responsible for working toward defined goals; and
- something more: whether profound, transcendent, or God—our love for family and friends, our guiding values, our sense of connection to that which is bigger than ourselves.

One can argue that, at their best, religious congregations reflect these same values as a means of addressing their own theological missions. As such, congregations "have" what millennials are seeking—although obviously not all congregations naturally address all seven themes at the same time. Individual congregations have individual strengths that would lead them to address some themes with greater ease than others. Nonetheless, organized religion rightfully understands itself as holding that which people seek.

What is at issue in the new and changing landscape, however, is that increasingly individuals are not seeking, or not exclusively seeking, to pursue these values through organized religion—through already established congregations. What Thurston and ter Kuile enable us to see is that meaning making is being pursued in the current culture with considerable energy despite the seeming threats of secular humanism and individual consumerism. To support their argument, Thurston and ter Kuile point to an array of organizations and initiatives quite dissimilar from congregations: the Dinner Party, CrossFit, SoulCycle, CTZN-WELL, U.S. Department of Arts and Culture, Millennial Trains Project, Live in the Grey, Juniper Path, Camp Grounded, and the Sanctuaries. Any or all of these newer organizations or initiatives do not easily address all seven of the themes identified by Thurston and ter Kuile, just as any or all congregations do not address them fully. However, millennials and an increasing number of people from other generational cohorts are finding satisfaction for their questions in these different places on the landscape. The new information here is that the "competition" for the hearts and minds of people that established religious institutions now face is not limited to other religions, other denominations, or upstart millennial congregations. People are actively seeking the truths held by our faith traditions but are seeking much more widely and in curious places for the very things for which congregations were once the "one-stop shop." I can only say that as an early baby boomer who has been involved and a leader in organized religion all of my life, the landscape uncovered by Thurston and ter Kuile's work surprised me deeply as I looked at these new additions through their eyes.

I am more convinced than ever that there is no going back. The good news is that we are now freer to move ahead. Leaders, however, will need quiet, purpose-driven courage in order to walk into these new and difficult waters trusting in God's promises.

Part II

The Assumptions

Assumption (definition): a thing that is accepted as true or as certain to happen, without proof.

Assumptions live at the tacit level. They are not deeply hidden from us in the unconscious where we cannot pull them up to inspect and consider them. Rather, they dwell at the tacit level right below our conscious awareness, where they powerfully direct and influence our behavior without being questioned.

3

A WORD ABOUT HOW

Assumptions about Change

In the previous chapter the focus was on significant changes in cultural values that cause institutions such as organized religion to become countercultural. I argued that we cannot recapture the aberrant time, so the current work of leadership will not be supported by the conditions that once favored institutions. We cannot go back again—a reality that leaders must accept in order to move forward, but under vastly different conditions.

In this chapter we need to pick up another fundamental shift—a change in our experience of time. Over the past decades technology and communication have changed time from a linear experience to an instant experience, from progressive to disruptive, and changed responses from sequential to networked.

Change is tricky. It is often hard to know what is actually changing and what is not—hard to determine which perceived changes will produce actual disruption and which are only novelty. I now read a digital newspaper each morning that I download through an Internet subscription. I have changed how I receive my newspaper, but it is not a significant change because it is an extension of an ongoing daily sameness tapping into a source and style of information with which I am familiar and trust. However, if I have a question after reading my newspaper I can type the question into the search engine of my computer and within nanoseconds be provided with literally hundreds of responses and opinions connected to my question. Here the daily sameness of simply wanting information is met with a deceptively deep change in which information is shared without filters, without credentials, and even in support of the provider's own agenda. No longer is this the sameness of familiar, trustworthy information but unfiltered information with potentially behavior-influencing bias. Getting my newspaper on my laptop serves me more as a convenient novelty than as a significant change, but having access to unfiltered, unvetted information through that same laptop has the potential of deep changes in my worldview. What is real change, and what is tactical adaptation to keep things pretty much the same? There are times in which it is important to make the distinction.

A helpful simile was used by Daniel Yankelovich in the last chapter's discussion of cultural values. Yankelovich distinguished between the deeply embedded and hidden "tectonic plates" of cultural values that rest well beneath our daily awareness (like the huge rock plates far below the surface of the planet on which our continents lie) and the daily, easily observable surface behavior that we all witness continually. The simile helps us to understand that when deeply embedded cultural values shift, usually without our ongoing awareness, what we see and experience in the immediate moment in our daily lives can easily be disrupted with earthquake-like force. Changes that disrupt and disturb us at the hidden, tacit level of our assumptions can actually have reordering consequences.

It is here that we need to walk into one of the key shifts in reality that has challenged and changed some of the deepest assumptions about change that guide my work and my understanding of leadership. If the previous chapter was about shifts in cultural values, in this chapter we need to give attention to the shift that has happened with time and the way in which change advances. I can no longer assume that time and change are only linear (progressive, ordered, and controllable) but now must assume that time and change can also be disruptive. I now believe that both linear and nonlinear leadership must be practiced—that leaders need to know the difference and when to practice each or both.

TIME AND MODELS OF CHANGE

Zygmunt Bauman, emeritus professor of sociology at the University of Leeds and the University of Warsaw, introduced the notion of "liquid" modernity in which the context of our living is no longer solid, no longer slow changing and based on certainty. Like postmodernism, which no longer assumes continual, linear progression in the sciences, Bauman reflects a much less solid, malleable, or controllable world related to time. He writes of the passage from the "solid" culture of the past to the "liquid" phase of modernity,

> The condition in which social forms (structures that limit individual choices, institutions that guard repetitions of routines, patterns of acceptable behavior) can no longer (and are not expected) to keep their shape for long, because they decompose and melt faster than the time it takes to cast them, and once they are cast for them to set. Forms, whether already present or only adumbrated, are unlikely to be given enough time to solidify, and cannot serve as frames of reference for human actions and long-term life strategies because of their short life expectation.[1]

The shift to liquid modernity means that the structures and institutions that we use to order our lives no longer serve individuals with stable frames of reference for establishing life projects such as marriage, family, community, career, security, or meaning.

To the point of organizational leadership, consider the impact of liquid modernity on planning, that is, how an organization will order its purpose, goals, and behaviors as it moves into the future. In the solid time of only a few decades ago (the aberrant time of cohesion and convergence) full-blown strategic planning in an organization would, with some confidence, consider five-, ten-, and even fifty-year time-frames for projecting their structure and outcomes. A futurist friend of mine used to say that it isn't hard to be a futurist as long as you don't mind eventually being wrong. In solid times it was possible to be a futurist and be right for at least a while by extending current trends and patterns assuming some level of sameness would continue between the present and the future.

In contrast, it is currently estimated that even massively complex multinational corporations involved in strategic planning will need to redo their work within eighteen to twenty-four months—months, not years. Current realities no longer consistently extend themselves forward. Ongoing work in strategic planning is needed in multinational corporations even before the most recent planning is stabilized. Strategic planning is no longer an *event* (an occasional project of inquiry used to set direction), it is now a *function* (an ongoing conversation necessarily structured into the very fabric of the organization). Said another way, for both individuals and organizations episodic learning is no longer sufficient. In a liquid time, learning must be continual. It is here that we begin to address one of the key shifts in reality. Time and change are no longer only linear. They are also disruptive.

Linear Models of Change

I was born into a linear world and trained in linear leadership. The models of change that I held allowed me to assume some level of control over my future. And models of change are very powerful. Models of change are assumptions about how the world works—assumptions that live at the tacit level without daily inspection or consideration but fully capable of influencing my behavior. The assumption of linear time and of linear change means that one can assume that there is a "right way" to be in the world and that one's current path can be corrected (problem planning) or progressively projected (developmental planning). In my consulting work I would help leaders first determine their goals in planning using the following descriptors.

Type 1: Problem Planning

- Short-term planning
- Problem-solving methodology designed to fix things
- Goal: to return things to the way they were before the problem
- Timetable: immediate and short term

Type 2: Developmental Planning

- Long-range planning
- Asks the questions, "What's next?" and "What do we do now?"
- The assumption is that things are good and that what we are currently doing in ministry is faithful and appropriate

- Goal: to determine the next steps, building on what is presently being done
- Timetable: takes three to six months to complete; commonly revisited or revised every one to two years[2]

In both of these cases, types 1 and 2, there are assumptions of linear progressivism—that given the current situation leaders can either correct what is not right (problem solving) or extend what is already working (developmental). Progressivism is a mode of social reform that assumes that the future can be shaped gradually or in stages, proceeding step by step. In terms of leadership, the leader (1) takes a measure of where the organization is at the current moment; then (2) projects or develops scenarios of the preferred future state; (3) measures the difference between the current moment and the preferred future; and then (4) identifies the steps or actions necessary to move from one to the other. Functioning as a leader in a linear mode is highly dependent on logic, assumes stability and continuity, and allows for the assumption of control. The linear model of change also moves rapidly from planning to action in its four progressive steps.

I was trained in and practiced linear models of change because they work. They worked well in the past. They continue to work well in the present. Under certain circumstances.

Conditions of a Steady State: Clear Problems, Shared Consensus

Linear models of change work well *when the leader is faced with a problem.* In chapter 2 we began with the distinction between technical and adaptive work, a critical difference described by Ron Heifetz in his work on leadership. Technical work is the application of known solutions to known problems. Leaders in congregations are very familiar with these kinds of situations. If you are a leader in a congregation in New England and your sanctuary heater fails on a Tuesday in February, you have a clear problem and you turn quickly to the steps of the linear change model in order to get heat back long before the Sunday morning worship service. If, looking ahead at program development, you see that you have a growing youth group but lack trained leaders, you move quickly with your newly defined problem, with linear steps, to find a solution. When the problem is clear and the solution is known, leaders move directly to action. (Clear problem > known solution > action.)

Similarly, linear models of change work well *when there is a clear, shared consensus on outcomes* by the people involved. This is Charles Handy's convergent situation, also described in chapter 2. A convergent situation is one in which both the question and the answer are the same for the people involved. "What is the shortest route to Bath?" is the example used by Handy. If all the people faced with this question are standing in the same room, the answer is obviously the same for all. The leader moves quickly to the steps of the linear model and soon the shortest route is determined. For a convergent question, there is a "right" answer. Convergence supplies direction and energy, even when there are multiple opinions among those involved. It may not be as clear as the known solution to a familiar problem, but leaders can follow a linear path to a convergent agreement seen as a "right" way to move ahead. For example, if a congregation has energy and agreement that in planning the next chapter of their life together they need to focus on outreach and growth among new and younger people who, they have learned, do not find the current sanctuary space, liturgy, or music inviting, there is already a convergence that allows direct movement to linear action. Leaders can project scenarios of different space, liturgy, and music that will accompany (not replace) the current practice of the congregation and move to the most plausible action plans. There may still be multiple opinions and preferences among church members, but the convergence around the importance of these next steps for the congregation allows for linear action that moves to action as the right thing to do.

While linear models of change can be described in relatively simple ways, they are effective in remarkably complicated situations. *American Icon* is the 2012 bestselling story of the turnaround of the Ford Motor Company.[3] By 2008 Ford was in a cash crisis, facing rising gas prices and growing Japanese competition while still reeling from their 2001 third-quarter $6 billion loss. Internally they were hampered by a deeply ingrained careerist culture that pitted leaders against one another. Offered a government bailout, Ford decided to save itself and new CEO Alan Mulally began the work of problem identification and problem solving, building a convergent leadership team as he moved ahead. A clear vision and polestar guide for company goals were developed. Regular and required points of accountability were installed through weekly BRMs (business review meetings) and SARs (special attention reviews).

Ten clear rules of leadership behavior were established. Data, specific targeted data, were used to measure and direct each step forward. More complicated than a broken sanctuary heater or a youth group without trained leaders, nonetheless there is similarity in the leadership model followed by new CEO Mulally, who saw clear problems that he could recognize from his previous work at the Boeing Corporation.

Moving Beyond Linearity: Complicated or Complex

"Complicated" is described by General Stanley McChrystal as having "many parts, but those parts are joined, one to the next, in relatively simple ways: one cog turns, causing the next one to turn as well, and so on. The workings of a complicated device like an internal combustion engine can be broken down into a series of neat and tidy deterministic relationships."[4] Simple or complicated, clear problems in a convergent situation respond to linear models of change.

McChrystal is the retired four-star general whose last assignment was as commander of all American and coalition forces in Afghanistan. McChrystal went to war with the highly organized chain of command tools of an army learned and skilled in linear history, linear strategies, and linear tactics. Now retired, he is a senior fellow at Yale University's Jackson Institute for Global Affairs and writes about the changed realities of leadership. McChrystal is clear that leaders increasingly face not *complicated* but *complex* situations. In his leadership role in Afghanistan he learned that even the nature of war had changed. "The war we had to wage was not only different from fighting a nation-state," he wrote, "it was different from any kind of war waged in the twentieth century. Insurgency, terrorism, and radicalization are as old as conflict itself, but by 2004 those phenomenon had been coupled with new technological variables to create an entirely new problem set . . . we came to understand that defeating AQI [al Qaeda in Iraq] would necessitate learning from them."[5] More than a war complicated by a different enemy in an unfamiliar terrain, McChrystal identified the shift from complicated to complex.

Different from complicated, "complexity . . . occurs when the number of interactions between components increases dramatically—the interdependencies that allow viruses and bank runs to spread: this is where things quickly became unpredictable. Think of the 'break' in a pool game—the first forceful strike of the colored balls with the white cue ball. Although there are only sixteen balls on the table and the physics is that of simple mechanics, it is almost impossible to predict where everything will end up. . . . The density of interactions means that even a relatively small number of elements can quickly defy prediction."[6]

Liquid, Nonlinear Realities

Yes, there are still known problems with known solutions. Yes, it is still possible to form convergent consensus that, despite differences and opinions, can move ahead with agreement. Yes, there are still situations that are merely complicated and that with patience can be tackled. However, it is increasingly the case that leaders are confronted with the complexity of uncontrollable and unpredictable interactions. It is increasingly the case that leaders are faced with divergent disagreements over the structure of the question, even before considering what an appropriate answer might be.

For example, many of the U.S. denominations have been in protracted discomfort, up to the point of conflict, over issues of homosexuality, particularly as it relates to the Christian understanding of human sexuality, same-sex marriage, and ordination of gays. As leaders wade into these waters they discover that

- some approach scriptural texts literally, while others approach texts historically, while others approach texts interpretively;
- some acknowledge current polity as authoritative, while others consider current polity as outdated;
- some lift issues of sexual behavior to the status of definitive of faith, while others see sexual behavior as life options that they may or may not agree with;
- some see homosexuality as sin, while others see homosexuality as within the normative human continuum of sexual response;
- some would limit homosexuals only to membership in the church, while others see social injustice if homosexuals are not offered full inclusion into leadership;
- and the differences go on . . .

All of these differences are commonly found at some level within all denominations, particularly those large national or global denominations that range across red and blue states or cross global cultures, where in some nations homosexual and transgender individuals are being elected to national offices, while in other nations homosexuality is illegal and punishable by a prison sentence. This is more than complicated; it is complex. Consider the possible interactions that will leap about unpredictably and can be quickly coupled with technology to organize people of one opinion against all other opinions.

It is in such a situation that leaders in the new liquid world need the wisdom to know when something is not a problem. This is the nonlinear world of Ron Heifetz's adaptive leadership. If technical work is the application of known solutions to known problems, such nonlinear situations do not fit the form. At heart is the reality that leaders cannot move to answers when there is no problem. By definition, something cannot be a problem if there is no real solution. Unlike the simple problem of a broken bone, the interactions of differing and competing worldviews such as those driving the contest over homosexuality have no simple answer but are, in fact, a *condition* that now lives within faith communities. That which is not a problem is a condition. Complex situations with unpredictable interactions have no solution and do not respond to the action-oriented progression of problem-solving steps. Indeed, Heifetz is quick to point out how leaders actually do more harm by using problem-solving, technical models in adaptive situations. He writes, "Indeed the harsher the reality, the harder we look to authority for a remedy that saves us from adjustment."[7] The more anxious the people are in our changed liquid reality, the more they look to leaders for clear, simple, linear solutions that reduce anxiety even when they don't help move to the future. However, complexity and unpredictable interactions that defy linear planning or clear solutions are increasingly the conditions of a liquid culture. We continue to move farther away from our linear, predictable, controllable past.

We are now living more fully in Handy's divergent world in which no question has a single answer and in which each question must be viewed from the perspective of the holder. We are now more fully in Heifetz's description of adaptive work, which does not move directly to action but rather to learning.

Linear: (Clear problem > Known Solution > Action)
Nonlinear: (Presenting Issue > Complex Interactions > Learning)

Note the critical distinction. Linear models lead us directly to decision making and action. Nonlinear models lead us to learning. If a broken bone is a clear problem, chronic asthma is not—it is a condition. It is not a problem because it is *chronic*—by definition it cannot be solved. The appropriate response requires everyone involved to learn. The patient, as well as family and friends, must learn new limits and capacities, must learn helpful and harmful responses, and must learn new definitions of a satisfying life. In turn the physician must learn how much information is helpful to the person, how the person responds or doesn't respond to treatment and lifestyle changes, and how to work with insurance and family and community resources. Linear assumptions, in such situations, move us much too quickly to action—a temptation we will take up later. Do not miss the key insight of General McChrystal noted earlier; he needed to come to understand that if his army was to defeat al Qaeda, it would necessitate learning from them.

Leading in a Culture of Change

There are many books written about leading change. Many, if not most, identify linear steps and stages of work for leaders to follow in order to produce (manage, control) change within their organizations. Much more realistic for the current liquid time is Michael Fullan's book on leading *in a culture of change*. In many situations leaders are not faced with the need to create or control change but rather how to manage themselves and their organizations in the swirling change that is already happening within and about them in ways that seem to defy control. Fullan is a leading international authority on educational reform, working in educational institutions that, like religious institutions and so many other long-established organizations, find themselves to be stable (rigid) to the point of resisting change while living in an environment of constant change that buffets them about. Rather than encouraging leaders to find solutions, Fullan encourages leaders to find ways to disturb. Drawing on the work of Pascale, Millemann, and Gioja, who look at leadership in relationship to chaos, Fullan notes that living systems (like schools, churches, and businesses) cannot be directed along a linear path because of the complexity that makes unforeseen conse-quences inevitable. Instead leaders must learn how to *disturb their systems* "in a manner that approximates the desired outcomes."[8] Philos-opher Ken Wilber makes a similar point with his wonderful language suggesting leaders "work to trim-tab (or adjust through leadership)" in order to steer closer to the truth needed or the change desired.[9] Trim tabs are the much smaller, adjustable parts of the larger rudder on a ship. By moving the much smaller trim tab, a negative pressure builds up, pulling the much larger rudder in the needed direction. When direct control over the system is not possible, the much smaller but strategic effort of disturbing the system, the negative pressure of a trim tab question, or intervention by the leader can dramatically influence the system's direction, if not completely control its course.

For leaders to intentionally disturb their systems may seem both counterintuitive and unsatisfying at a time when people are already anxious about their future. Nonetheless, there are conditions under which we can only move ahead with right questions that disturb rather than satisfying answers that produce unproductive calm. Earlier in this chapter I noted two types of planning that I followed in my consulting work: problem planning and developmental planning. Appropriate to linear situations, these forms of planning searched directly for answers and next steps. However, as I worked with leaders I also searched for type 3 situations and encouraged leaders to consider whether or not this nonlinear approach was more appropriate.

Type 3: Frame-Bending Planning

- Asks essential formation questions, "Who are we?," "What are we called to do?," and "Who is our neighbor?"
- The assumption is that things are not working and that what we are currently doing in ministry is not faithful and effective
- Goal: to go back to the beginning and examine our purpose and call from God
- Timetable: takes twelve to eighteen months to complete, com-monly revisited or revised every three to five years[10]

Over the years I have learned so much more about nonlinear leader-ship, its effect on any form of planning, and the timelines involved. But note that such frame-bending work hangs on questions that disturb. To ask "Who are we?" is a deeply disturbing question because it challenges us with a question for which we actually think we have an answer. Subsequently I have learned to approach this question in a slightly different form, asking, "Who are we *now*?" Consider that most people think of themselves as younger than they actually are. It is a common experience that sets groups of people to laughing if you ask how many people think of themselves as younger. But thinking of ourselves as younger than we are suggests rather directly that we consciously know more about who we *once were* than more realistically about who we currently *are*. Similarly, congregations, denominations, and all other well-established organizations and institutions know much more about who they once were than about who they are. Such a deceptively simple question can be deeply disturbing. Such disturbing questions open the door to nonlinear change.

A Nonlinear Model of Change

For more than twenty-five years I have carried with me a simple nonlinear model of change to help guide my thinking and my steps when problem-solving models could not help. The model comes from John Scherer, president of John Scherer Associates and former president of the Association of Creative Change.[11] While much more has been learned about nonlinear conditions during this twenty-five-year period, this model has provided the basic building blocks I have used to both diagnose a situation and guide my responses.

To begin as a point of contrast, let's recall the *linear model* described earlier in this chapter. The linear steps are:

1. take a measure of where the organization is at the current moment;
2. project or develop scenarios of the preferred future state;
3. measure the difference between 1 and 2; and
4. identify the steps or actions necessary to move from 1 to 2.

Quite different, a *nonlinear approach* includes leadership steps that make the organization's work more difficult and more anxious—preconditions for deeper change. The stages of a nonlinear model are:

1. connect the organization to its realistic pain;
2. help the organization capture its possibility;
3. challenge the organization to step out of its box;
4. accompany the organization into its subsequent chaos; and
5. support the learning and reordering that will come from the work.

Connect the Organization to Its Realistic Pain

Scherer defines pain as the "awareness of an unacceptable disequilibrium, or a significant discrepancy between the way things *are* and the way things *could be*."[12] This is the "disturbing the system" that Fullan points to. It is the first step of providing the honest picture of the current reality of the organization in a way that is not deflected or denied. It is the pastor or lay leader helping the church see that as much as they talk about being part of the community, they do not know the people living around their building and have not participated in any community events or issues for years. It is the middle judicatory executive pointing out that the continual emphasis on numeric growth in congregations has reinforced an internal focus on the viability of the congregation without any encouragement for the congregation to focus on the needs of others in their community.

Data and discovery are the tools of introducing appropriate pain. The leader must help the organization use its own information to draw a different picture of itself. Such pain is the adaptive gap between what an organization says it does and what it actually puts its hand to. The first step of a nonlinear model of change is the introduction of conscious discomfort into the system because within that pain is the motivation to be different. I have long appreciated the aphorism that "you can't steer a parked car." There must be movement within the organization, emotional or purposeful, positive or negative, to have any hope of thriving in change. Such movement can be the product of discomfort with what is. The only deadly posture for an organization is stasis—the equilibrium that comes from a satisfaction that clings to an earlier time.

Help the Organization Capture Its Possibility

If pain is the awareness of an unacceptable state, possibility recognizes that something better can be achieved. As Scherer described it, "The overweight person must actually see himself leaner and more healthy. The work team or organization must see the possibility of the situation resolved, productivity at peak levels, the crisis yielding to break-through."[13] If pain provides motivation, possibility provides direction. The reality is that pain without possibility is debilitating. To face into one's pain without any hope to move beyond it incapacitates both the individual and the organization. Yet false hopes and easy answers to pain short-circuit the future by allowing the organization to recognize its situation but remain complacent, believing that the situation will be cared for simply with patience or easy steps—it is denial and work avoidance. Leaders must carefully shape possibilities, not as answers to the organization's pain but as worthwhile paths of learning, experiments to explore, or investments that will make a critical difference—but always as something that the organization does not currently understand or know how to do. The possibility must bear some cost to the organization.

Pain plus possibility. A nonlinear approach needs to hold these two together at the beginning. Together they are identified by Scherer as the "parents" of change—both motivation and direction must be present if change is to be birthed.

Challenge the Organization to Step Out of Its Box

This is perhaps one of the more difficult of the requirements of a nonlinear approach because leaders live in the same box as others in their organization. The box referred to is established by the norms and assumptions that live at the tacit level of our awareness—in between the conscious world we are constantly aware of and the unconscious world that we cannot access. We can understand this tacit level, but the fact that it is daily hidden from us by our assumptions and established practices makes it very difficult to "think outside" its established limits. If congregations are still membership organizations in which "belong-ing" is seen as the condition of full inclusion marked by a membership ritual with membership vows, it is difficult for the congregation to step out of the box to find ways to build relationships with people who want to participate in other than membership terms. If worship is the prime (and, in an increasing number of congregations, the only) time of the gathering of the community, it is difficult for the congregation to wel-come those who want to be part of their mission but may not want to be involved in worship beyond occasionally. If ordination and assignment/ appointment/call are the terms of clergy relationship with the denomination, it is difficult for the denomination to relate to and support the ministry of nontraditional pastors who may be effective in reaching others but eschew ordination and formal connection.

The role of the leader at this stage in nonlinear change is simply to challenge old assumptions and ways of thinking (difficult enough for leaders also marinated in the box of those same assumptions and ways of thinking). This is the stage of asking "what if" questions without knowing how to move beyond the "what if" stage. It is not an exercise of leadership that is highly rewarded because it introduces additional levels of frustration to others rather than the clarity and action that is desired.

Accompany the Organization into Its Subsequent Chaos

If stepping out of the box with questions is difficult for leaders because of their own boxed-in condition, accompanying the organization into chaos is the most threatening stage of nonlinear work. Managers help organizations do things right; leaders help organizations do right things. When the conditions confronting the organization cannot be solved, then stepping into the unknown to learn new ways of thinking, new ways of being, and new ways of doing is the right thing to do. However, as noted from the beginning of the book, it is not rewarded. People in organizations do not want their leaders to make their work more difficult and to add to their anxiety by producing questions without answers. It is often easier for consultants to do this work because they are not fully in the system and subject to the full reward processes of the system. At their best, consultants are trained to stand with people as the people do their own work without allowing the people to turn to the consultant as if he or she is an "expert" with answers in hand. As leaders who are fully in the system step in to do this work, it is helpful for the others in the organization to at least be helped to understand why their leader is pursuing questions without knowing the answers.

Stepping into questions without answers produces chaos, and chaos is the right condition in which deep change can happen. It is a form of change that can neither be predicted nor controlled. More will be said about this chaos because, especially for religious organizations and religious people, this chaos is a primary medium for the hand of God. But for the moment I simply want to recognize that the appropriate role of the leader is simply to stand with the people in their confusion and discernment in their chaos. It takes courage to stand with people as they face into questions for which there are no known answers—quiet courage. And so this part of leadership in nonlinear moments following an aberrant time is very much the subject of the larger book and much more than a posture or technique for leaders to learn.

Support the Learning and the Reordering That Will Come from the Work

What comes from a willing, purposeful wandering in chaos are new insights, changed perspectives, untried ideas, and corrected directions. The task of the leader is to help the organization capture and use these new, changed, untried, and corrected insights and to test them against their purpose.

Any organization can create more work for itself. The old adage "When we don't know what to do, we do what we know" describes the busyness that can be created by an organization addressing its anxiety by doing more of what it already knows how to do. What leaders in nonlinear situations need to continually scan for is "worthy work"— work that is within the capacity of the organization (we can do it) and that will also address our purpose in a new and untried way (it can make a difference). It is quite possible for organizations in the chaos of nonlinear times to learn things without knowing it. The leader needs to assume that quiet, dispassionate place of reflecting on what of value is being learned or discovered in their wanderings and then reflect it back to the people, asking, "What now will we do with this?" It is from this reflecting and questioning that next steps will be formed. It is from experimenting with next steps that new paths can be found. Not clear, not controlled, not predictable—nonlinear processes raise anxiety and risk. Hence the need for quiet courage. Such processes, however, are fundamental to liquid times.

More about Chaos: "Then Something Happens Here"

To walk willingly into chaos is to accept mystery. A long-remembered cartoon pictures two mathematicians standing in front of a full wall-sized blackboard filled from top to bottom with a single, exceedingly complex equation that ends at the bottom with the solution = 0. One mathematician is explaining the equation in all its preciseness to the other by pointing to an empty box at the end of the equation that immediately precedes the solution of 0, saying, "Then something happens here."

This is the chaos that is creative—to take all that you know and still accept that something will happen that you can't explain, predict, or control. It is willingly standing at the edge between the known and the unknown. We have known about this edge for a long time. It had been around for long enough to be captured in the 1995 novel *The Lost World* by Michael Crichton:

> Complex systems tend to locate themselves at the place we call "the edge of chaos." We imagine the edge of chaos as a place where there is enough innovation to keep a living system vibrant, and enough stability to keep it from collapsing into anarchy. It is a zone of conflict and upheaval, where the old and the new are constantly at war. Finding the balance must be a delicate matter. . . . Only at the edge of chaos can complex systems flourish. [14]

This is creative space. Through the work of Nobel physicist Ilya Prigogine we learned the phenomena of self-renewal and self-transcendence as principles of self-organizing systems. [15] Any system (like a congregation or a denomination) held in chaos long enough will self-organize. It will renew itself and transcend beyond its former self to accommodate and relate much more effectively with its new environment. Beginning in the 1970s the lessons of the new physics caught the eye of both philosophers and scientists as writings began to appear comparing the complementarity of the new teachings of physics and the ancient teachings of world religions, Buddhism in particular. The world of understanding (science) and the world of meaning (faith) were finding new attractions and similarities.

But much more to the point of the Christian community and the difficulty of leaders standing in the liminal space at the edge of chaos is that Christianity has long understood (if not practiced) the power of chaos to form and reform. God created out of nothing and formed the world from chaos. The ongoing metaphor for chaos in both the Hebrew Bible and the New Testament is the "wilderness." It is in the wilderness that one gives up control and is reformed/transformed. Alan Roxburgh reminds us that God is the active agent of change in his review of the depth of cultural change facing the church.[16] The story of Exodus is formative to the Judeo-Christian faiths. Yet in this foundational story of the saving and the reforming of God's people, the only character in the story with agency is God. Moses, who seems at first to be the main character in the narrative, understands that he cannot accomplish what God asks, and he tries to withdraw, asking, "Who am I to go to Pharaoh and to bring the Israelites out of Egypt?" (Exodus 3:11). Then, asking who this God is that sends him on such a task, Moses is given the nonanswer of "I am who I am" (Exodus 3:14), which offers no information or control for Moses to use in his negotiations for the future. Sent into the wilderness with no directions, Moses gets no answers about how to live there until he gets to the mountain (Exodus 3:12). Unsure how to sustain the people, Moses must depend on the fragile appearance of manna and quail (Exodus 16). Not sure how to move ahead, Moses must follow pillars of cloud and fire (Exodus 13:21–22). As Roxburgh appropriately notes, "at each step of the negotiations God gives Moses a way forward but no control."[17]

Problems lend themselves to control. Liquid time in which we are faced with conditions built on divergence do not respond to control, but they do provide new ways to be and to act in the world if we willingly stand in the chaos open to change. So should leaders pursue the problem solving of linear change? Or should leaders risk standing with people in their chaos to be open to nonlinear opportunities? Yes. If the models of change that we carry direct our behavior, then this is clearly a moment in which leaders need both—and need to know when to apply each. Leaders need to know how to exercise structure and control in the linear moments. Leaders must also know how to step into the open posture of learning when facing nonlinear conditions. And, assuredly, leaders stepping into nonlinear change in liquid times need quiet courage.

4

A WORD ABOUT ENOUGH

Assumptions about Resources

Assumptions powerfully direct and influence behavior without being questioned. Despite all that is being said about the *shrinking* middle class in America, the majority of Americans continue to self-identify as part of that middle class. "Cognitive science teaches us that we learn to make sense of the world by putting things into categories," notes Anat Shenker-Osario, independent researcher and communications consultant.[1] In order to identify what category they fit, people naturally turn to popular depictions of wealth (Real Housewives, pop stars, the Kardashians, the Gateses, Fortune 500 CEOs) and of poverty (urban blight, breadlines, homelessness), and, not finding themselves in either, they assume they must be in the middle—that is, middle class. However, such assumptions direct behavior. If people actually fall at the lower end of the economic scale, a complacency about being middle class may inhibit behaviors such as taking advantage of a 401K retirement plan that could help to secure their future. If people actually fall on the higher end of the economic scale, a fear about their security as part of the middle class may hamper a more effective use of their resources to contribute to a saner, more equitable world.

Assumptions matter because they direct behavior. To check assumptions they need to be drawn up into the light from their hidden, tacit level of consciousness where they do their work. While this book will explore four sets of assumptions that need to be challenged in order to form the quiet courage of leadership needed in this postaberrant time, the two that need to be most directly challenged are assumptions about how change happens (chapter 3) and assumptions about resources. These two sets of assumptions are most influential on how institutions and their mission will or won't move ahead.

LIVING UNDER THE MYTH OF LIMITED RESOURCES

Growing up in the aberrant post–World War II period shaped a memory of growth and strength for many of our current institutional leaders. There was a demographic burst of growth as soldiers returned from the war and created a baby boom. There was economic growth as the United States shifted from a war economy to a manufacturing economy that, as the only major nation that exited the war with its economy intact, allowed the United States to capture the major share of global manufacturing. People were pushed toward membership organizations such as churches, so there was no lack of people power and volunteerism in local churches. As pointed out earlier, church construction in the short period of fifteen years following the war increased by more than 350 percent. In addition there was a platform for the voices of the church to have public impact, from Reinhold and Richard Niebuhr's theological influence, to George Buttrick's pulpit presence, to Billy Graham's evangelical fervor, to Archbishop Fulton Sheen's ecclesiastical popularity.

With a constant flow of resources, the generational cohorts following the war operated on the assumption of always having resources available—resources needing to be managed, to be sure, but always available. Additive decision making became a somewhat addictive behavior that later proved hard to break. Additive decision making is simply the assumption that decisions always come down to "yes." If someone comes up with another idea or need, then yes, it can and will be added to the list because there is always a way to direct attention and resources to one more thing. Middle judicatories routinely set priorities in additive ways in the decades of the 1950s, 1960s, and 1970s.

A priority is meant to be the thing that is to be given attention over other things. Priority suggests limiting the number of things to which attention is given. However, the assumption of a continuing flow of resources encouraged leaders to approach a priority not as that which is more important than others things but rather as one of a growing list of issues or needs that constituent members were concerned about—all of equal importance and all able to be addressed because of the people, dollars, and influence that continued to flow. Additive decision making increased the complexity of congregational and denominational structures as each new issue or group was given a committee and budget in order to take their place in the line of important things for the church to address. Additive decision making meant there was something for everyone. The resource lessons of those postwar decades supported the spending of money because in an expanding economy you can spend money today with the assumption that there will always be more tomorrow—and with inflation it is better to spend money today because it is worth more than it will be tomorrow.

If *having* resources was assumed, the corollary assumption that was spawned was of *needing* resources in order to address the issues and priorities of the mission of an institution. If resources of people, dollars, and influence were the way in which ministry happened, then in order to make ministry happen leaders needed to produce people, dollars, and influence. Instead of believing in the manna that came from God's hand, the church learned to set its own table and provide its own feast. Friend John Wimmer of the Lilly Endowment, Inc., was the one who most helped me to understand the functional atheism that so many leaders in the church began to practice. The functional atheist is the one who speaks about God as the active agent of salvation in the life of individuals and in producing a wholeness in the world but who then assumes that nothing is going to change unless and until he or she puts his or her hand (and resources) to it. Mystery does not operate in the mind of the functional atheist because the empty box of the cartoon mathematicians where "something happens here" always has to be filled in with the knowledge, resources, and leadership of the functional atheist. While speaking of depending on God, the functional atheist actively depends on his or her own agency and the resources that can be produced—again missing the point of Bill Coffin's prayer about our more complicated blessings that include our lack of resources, "which points to the only truly renewable resources, the resources of the Spirit."

With an earlier remembered time of abundant resources as the baseline against which other times are measured, the current moment of declining memberships and budgets has been reshaped with assumptions of scarcity. People no longer naturally flow into congregations supported by cultural messages of the importance of belonging. Time and dollars are subject to intense competition in an age of consumerism and technology, and neither volunteerism nor dollars flow so naturally toward congregations or other institutions that don't offer direct services in return. In a convergent postwar period there was sufficient public consensus about values and behavior that supported the few articulate voices of influence like the Niebuhrs, Buttrick, Graham, and Sheen, assuming that they spoke for all, or at least for many. In the present divergent time voices of influence have no singular platform and so become reduced to competing voices representing their much smaller, segmented audiences. People, dollars, and influence seem to have evaporated, producing a myth of scarcity. It is, however, a myth because the scarcity that now directs the behavior of so many leaders is built on old assumptions that can be challenged and reshaped. The reality is that the church could once again authentically pick up the words of Paul, who wrote to the Philippians, saying, "My God will meet your every need out of his riches in the glory that is found in Christ Jesus" (Philippians 4:19). However, confronting our present myth of scarcity will take the quiet courage of leaders to face into their addiction to additive decision making and require them to come to terms with understanding "enough."

Additive Decision Making and Learning to Say No

If additive decision making is the constant "yes" of adding multiple ideas, needs, and concerns of constituents to the laundry list of priorities that demand attention and resources, then breaking the addiction requires making choices: choosing "yes" for only the most important and "no" for all others.

A rising tide raises all ships. That well-known aphorism gives reason to the earlier additive lists of priorities that made everyone happy by seeing their idea or issue on the list of priorities on which the local church or middle judicatory was going to spend its time, people, and dollars. In 2011 journalist Thomas Friedman and foreign policy professor Michael Mandelbaum collaborated on their book *That Used to Be Us*, which describes how the United States is beginning to collapse under the many prior decisions and commitments of its own addictive decision making that can no longer be sustained. In a chapter about how the United States is compromising its future, they wrote, "It may be possible to grow effectively without a plan, but there is no way to shrink effectively without a plan."[2] Businesses, congregations, and nations can grow without a plan if they are living in an aberrant time that supports growth of all things. A rising tide raises all ships, whether there are plans to rise or not. Decisions are easy to make because so many of them fall into the category of "yes." Unwise decisions are hidden because the loss created gets filled quickly by the people, dollars, and influence that continue to flow.

However, when the aberrant time is over, a plan is needed and decisions take on a different character. Decisions in such a time represent actual choices. The leader must help the people say that "this" is more important than "that." Additive lists of priorities and preferences can no longer be sustained and choices must be made. To break the addiction of making everyone happy (and being subsequently rewarded as a leader), the leader must have a reason for making a choice. Such choices can be made only when the leader has first helped the people shape and form themselves around a purpose. Having a purpose that is held with greater value than people's preferences and personal interests allows for actual decision making in which real choices assign yes to "this" and no to "that."

Enough

And then there is the understanding of "enough." If breaking addictive additive decision making is necessary to see past the myth of scarcity, understanding the importance of enough is the supporting counterpart. Of the favorite novelists that I carry with me from my younger days, Kurt Vonnegut is certainly on top of the list, and Joseph Heller comes quickly behind. Somewhere I picked up the story about these two writers who were attending a party together that was hosted by a billionaire whose extravagance was widely known. Vonnegut was to have turned to Heller and said something to the effect of, "Joe, how does it make you feel to know that our host made more money in the time we have been at this party than all of the royalties you got from *Catch-22*?" To which Heller responded, "That may be. But I have one thing that our host will never have. Enough."

Having built the current versions of our congregations and denominations in a time of growth in which resources flowed, those congregations and denominations now have complex structures and practices, properties and assets demanding maintenance, multiple programs and initiatives that exist apart from any accountability to what they are intended to produce, all of which are staff dependent. With the stemmed tide of resources of people, dollars, and influence it is easy to see that these institutions no longer can afford to sustain what was earlier built. What is currently being learned is that there is no longer what is needed to continue what has always been done but that there are sufficient resources for what we are now called to do. There is enough.

SCARCITY, ABUNDANCE, AND SUFFICIENCY (ENOUGH)

"Money is like an iron ring we put through our nose. It is now leading us around wherever it wants. We just forgot that we are the ones who designed it."[3] So begins Lynne Twist's important conversation about money as she quotes Mark Kinney. Twist is a global activist and fundraiser whose understanding of resources and money is framed from a lifetime of working side by side with both the wealthiest and the poorest people on our planet. She calls scarcity "the Great Lie," even when she is in the poorest of the undeveloped areas of the world. In particular, scarcity is a lie in North America, one of the richest pockets of the globe. "Yet, surprisingly," she writes, "in that world of overabundance, too, the conversation is dominated by what they don't have and what they want to get. No matter who we are or what our circumstances, we swim in conversations about what there isn't enough of."[4] She notes how often conversations revolve around not getting enough sleep, not having enough time, or not having the "right" clothes. While living in the midst of abundance, people still measure their lives by what they don't have. It is not an issue of money. It is the condition of living with the assumptions chosen. It is a mindset.

If their anxiety and their conversations center on scarcity, people's aspirations gravitate toward abundance. Particularly in the church, people resonate to God's abundant hand, developing liturgies of thanks for God's abundance and theologies of abundance to explain God's creative richness. However, Twist points out that stretching for abundance to counterbalance scarcity is belied by the way in which people cling to the toxic myth that more is better. In a consumer-driven society there is always "more"—a more that is presented without ceasing through the delivery systems of TVs, computers, and the growing insidiousness of technological marketing that tracks how any and every product that catches an individual's attention can be followed with personal deals and offers that match his or her longings. Twist notes, "When we buy into the promise that more is better, we can never arrive."[5] Living in a mindset of scarcity, people seek abundance. But by defining abundance as "more," people are back to measuring what they don't have—because there is always "more."

"Sufficiency resides inside each of us," Twist continues, "and we can call it forward. It is a consciousness, an attention, an intentional choosing of the way we think about our circumstances. In our relationship with money, it is using money in a way that expresses our integrity; using it in a way that *expresses* value rather than *determining* value."[6] Like all assumptions that live at the tacit level, assumptions of scarcity can be examined and transformed, allowing people to connect in a new way with the sufficiency that is already at hand.

For example, beginning with the work of David Cooperrider of Case Western Reserve University, the quest for "appreciative inquiry" has been a strategy for searching and using the sufficiency that already surrounds us.[7] Consider the difference made if leaders simply adjust their normative problem solving by choosing to revise their assumptions and subsequently their questions.[8] In normative problem solving people operate on the assumption that there is something missing—and it calls for a fix.

Problem solving:

- What problems are you having?
- How will you fix them?

Fixing something calls on the expenditure of resources, and the agency remains within the problem solver. A problem assumes that something is missing, and a fix assumes that what is missing must be supplied. Something more is needed. The leader must supply resources to make the something more happen.

However, in appreciative inquiry the assumptions shift and instead of searching for what is missing, the search is for what is already provided.

Appreciative inquiry:

- What problems are you having?
- What is working around here?

Instead of looking for what is missing, this different assumption allows the leader to go in search of what is already provided. It is not an assumption of scarcity that sends people in search of missing answers and resources. It is an assumption of sufficiency that sends people in search of what is already available so that they can learn from and extend what already is. At a time when the aberrant flow of resources has been stemmed, people are fully free (without any Pollyannaish naïveté of any kind) to change their assumptions to depend on what God has already given and what God is already doing. It will be enough.

WHAT WE NEED TO WRESTLE WITH IN ORDER TO BE ENRICHED WITH ENOUGH

The hard work of challenging and changing the assumptions that drive people's behavior requires not only that old assumptions be brought into the light of day for examination but also that alternative ideas and insights be found to free people from the constraints of the old assumptions. There are three newer ideas and insights that are most helpful.

Understanding the Difference between Outcomes and Resources

W. Edwards Deming was an organizational consultant who is credited with turning Japanese manufacturing around following World War II. Prior to the war Japan was globally recognized as producing "junk"— inferior products of questionable worth. During the war Japan's manufacturing cities and factories were destroyed. As Japan's leaders began to rebuild they called on Deming, who described himself as a "statistical philosopher," for help. In the process Deming did not just help the

Japanese rebuild what they once had. Rather, he helped them transform their manufacturing into an industry that, to this day, leads other nations in technology, quality, and inventiveness.

Deming had a rather simple philosophical approach to understanding human systems, to which he added strict statistical measures and guides for productivity and continuous improvement.[9] The basic Deming model will be picked up again in chapter 9 in a more thorough manner when we explore the temptation of tiredness. For the present it is sufficient to begin with a rudimentary outline of the basics of any system as defined by Deming.

Deming's idea was that any system can be understood as constructed of three component parts: the input (that which goes into the system), the throughput (that which the system does to, or the way the system uses, the inputs), and the output (or outcome, that difference that the system is trying to make).[10] A simple diagram of such a system is shown in figure 4.1.

At the heart of the church's struggle with resources is the common dilemma that nonprofits routinely do not know what clear difference they are trying to make. In other words, nonprofits (of which churches and middle judicatories are clear examples) do not know what their intended and intentional outcome is. Rather than thinking in terms of outcomes, nonprofits more commonly think in terms of aspirations—again, a topic to be further addressed in chapter 9.

The church thinks of its work as changing lives, changing communities, or changing the world (all of which are aspirations) without saying specifically what must be intentionally made different (a clear outcome) in order to make a person's life, community, or world changed in a better or more faithful way. Because the church and other nonprofits

INPUT	**THROUGHPUT**	**OUTPUT/OUTCOME**
RESOURCES	ACTIVITIES	THE DIFFERENCE OR
(NOUNS)	(VERBS)	CHANGE TO BE
		ACCOMPLISHED

Figure 4.1.   The Simple Deming Model

are not clear about what they are trying to produce (what clear difference they are called to make), they cannot measure their intended outcome. Not being able to measure their outcome, the church and other nonprofits end up measuring what they can—their resources and activities (their inputs and throughputs) that are much more easily counted. How many members do we have? How large is our average attendance at worship? How many baptisms, confessions of faith, young people in our youth group, children in Sunday School, or volunteers in mission programs? How much is our per capita giving, our budget, or our debt? These are all questions of resources and activities, and they are all very countable—they are nouns and verbs. Reggie McNeil has said that the primary dashboards for the mainline church are all about how many, how often, and how much.[11] These dashboard counts are commonly much more related to inputs and throughputs, the resources and the activities, than they are to outcomes. They measure what the church or middle judicatory has and what they do. They do not measure the intentional difference a church believes it is called to make in the life of a person or community. And even after all the counting of resources and activities, many churches come up wanting because their aspirations have not been fulfilled and the differences they hoped for have not appeared. Aspirations unfulfilled then lead to the wish for "more" (more resources and activities) as leaders assure themselves that with more their aspirations would certainly be fulfilled. Scarcity intrudes again, especially as resources dwindle.

To add to the dilemma, nonprofits such as churches and middle judicatories are often encouraged to think of themselves as businesses, or they are encouraged to behave in a more businesslike manner. Jim Collins, business consultant and author of both *Good to Great* and *Good to Great in the Social Sector*, notes the confusion involved when he addresses issues of organizational greatness in the social sector—the arena of public life in which nonprofits operate. He writes, "The confusion between inputs and outputs stems from one of the primary differences between business and social sectors. In business, money is both an input (a resource for achieving greatness) and an output (a measure of greatness). In the social sectors, money is only an input, and not a measure of greatness."[12] Businesses use money to purchase the resources, personnel, facilities, and credit needed to do their work. Money is fundamental to the input. Then the business transforms those resources (their throughput) into automobiles, toasters, or services needed by consumers. The business then measures its productivity and success once again with money, defined as the output of profit and/or investor return. The process of the business may be exceedingly complex, but the measure is simple—money in (resource)/money out (outcome). The goal is to have more money at the end than at the beginning. The point, however, is that both resources and outcomes can be quantified in a clear way.

Businesses measure their greatness, in part, by the increase of dollars gained by doing business. Not so for nonprofits. Nonprofits commonly end up giving attention to how difficult it is to increase their resources because they are resources only, not outcomes. Once again, the measure is commonly one of scarcity—or at least a measure of difficulty.

Without clear outcomes, measures of resources for nonprofits will always be subject to scarcity because there could always be "more." However, the deeper understanding from Deming's simple construct of a system is that the resources actually needed cannot be determined until clear outcomes are established. In other words, such systems need to be built backward. Even a business doesn't know what resources are needed until its specific outcome is established. A business needs to understand that it makes cars, not toasters—and, if cars, specifically what kind of cars—before it can determine what manufacturing facilities it needs, what design work will be required, what workforce, what materials, what dollars, and so on. Deming's insight is that systems need to be built backward in order to determine the inputs and throughputs needed. The leader must begin with a clear outcome in order to determine the resources and activities needed to produce that outcome. This is a shared insight from Stephen Covey in his work on the habits of effective people in which a guiding principle is to "begin with the end in mind."[13]

Without clear outcomes nonprofits will all feel the scarcity of resources that are diminishing or difficult to find. In fact, as noted, in many such nonprofit systems leaders have already convincingly proven that they do not have sufficient resources to continue doing what has always been done. However, the more promising reality may well be that it is not until clear outcomes are established (that is, until leaders accept the fact that our systems need to be rebuilt, and in the rebuilding "built backward" specifically to accomplish the specific differences to be made) that they will be able to determine what resources are actually needed. What if leaders are surprised to find that they actually have enough?

Reversing the Field: Trusting in God's Agency

What if God has already provided, and has activated, what is feared to be missing? The second idea that I find helpful in breaking past assumptions of scarcity is that leaders can trust in God's agency to have already put in place what is needed to fulfill their purpose of changing lives and communities in vital and faithful ways. To pursue this idea leaders must reverse the field. Instead of constantly asking how a person or congregation can be an agent of God's Spirit, leaders also need to ask where and how God's Spirit is already at work—and then ask how they can get behind that work and help. It is a challenge to functional atheism through which people have convinced themselves that they are the (only) hands and feet of God, and unless they get up and about with their own doing they believe that God's Kingdom will not advance.

Such functional atheism in the postaberrant time when the usual, dependable resources are no longer free flowing leads to conversations of impoverishment. Local churches, many of which are struggling with their own budgets, buildings, and dwindling levels of energy, look out into their congregations or communities asking what need they can meet. It is scarcity talking to scarcity in which congregations (or denominations) believe they do not have enough for themselves, yet ask if they can meet the needs of a community that is not providing enough for its citizens.

To challenge such assumptions of scarcity, agency must be reversed so that churches and denominations begin to ask where God's hand is already at work (the agency being with God) and how can the church get behind that work and help (the church/denomination as resource, not as agent).

One United Methodist bishop noted his own deliberate choice when looking over the annual conference where he was the assigned leader. He said that he could choose to look at his area as a *geographical map* in which he could locate his congregations and leaders. In looking geographically he could locate some strengths but also considerable weaknesses and a host of problems to be solved. From this perspective he felt weighted down with the responsibilities of his own agency and his lack of resources to do what was needed. However, he could also look at his area as an *energy map* rather than a geographical map. Looking at his area as an energy map, he could ask where there was already movement, where there were already differences being made, where there were already experiments and initiatives building up, and where there were already people excited by their purposes. In other words, he was asking where God's agency was already at work in ways that the energy showed up. Getting behind energy that is already flowing is not an act of scarcity but rather lending oneself to an "enough" that is already at work.

Mike Mather is pastor of Broadway United Methodist Church in Indianapolis, Indiana, and he is a master of reversing the field. In serving communities where people have great needs, he realized that the outreach programs of his church were focused on what was missing. During intake, people who came to the church for help were asked about their level of poverty and what was missing from their lives— food, clothing, shelter, health care. Then his church would struggle mightily with their own dwindling resources to meet what needs they could. However, reversing the field, his church began to learn how to ask people what they had, not what they lacked. People were asked what they knew how to do well and what they could teach others to do. In one case a woman claimed to be an excellent cook—which proved to be the case when Mike asked her to cook a meal for his full staff. Having tested her gift and found it substantial, Mike's church then had her cook meals for community groups using the church facilities—all efforts that were parlayed into the woman developing her own catering business and then opening a restaurant using her own gifts with the lending hand of the church. The church did not give the woman resources. Rather, she was given opportunity to use the resources she already had. Where many congregations structure themselves around programs (councils or committees that use church resources to plan programs or events for others), Mike's church structured its mission around "encouraging the Spirit" (leaders who went out into the congregation and community, asking where God was already at work, and then asking how the church could help).

Describing the power of reversing the field and trusting in God's agency is not as powerful as hearing the stories.[14] Consider further the stories of what is being discovered in the Fresh Expressions movement that began in Great Britain and is moving into the United States. In Fresh Expressions, generally atypical faith communities (meaning not heavily dependent on the resources needed by traditional congregations) are gaining traction.[15] These Fresh Expressions depend less on denominational agency and resources and more on the energy of God's Spirit. Going further, consider the discoveries of Casper ter Kuile and Angie Thurston, Ministry Innovation Fellows at Harvard Divinity School, mentioned in chapter 1. They found extensive examples of young millennial adults and a growing assortment of "non-organized religion" folk of all ages who are finding their own communities of spirit, purpose, and transformation in rather surprising places.[16] Again, these are energy, agency, and resources that are not dependent on organized religion but are aligned with the purpose of the church in some way. The church does not need to (does not have the capacity to) create these communities. The church, however, could get behind what is already happening and support the Spirit's movement.

Courageous leadership includes challenging assumptions of scarcity that people live with in order to risk looking for the "enough" that is already at work but that looks deeply unfamiliar and unlike traditional ministries and established practices. Leaders would have to change their own familiar practices and established rules to join with the "enough" that is already bubbling up. It would, however, let leaders escape the assumptions of scarcity that they allow to bind them.

The Third Law of Power

The final newer idea to challenge our old and confining assumptions about scarcity of resources has to do with power. Power has long been understood to live at the center and be a tool of the "large." Resources and decision making have traditionally fallen to the elected, appointed, or employed leaders who oversee from the central (or top) positions of their institutions, businesses, or government. Power then further amasses to the larger of these institutions, businesses, or governments as they use their size and position to fend off rivals. In the aberrant time, institutions were highly regarded for their power and their ability to influence from the center of the cultural marketplace. In particular, the mainline Protestant denominations once enjoyed power that could be exercised from that position. However, now with a divergent culture that has fragmented any public platform and with diminished members and dollars, organized religion feels the scarcity of its influence along with the assumed scarcity of other resources.

Once again, the postaberrant time is not a turnaround situation, and congregations and denominations will not go back to a time when any faith tradition(s) would hold power over a convergent culture. Not being able to go back allows leaders to move forward but simultaneously requires a new understanding of resources—including power.

The dilemma of deep cultural changes is that such changes are directly felt by those living in the midst of them but are simultaneously extremely difficult to understand because living in the midst of the changes is too close to allow any perspective. So at this stage it is at least clear that *something* is happening to the distribution and use of power as populism contests with established governments and as movements contest with institutions. What is clear is that power is morphing in shape and location.

Moisés Naím has served as editor in chief of *Foreign Policy*, as Venezuela's trade minister, and as executive director of the World Bank. Currently a scholar at the Carnegie Endowment for International Peace, his is a global perspective from which he explores power used by the largest to the smallest entities. He argues clearly that power is changing and becoming more feeble, transient, and constrained. The change is prompted by the breaking down of barriers that could once be used by large nations, corporations, and institutions to fend off competitors. The breaking down is enabled by technology, communication, and international, transglobal relationships. He writes, "There is much more going on than a simple shift of power from one coterie of influential powers to another. The transformation of power is more total and complicated. Power itself has become more available—and, indeed, in today's world more people have power."[17]

He identifies the rise of a new kind of power, which he calls "micropower," with new capacity to challenge both old ways and the former large holders of established power. Micropower can be accessed by small groups and organizations that can use technology and their agility to escape the barriers once presented by large organizations and government. Power is no longer confined at the center of large organizations, which is the first lesson denominational and congregational leaders must learn in this deeply changing landscape. For example, well-developed, full-institutional plans and initiatives of denominations can now be quickly disregarded by the very people they are intended to influence as new power sources arise in contest with the leaders who are expected to be "in control."

"This is a moment of citizen power," writes Eric Liu, executive director of the Aspen Institution Citizenship and American Identity Program. "Citizens today no longer have to accept the bundles—the one-size-fits-all packages—that the monopolies of politics and business have long forced upon us. Unbundling is everywhere, from how we get the news to how we listen to music or watch television to how we catch a ride across town to how we label ourselves by party, gender, or race."[18] In other words, power also responds to Bauman's "liquid modernity" by constantly reforming itself in shape and application, just as institutions and organizations must constantly reform themselves.

Liu identifies three laws of power. The first is that power concentrates. It feeds on itself and compounds. In other words, those who have power seek to use it to play a winner-takes-all game. The second law is that power justifies itself. People invent stories to legitimize the reasons they have power (or lack it). These first two laws lead to zero-sum assumptions that make people believe that power has a finite limit and that if you don't have any, you can't get any. This is the realm of scarcity. Congregations and denominations, many of which once felt the power and influence of their cultural and organizational positions, now feel impoverished in the postaberrant time.

However, Liu points to a third law of power: that power is infinite.[19] There is no inherent limit on the amount of power that people can create. As power shifts, people create new centers of influence, many of which do not have the organizational or formal structure once thought necessary to house power. And so there are multitudes of populist subgroups, social justice movements, crowdsource funding, social media influence groups, and a host of new expressions of faith communities no longer asking permission or seeking the certification of organized religion to exert their power in pursuit of faithfulness and meaning.

Power is infinite. It cannot be contained. The people of the biblical text should be the first to recognize this. When Moses confronted Pharaoh with the word to "Let my people go" (Exodus 5:1), it was a reconfiguration of power. Pharaoh owned the land and the food of the land. He had armies and sat at the center of government. He embodied power only to be confronted with a different truth from a singular fugitive. "The truth to be told and visibly enacted is that Pharaoh is exposed as a fraudulent authority," wrote Walter Brueggemann.[20] Where power was ensconced at the center and within the large, God quickly enabled the creation of new power to be embodied by slaves and fugitives.

The lessons of power in our current postaberrant time are not yet clear. What is clear is that power is no longer confined within our institutions to be used only by elected or certified leaders. What is clear is that there is no scarcity of power. What is yet to be learned is what is enough. What is yet to be learned by the church, as a religious institution, is how to connect our purpose with the new power that God is redistributing to the multitude of new forms of faithfulness that dot the landscape.

Stewarding Potential

One final challenge to our assumptions about the scarcity of resources has to do with tense—the forms of our verbs by which we indicate time. In my role with the Texas Methodist Foundation (TMF) over the past years I have been involved with a very vibrant, ongoing examination of the purpose and outcomes of this marvelous organization, which began over seventy-five years ago out of a need to address the financial challenges of churches. In the past fifteen years TMF has grown in purpose and capacity to focus on leadership, along with finances, as the resources needed by the church in order to accomplish its God-ordained mission. During the most recent years, as TMF continued to pursue its own purpose and outcomes, the conversation shifted to the meaning of stewardship—and what it is that TMF is actually called on to steward.

In the minds of most in the church, stewardship is most directly connected with some form of property. Deriving from the seventeenth-century Old English, "steward" refers to the ward of the house or the ward of the hall. The idea of stewarding is to care for property (physical or financial) that is owned by another. The connection of stewardship to property is also a connection to that which already exists—to the present and to the past tenses. Churches steward what they already have and what is currently available to them. In stewardship campaigns churches seek resources, in the present tense, from the resources available to their members and participants. In the stewardship of their facilities, their investments, and their endowments, churches protect and seek to use what they carry with them, from the past tense, that comes from those who have gone before. Stewarding, in these forms, focuses on the past and the present. In the postaberrant time such stewarding is most often cast in the shadow of scarcity. Leaders worry about protecting from loss that which they already have, worry about competing in an ever-complicated and competitive environment for that which they think they need, and continually focus on "more." Stewarding often takes on the feeling of facing into scarcity.

However, as the conversation at TMF matured, it took on a different twist, producing the notion that perhaps they were not just to steward resources (that which they already had or had access to), but that perhaps they were also called to steward *potential* (that which is not yet). Stewarding potential shifts the tense of one's work and one's attention. Stewarding potential is work aligned with the future, not limited to the present and past. This is work aligned with God's agency (what God is yet to do that we don't yet see) and not just with our own activities. Because it is aligned with the future and with God's agency, it is an institutional risk. It requires loosening control, intentionally learning about a future that is not easily understood, and continually experimenting. Experimenting risks failure, misdirection, and false starts to discern where God's Spirit leads.

In its identity and purpose TMF has now taken on the tagline of "stewarding potential" in order to tell others, and to remind themselves, that this is what they have been called to do. It is a new role in these past few years, so it is still in the early stages of being lived into. It does, however, invite people to step beyond the assumed limits so commonly attached to resources. Leaders do not need to be limited by time, neither the present nor the past. They do not need to be limited by what they already have or have access to. That which people and institutions steward is not limited—it is exponential. Reality is defined by our assumptions. Assumptions can be changed.

5

A WORD ABOUT STRUCTURE AND PROCESS

Assumptions about Fear, Organization, and Democracy

Strength overused becomes weakness. Successful strategies that go unchanged become the pathway for losses.

George Washington has been described as a stiff and formal man who was most comfortable at a distance from others and was perceived as being aloof.[1] With his height well over six feet, his courage attested to in revolutionary battle, and his quiet reserve (to the point of being taciturn) amid the heady debates of the founding fathers, he was a formidable, proven leader, more easily revered than approached. Historians attest that a fledgling republic, still unformed and unsure of itself, required such a powerful and substantive person to stand at the center and hold all together lest it fly apart. It was with reason that he was so quickly called the father of the country and that the federal city built to house government was named after him.

However, strength overused leads to weakness. In Chinese philosophy the dark and the bright (feminine and masculine, negative and positive, weakness and strength) are interconnected and interdependent in the principles of yin and yang. In the concealing side of one is the exposing nature of the other. The opposite of each is embedded in the other, and too much of one exposes the other. So too much talk leads to meaninglessness, too much information leads to confusion, too much rigidity leads to fragility. In George Washington's case, too much

of his regal character projected by his presence, aloofness, and definitive silences led to the charges in his second term of office that he had
become monarchical. He was accused of becoming the very thing that
the revolution was meant to unseat. He himself had not changed from
his first to second term of office. Still authentically himself and living
out of his well-developed character strengths, being too strong and
unchanging led to the taunts of being King George instead of President
George as the republic matured and became less dependent on him.
The overuse of strengths leads inevitably to weakness as the surrounding conditions change.

Always going to the tried and true, always operating out of strengths
and practices that are known and comfortable, are the "too much" leading to weakness that will be explored in this chapter. In the previous
two chapters I challenged assumptions about how change happens and
assumptions about the availability and use of resources as the most
threatening sets of assumptions. Without recalibrating models of
change and dependence on a steady stream of resources, leaders will
not move forward. In the present chapter I want to lift up a secondary
subset of assumptions that have to do with a debilitating oversensitivity
to fear (assumptions about our reward systems), the unthinking assumptions about the importance of the present institutional structure,
and the need to rethink the use of democratic practices as the only way
to be community. These practices have all been strengths well used in
the past but are increasingly becoming weaknesses. Here again, assumptions that dwell at a tacit level need to be lifted, examined, tested,
and changed.

A DEBILITATING OVERSENSITIVITY TO FEAR: ASSUMPTIONS OF A REWARD SYSTEM

John Wayne is to have said that courage is being afraid but saddling up
anyway.

Such a notion from such an iconic American fits well into the idea
that courage is a feeling to call up at a time when fear needs to be
pushed down. This is the courage defined by boldness and battle. I
want to be clear that this is not the courage necessary for this postaberrant time. What is now needed is a much quieter form of courage.

In order to see our way into a quietly courageous leadership that is less constrained by overused strengths, it is necessary to redefine courage as a choice to be made rather than a feeling to be controlled. Consider this different definition of courage from philosopher John Silber: "Courage is very often misunderstood as a capacity to suppress emotions of fear," he wrote. "Plato had a far more important and profound understanding of courage. He said that courage was not to be understood in terms of the emotions, but rather as the knowledge of what is or is not to be feared."2

Courage is less the response of the stirred heart than of the discerning mind. Courage is *knowing* what to be afraid of. This knowing takes a considerable amount of work, particularly in highly relational systems.

To begin, consider an example of quiet courage. A consultant friend sent me an email describing a planning session he observed in a local church. My friend reported that in the midst of the meeting,

> a powerbroker in the congregation tried to hijack the session when he stepped to the front of the room and said, "We have seven problems here, and I have seven solutions." Though the people were not rude to him, when he was done and had taken his seat, we picked up right where we had left off with people giving really powerful answers to the question at hand. The pastor is handling that powerbroker really well, and that's not easy since he's 70 and a former member of the [local] school board and several task forces of the mayor. She listens carefully and respectfully and thanks him for his advice and says that there is lots of good stirring in the congregation.

Courage need not be confrontational, pushing to win. The pastor did not have to subdue her fears in order to "take on" the powerbroker. In most settings leaders don't need to win the day; they just need to know to be more afraid of easy answers and safe responses that do not lead to change than to be afraid of displeasing the person who comes with the easy answer or a need for attention. Courage requires the leader to make a choice between satisfying the person immediately in front of her or him or satisfying the longer-term mission or purpose at hand. The dilemma that requires such a choice arises when we understand the two most basic poles on which all vibrant organizations are built, as well as the tension that is created by the contradictory pulls of the two poles and how organizational reward systems influence leaders' responses.

The Polarity of Purpose and Relationship in Healthy Organizations

Let's begin by describing the two fundamental poles on which thriving organizations are constructed. On the one side is the *purpose* of the organization, expressed in its mission, goals, and outcomes. This is the reason for which the organization exists, the difference it intends to make. If you wander into a bookstore and browse books on leadership, you will find shelves about visioning, management, and metrics. These are all books about fulfilling the purpose of the organization. In that same section you will find other shelves on team building and personnel management. These are books on the other side of the polarity, about managing the *relationships* in an organization. Purpose and relationship: effective leaders are to help identify and shape the purpose of the organization, from its overarching long-term vision all the way down to the specifics of the outcomes that identify what has to be accomplished in the next six weeks and then work to align the people around that vision and its outcomes in order to make it all happen. Both purpose and relationship are required. They are the two poles on which healthy organizations are built. One does not thrive without the other.

Purpose needs to be connected to relationship, and relationship to purpose. At any given time leaders commonly need to give one of the poles in this polarity more attention than the other in order to keep the organization within a healthy balance. However, there are some types of organizations that by their nature lean more heavily into one of the poles than the other, *in which case the leaders must pay attention to not overuse the organization's preferred strength to the detriment of its overall health.* Military and police organizations lean more heavily into their purpose and their tasks than their relationships and can suffer greatly when the needs and rights of people are not respected. On the other side, churches and church systems lean more heavily into relationships, as do any organizations that rely on voluntary associations within the organization.

It is here that leaders need to understand the overused strengths of highly relational organizations like congregations and denominations and the capacity of the reward system to constrain leadership that is not courageous. Membership or participation in a voluntary association is a choice, and in most voluntary associations the threshold to get into the organization is relatively low. In the case of the local congregation, one needs only to show up and be tenacious enough to be recognized and included. Churches that have been losing members and participants for decades (as well as denominational systems that are hard pressed to recruit an adequate stream of good, healthy leaders) rejoice when someone shows up and crosses the very low threshold of just being present. However, if the threshold to get into such voluntary organizations is low, the threshold to get out is even lower. A disenchanted voluntary participant can simply stop coming and in most cases will never face a conversation about why. This puts the leader in the position of encouraging people to step over the low threshold to enter the organization—and then feel strong pressure to satisfy people so that they don't step back over the even lower threshold of leaving (that is, a pressure to work hard to keep people happy).

We have been describing a postaberrant time in which the culture does not support membership in institutions and, in fact, pushes people away from organizations. At the same time there is a great anxiety about the capacity of churches and denominations to attract participants, leaders, and future clergy. These conditions ripen the moment for overusing the relational strengths of voluntary organizations like churches by seeking to oversatisfy the personal needs among those who are a part of the organization. Leaders in congregations so rejoice in someone showing up and are so aware of how easily someone might simply stop coming that they easily become what pastor and seminary professor Richard Lischer described as "a quivering mass of availability" in his memoir of his early tenure as pastor of a country church.[3] Leaning too far toward the relational pole of the organization, the pastor is tempted to satisfy the individual who is standing right in front of him or her in whatever way necessary and in the process step further away from the purpose or the mission of the church to change lives and to change communities.

The leader faces the temptation of being a quivering mass of availability who is willing to do what is needed to satisfy the other person because the reward system in a voluntary association measures satisfaction and dissatisfaction. The metrics used in such a highly relational system to evaluate leadership focus heavily on how many people participate, how many people drop out, and how many complaints have to be dealt with. True leadership that asks uncomfortable questions and seeks to disturb the organization in purposeful ways does not fit well into highly relational systems in which comfort and satisfaction are valued and are so closely monitored by the reward system. Many stories have been told of pastors whose salary checks are late or even withheld because the church treasurer is angry. Pastors, their spouses, and even their children know what it is like to receive an angry word, a cold shoulder, or even an absence of a familiar invitation to a gathering because the pastor's leadership disappointed or disturbed equilibrium. United Methodist bishop Will Willimon, now retired, shared his reflections of facing into this polarity between purpose and relationship in his memoirs.

> My job could be unmanageable were it not for the Vision. When some dear soul makes the hackneyed complaint, "Clergy morale is low in our conference," or asks, "What have you done to end stress coming over our overburdened pastor?" what joy there has been to shove this sentence before them with, "Sorry. Not my job. Here's what is expected of me (and you)." The test of my ministry is how well God uses me to challenge and to equip every church to make *more* disciples for Jesus Christ by taking *more* risks and changing lives.[4]

Willimon is known, and cherished by many, for his provocative bluntness, and he does put the tension between purpose and relationship into sharp relief as he responds with reminders of purpose when asked questions of relationship. It is easy to imagine how he could suffer *negative* rewards as he so willingly steps away from the expected nurturing kindness always concerned for the feelings of others in the sphere of his leadership. All organizations have reward systems that offer both positive and negative rewards depending on whether the leader is able to address the values and outcomes most prized. In systems that so highly reward relationships, leadership requires a quiet courage to choose to stay connected to purpose.

Leading in Community

Let's deepen the understanding about the reward system and its connection to fear by examining the contract for leadership under which many leaders in nonprofit and voluntary associations work. Keep in mind that all leaders of organizations of any kind must manage the polarity between purpose and relationship, and at no time is any leader free from being aware of and responding appropriately to the feelings of the people who work in their system. However, in voluntary associations and particularly in religious organizations, leaders must lead *in community*. Leading "in community" means that pastors and denominational executives are leading in systems *in which the terms of employment are set by the very people to be led*. This is a subtle but critical distinction that employment-based systems commonly miss. For example, business leaders or professionals such as lawyers or physicians will assert that they too must attend to the needs of the people that work for them but that clergy should—as they do—simply tell people what must be done. Leaders in employment-based systems do, in fact, need to manage the balance between purpose and relationship and in the process be aware of the needs of the people who work with them. However, what they miss is that their employment-based contract for leadership is formed around and rewarded for specific outcomes for which they are accountable to their employer, not to the people that they serve or interact with. Very differently, leaders (clergy and laity) in volunteer-based systems like congregations work under contracts formed more around relationships and are accountable to the very persons who both employ them and whom they are expected to lead.

In such volunteer-based systems, exercising leadership that disrupts or disturbs jeopardizes both the security and the relationships of the leader. In his compelling history of clergy in America, Brooks Holifield notes this distinctly American phenomenon that began centuries ago in the earliest settlements:

> No trend affected the status of the clergy in early America more than the resolve of congregations to set the terms of employment. In the absence of a bishop, the Virginia assembly in 1643 authorized local vestries to choose their rectors and then present them to the governor for induction. Since induction virtually ensured tenure, the parishes soon learned to offer ministers annual contracts, ignoring the governor and keeping the clergy under their control. . . .
>
> Not all the clergy found the arrangement satisfactory. Morgan Godwyn protested in 1680 that the vestries reduced the ministers "to their own Terms; that is, to use them how they please, pay them what they list, and to discard them whensoever they have a mind to it."

Commissary James Blair bemoaned the "contrary Custom of making annual Agreements with the Ministers, which [the parishes] call by a Name course enough, viz. Hiring of the Ministers, that they may by that Means keep them in more Subjugation and Dependence." He thought that the practice drove good ministers away and dissuaded them from preaching "against the Vices that any great Man of the Vestry was guilty of."[5]

Having the terms of employment set by the very people being led is a constraint on leadership, creating an ongoing fear of the ensuing reward system. Setting the terms of such in-community contracts can be done very *formally* through the use of polity. For example, the initiatives or decisions of a denominational executive can be challenged as stepping over the lines of established rules by any member of the organization whenever the leader disappoints or disturbs beyond comfort. Setting the terms can be done very *informally* by, for example, a personnel committee measuring a pastor's performance by how satisfied members are with their own congregational experience as opposed to whether ministry outcomes are being produced. Setting the terms is done regularly by executive evaluations and annual pastoral evaluations that ask if the people want their leader's tenure extended without asking if outcomes of ministry are being accomplished.

Leading in Dual and Conflicting Reward Systems

Stepping beyond the congregational level, a similar but more complex dynamic is at work in denominational organizational reward systems. It is important to understand that leaders in church systems commonly operate in multilevel organizations that have at least two different reward systems. At the local congregational level, clergy and other local leaders lead "in community" in a highly relational system, as described earlier. However, these same clergy and local leaders are also a part of and accountable to a larger middle judicatory regional system known variably as a conference, presbytery, synod, diocese, or region. A middle judicatory is that part of the denominational structure that exists between the local congregation and the larger national or global denominational body. At the head of the larger middle judicatory part of the system is an elected or employed leader who is commonly less tied to the dynamics of leading in community and more responsible for purposeful goals. These regional executives more commonly have the terms of their contract for leadership defined by the polity and practice of the denomination rather than by the people that they lead. This difference leads to a certain tilt within the denominational organization in which there are interacting levels of leadership with different constituencies and with different standards of reward. Using the work of sociologist Peter Takayama, David Roozen points to a generally accepted sociological generalization that differentiates regional and national staff from local congregation staff and leadership.[6] Given the polarity between purpose and relationship, it is generally accepted that denominational staff (including seminary professors and other church professionals) tend to lean more toward the pole of purpose and speak more easily about vision, mission, and outcomes. Denominational leaders are, as it were, more distant from the reward system dominated by relationships in the local congregation. Local congregational clergy and leaders, however, tend to lean more toward the pole of relationship because, as described earlier, they lead in community where the contract for leadership is held by the people to be led and where satisfied people are a default measure of leadership.

In the necessary tension between purpose and relationship *denominations tend to be more purposive, and congregations tend to be more relational.* The real pinch point is that clergy in such religious systems are caught between two different reward systems. Clergy depend on their denominational system for their certification and deployment in order to have a job and then depend on the local congregation for the paycheck and benefits that come with that job. Clergy in such situations are then subject to two reward systems that can easily compete with one another. The regional unit or denomination identifies missional outcomes and changes that the clergy are to lead (the purpose pole), while the local congregation continues its sensitive concern for the satisfaction of the people who are already in the congregation (the relational pole). Each of these different levels of the same system will evaluate and reward the clergy and leaders caught in the middle based on the measures of their own preferred pole. The denomination will evaluate and reward based on whether the congregational clergy or leader is accomplishing identified changes. The local congregation will evaluate and reward based on whether the people in community are satisfied with the clergy or leader—a satisfaction that is more commonly measured by whether things continue as they are rather than whether things change. Caught in such a double-bind, it is not unusual for local congregational leaders to attend regional meetings or conferences and to verbally and willingly support the goals, outcomes, and need for changes identified by the denominational level. The support is, in fact, authentic because the local congregational clergy and leaders understand the need for change and are sitting with that part of the larger church most concerned with purpose. However, it is equally usual for these same local congregational clergy and leaders to return to their own local congregations where so much is measured by relationships and say very little about what might have happened at the regional meeting or conference related to change. Back in the part of the church most concerned with relationships, they choose not to disturb or disrupt. People naturally respond to the reward system in which they are sitting, and if the reward system changes, so does the behavior. This polarity between purpose and relationship will be revisited in chapter 8 around the temptation of empathy.

Leading without Regard for Reward

Far from offering an argument that denominational executives or pastors be given more unchecked authority or guaranteed tenures, I simply want to acknowledge that leadership takes courage. It requires courage to know to be more afraid of not stretching to be missional and purposeful than to be afraid that stability will be rocked and personal rewards and security will be threatened. It is a choice.

In my ongoing work with active United Methodist bishops, district superintendents, and clergy, I have regularly encouraged these leaders to exceed the level of authority that their system is willing to give them. The relationship between leader and the people is always, quite naturally, measured by whether the people feel safe and comfortable. Led out of slavery only forty-five days after leaving Egypt, "the whole Israelite community complained against Moses and Aaron in the desert" (Exodus 16:2) because they were unsure of having enough food. This is not hyperbole; this is normative behavior. Whenever we are unsure or feel threatened we turn to our leaders, not to encourage them to continue their purposeful path but to ask them to relieve our distress, to return us to comfort, even if the regain of comfort includes a return to slavery.

People only naturally extend the use of authority to their leaders up to, but not past, the point of discomfort. This is the major point that Ron Heifetz and Marty Linsky make in their book about sabotage that examines the normative consequences to adaptive leaders who ask purposeful questions rather than provide comforting answers.[7] If the leader does not act to reduce anxiety and return equilibrium and comfort to the system, or if the leader does not give the people a good reason for their discomfort, the people will quite normally and naturally look for ways to sabotage the leader. We naturally look for ways to constrain the very leadership we ask for. *If leaders truly hope to make a situation different, if they want change, they must be willing to exceed the level of authority that people willingly and easily give.* It then takes quiet courage not to be dissuaded by the reactions of the reward system.

In its relationship with fear, courage is knowing to be more afraid of not being able to move the church toward its missional purpose of changing people's lives and transforming their communities than to be afraid of our own anxiety and loss of familiar comfort as we face change. Indeed, one of the descriptions I have given to the work of courage is *being willing to lead without regard for reward.*

ASSUMPTIONS OF OUR PRESENT STRUCTURE

Turning our attention to the second of the subset of tacit assumptions to challenge in this chapter, we must also willingly question the importance and the permanence of our current organizational structure that is highly organized and rigidly constructed. By far, the preponderance of our current congregational and denomination structures is hierarchical, linear, and bureaucratically organized. In a 1992 essay, Craig Dykstra and James Hudnut-Beumler offer three metaphors for the historic development of American denominations: from constitutional confederacy (1780s), to the corporation (1860s), to regulatory agencies (1960s to the present).[8] Like other histories of denominational structures, Dykstra and Hudnut-Beumler reflect a primary, period-driven transition that took all of our denominational systems from an earlier American stage in which denominations were a loose confederation of local congregations linked by theological and immigrant origins but with few cross-congregation structural connections to a later stage in which denominations organized themselves into more corporate-like structures. The corporate-like structures were built of local congregations that organizationally became more like one another and were connected by denominational offices, officers, and denomination-based service providers such as general agencies, mission boards, and publishing houses. Denominations, if you will, went through a transition from a collection of similar but relatively independent "cottage industry" congregations to a corporately connected bureaucratic organization of identically structured and governed congregations linked not just by history and purpose but also by organizational design. Denominations were built as organizations that mirrored other organizations of the time, such as banks and businesses, that were thriving because they fit the cultural environment of that time. The move to a more corporate structure was culturally appropriate and effective. The shift enabled denominations to grow and congregations to spread.

However, a strength overused becomes a weakness. In a paper given at a denominational colloquy in 2017, Bishop Robert Schnase reflected the corporate, linearly structured nature of the United Methodist denomination that is a legacy of that historic shift. While born in the strength of its cultural compatibility beginning in the 1830s, the strength overused for too long a time birthed the beginning of its weakness. He wrote,

> The formation of the United Methodist Church in 1968 merged kindred branches and righted many wrongs, including the long-standing injustices of the Central Conference in the US, the fruit of blatantly racist strategies. But the shifts that took place between 1968 and 1972 erred in another way, less sinful but nevertheless deadening for our witness.
>
> We began to treat congregations, districts, and conferences like interconnected widgets that must all operate in uniform fashion or else the connection would suffer. This uniformity reflected corporate and governmental models that reached their apex ten to twenty years previously. The organization of the United Methodist Church required every church to have the same administrative board structure, the same council on ministries, the same work areas that perfectly aligned with similar work at the district, conference, and general church level. The *Book of Discipline* required the same structures with the same names for every church no matter how large or how

small, all internally focused, and with no variability derived from the mission field.

Context didn't matter. Unity relied upon common structures more than a common sense of mission.[9]

That which was appropriately built for strength in an earlier day, when practiced for too long and practiced too strictly, was a strength that turned to weakness. There are two things to quickly note as we move ahead. The first is that most current denominational structures are less than two hundred years old in their earliest forms and, in many cases, less than sixty years old in their present forms. The current denominational forms are not sacred in their origins or designs and not determined by theology or history. They are simply older than the present generations of the individuals who currently lead them and feel as if they bear the weight of the full tradition of the faith because they are older than current memory. The second thing to note is that they are forms and structures appropriate and effective to the earlier "solid time" that was less frenetic in change and divergence than the current liquid time that is driven by technology and communication. They were good and right, strong for their time. But in many ways these organizational designs and practices became strengths clung to for too long, strengths overused. The overused strengths currently present at least three major challenges.

Our Current Denominational Structures Are Increasingly Expensive to Maintain

As noted in the discussion about resources in chapter 4, the continual growth of our denominations in the first half of the twentieth century increased the complexity of the structure, the amount of staff, and the size of budgets needed to sustain the increasing size, complexity, and programming. During the earlier aberrant time when the culture pushed people toward membership organizations, the growth of resources kept pace with or outpaced the growth of the denomination. In the current postaberrant time this is not the case, yet it has been exceedingly difficult to shrink our organizational structures. As noted, a plan is not necessary for growth when that growth is culturally driven. A plan, however, is needed to shrink—and such plans for shrinking a denomination for missional reasons are exceedingly difficult to develop.

We can no longer afford the large, corporate institutional organizations that were once so appropriate and effective in their solid culture.
In a 2012 report to the United Methodist denomination, Donald
House, using the tools of a master economist, pointed to a number of
variables that were leading indicators of the shrinking size, resources,
and effectiveness of the denomination.[10] Variables in the study included
the increasing age of certified clergy, the large number of both clergy
and congregations in a system that has less membership and attendance, and the patterns of local church spending in areas of staff, programs, and debt. In addition, based on the data on membership in the
United Methodist denomination, Lovett Weems of the Lewis Center
for Church Leadership introduced the idea of a "death tsunami" that is
facing many denominations that both confirms and compounds the
analysis by House.[11] The death tsunami—a rapidly swelling and overwhelming wave of pending member deaths—is the product of the earlier demographic post–World War II baby boom and reflects the now
aging population of those people who are members in religious denominations. While the national death rate (deaths per one thousand people)
has remained steady over a period beginning in 2003 and continuing
through 2018, the rate of member deaths in the denomination is projected to continue to go up every year until 2050, with 50 percent more
deaths in 2050 than in 2010. House's conclusion is that by sometime
around 2050, in the absence of change and with an inability to influence
current trends, denominations such as the United Methodist Church
will no longer be able to afford their continuance as institutional denominations. If that is the case, and the current trends are not disrupted
and the organization of local churches and denominational structures
are not redesigned for a new and changed missional time, one strong
scenario is for the local churches of any tradition to revert back to some
new form of a confederacy in which they will hold together in a shared
identity without the connection, accountability, support, or resourcing
of a larger denominational body.

The Gridlocked Nature of Our Current Denominational Structures Makes Them Difficult to Change

Along with our diminished capacity to afford them, with their size and
complexity, current denominational systems are increasingly difficult to
change. This becomes truer as their public mission becomes increasing-

ly overshadowed by the private mission that develops around satisfying the strongest of the internal constituencies that make up the denomination. Competition among the internal constituencies produces gridlock in which purposeful decisions go unmade because of the countervailing interests of competing factions. Undergirding the arguments of competing factions is the elaborate and rich web of norms, rules, practices, and polity that has grown exponentially over time. Used selectively and strategically, these rules can be employed by constituencies to support their own interests while simultaneously used to constrain the interests of competing constituencies.

That elaborate and rich web of norms, rules, practices, and polity has been described by Gordon MacKenzie as a "giant hairball."[12] MacKenzie explored creativity within bureaucracy as part of his work at the Hallmark Cards company. With characteristic creativity, he noted that every new rule put in place, every legislative act, every agreement, norm, or policy established is like one more string added to a giant and growing hairball that in its growth is increasingly difficult to untangle or reduce. As the denominational "hairballs" grew (evidenced by the exponential growth of denominational books of polity fueled by resolutions, legislation, and policy statements), the focus of leadership increasingly shifted from the public mission of changing lives and communities to the private mission of caring for and satisfying the rules of the hairball and the demands of internal constituencies.

Indeed, internal constituencies shaped the terms of the gridlock that both stymied a focus on the purpose and the mission field of denominations and blocked organizational change. Church historian Russell Richey noted that Methodism divided structurally about every ten years in the first one hundred years of its American experience.[13] Like other faith traditions, Methodism is the product of schisms. On the one hand, those divisions spawned an even richer and, in some cases, a more just religious fabric in the United States. However, it came at the cost of diminishing the mission of the Methodists and their ability to grow. Richey noted that in the twentieth century Methodists dealt with the cost of schism by providing space within the denomination for all voices—space provided by giving factions organizational departments and/or caucus status within the structure, a space that precluded the need for schism. Rather than having to leave, constituencies were given more control over their own segment of the denomination. The unintended consequence was that over time the internalization of competing voices within a large and complex organization increasingly internalized the focus of the denomination so that the public mission of making disciples and transforming the world was given less attention and the private mission of competition among internal constituent voices was given more attention, time, and resources. Attention to mission and to the external mission field was significantly sacrificed to the gridlock produced by competing voices, each claiming importance, attention, and resources internally within the denomination.

The powerful insight from MacKenzie's metaphor of an institutional hairball is that many leaders (bishops, clergy, laity) clearly see the confusion and cost of the twisted complexity of rules, normative practices, and competing constituencies. Brave leaders willingly step to the center of the hairball, by election or appointment, with the intent of unraveling the hairball in order to return to the public mission. However, what most of those leaders miss is that by stepping into the center of such long-established, complex, linear, highly organized organizations that are guided by established rules, policy, and procedures, it becomes more, not less, difficult for insightful leaders to produce change. Stepping into the center does not invite a leader to unify the voice of the organization but to be more subject to the competing internal voices already within the organization. Stepping into the center of a hairball does not give one more influence on change but rather increases the accountability of that leader to maintain and uphold the rules, policies, and procedures and increases accountability to the competing internal voices. Achieving higher leadership rank does not increase the freedom to produce change but rather increases the accountability to maintain the hairball that already exists.

Learning Is Inhibited

The linear nature of hierarchical structures continues to assume that leadership and learning comes from the center/top and thus inhibits the capacity to be responsive to a fast-changing missional environment. Along with the difficulty to change, the other significant difficulty of such highly organized and constrained organizations is in learning new ways to adapt to the mission field. Walter Isaacson, CEO of the Aspen Institute, states,

Complexity at scale has rendered reductionistic management ineffective for solving these issues in our networked world. Efficiency is
necessary, but no longer sufficient to be a successful organization. . . .
Management models based on planning and predicting instead of
resilient adaptation to changing circumstances are no longer suited
to today's challenges. Organizations must be networked, not siloed,
in order to succeed. Their goal must shift from efficiency to sustained organizational adaptability. [14]

Highly organized, bureaucratic organizations are highly efficient when
well run. They control communication and decision making in an orderly manner that is directed from the center/top. They break down complicated processes into a division of labor that can be positively coordi-
nated to produce intended outcomes (but that also silos information
and decision making so that fewer, rather than more, have an overview
of the work of the whole organization). Leadership remains at the center. Expertise also remains at the center, as the few people who have
the larger perspective of the whole organization, mission, and mission
field are able to respond beyond the limited purview of a single department. Leadership and learning are confined to the center of the organization where officials and experts reside.

As noted, this design works well in an ordered culture in which
congruence and a steady flow of resources stabilize the environment.
However, in the postaberrant time when divergence reigns and where
change is both rapid and chaotic, the center (or top) of the organization
is actually the most distant from the change that needs to be addressed.
Learning happens at the edge of organizations, where there is actual
contact with the changing environment of the mission field and where
agility and adaptation become the tools of learning. If change is constrained at the center because of the hairball effect and the competition
of constituent choices, change is the norm at the edges, where the
organization encounters its environment. The day of the leader who
comes complete with "the answer" is over. The day of the expert who
can tell others uniformly what to do is over. Decision making and learning must happen at the edge, where institutions encounter the liquid
culture.

The assumption of the present structure that must be challenged is
that it is somehow "sacred" simply because it has some historic root and
is currently the known way by which work is done. These organizational

structures of both congregation and denomination were made by the hand of those in them and were appropriate to and highly successful in the aberrant time of resource-rich convergence. However, I have been arguing to reframe our purpose and practices in light of the postaberrant time of a highly divergent and rapidly changing liquid culture. Pointing in a more helpful direction, it is clear that as congregations and denominations move ahead they will be more effective in mission if they are

- simpler, not more complicated; looser, not tighter. More rules, policies, and standardized practices will inhibit agility and the learning that will produce adaptability. Increased prescriptions and more accountability with the intention to create uniform practice (not purpose) will constrain.
- agile, not organized. Neatness no longer counts in a culture that is constantly morphing. Rather than being rigid, organizations must become resilient. Resilience can be defined as "the capacity of a system to absorb disturbance and still retain its basic function and structure."[15]
- decentralized, not bureaucratically centralized. Decentralization means that, driven by shared and common purpose, decision making and learning are pushed out to the edges of the organization where they touch its missional environment. Change is experimented with at the edge, not directed from the center. Purpose is shared and followed by all, but decisions about practice are free to be made where implementation happens.

Writing about decentralized, "leaderless" organizations (in the sense that they are not *directed* by leaders), Ori Brafman and Rod Beckstrom are clear that "ideology is the glue that holds decentralized organizations together."[16] Identity and purpose are at the center. Results are what are measured. The means and practices by which one gets from purpose to results is agile, at times chaotic, and will help the organization to learn what to do next. Learning is not a product of the organization; it is a strategy.

In the curious ways of the world, two prime examples of such deep learning organizations are terrorist groups and drug cartels. The civilized world stands against their purposes. Nonetheless, we have much to learn from their assumptions and practices that lead to their agility, resilience, and continual learning. In his research on these organizations, Michael Kenney points out that their "success," which continues to withstand defeat from opposing military and police, stems from a practice of *mētis*. The concept of *mētis*

> comes from the ancient Greek poets and philosophers. Mētis refers to a broad range of practical skills that sailors, athletes, doctors, statesmen and others use to respond to "a constantly changing natural and human environment," including prudence, perceptiveness, ingenuity, elusiveness and deceit. This crafty intelligence "bears on fluid situations which are constantly changing and which at every moment combine contrary features and forces that are opposed to each other."[17]

As far away as the church stands from the purpose of terrorists and drug cartels, to live in a liquid, divergent world the church will also need to learn that any defeat is not a loss but rather a lesson to instruct what is to be done next to fulfill its purpose. Quietly courageous leadership will learn from the uncertainly of a situation, knowing to be more afraid of being constrained by old ways than to be anxious about new unknowns.

ASSUMPTIONS OF DEMOCRATIC PRACTICES: REFLECTING EARLY BEGINNINGS

The earlier argument was that American congregations and denominations ordered themselves by mirroring hierarchical organizational structures of government, businesses, and other institutions beginning in the 1830s. Reaching further back in their development, American religious organizations also reflected the revolutionary democracy birthed in the 1700s as a means of governance. At the heart of that revolution was the central value that, unlike in monarchies and aristocracies, everyone counted and had a say in their own destiny, either individually or by representation. Governance depended on and was subject to the wisdom and interests of the people. Historian John Wigger writes, "The system of religious economy that [Francis] Asbury and the Methodists were largely responsible for creating—churches unaided and not coerced by government interaction, operating outside the control of social elites—was far different from what had existed in colonial America. Most leaders in colonial America were relatively wealthy college elites."[18] Indeed, the contest between the wealthy college elites and the rapid populist expansion of religion beginning in the late 1700s spawned an argument about whether the credentials of preachers were to be grounded in education or in evangelical spirit—about whether ordained religious leadership was a profession or a calling.[19] It is an argument that continues episodically to this day.

Historically denominations, along with local, state, and federal governments, wrestled with the process of decision making and the locus of authority as they developed, all reflecting a growing democratic spirit that involved the voice of the people governed and ascribed both authority and balancing constraints on the elected leaders. Along the way highly democratic practices and values developed that continue to mark the current landscape of American religion.

However, by the turn of the twenty-first century American democracy was experiencing a duress that came from the challenges of polarized gridlock, global power shifts aided by technology and disappearing national boundaries, a diversity that confounded any unified voice, and a populous resistance to centralized authority. Academics, editorialists, and commentators currently give voice to a vibrant conversation about the future shape of democracy, making the practices and values of democracy fall under review in a new and startling way.

No doubt American congregations and denominations will follow, a decade or more behind, and conform to the changing paths and revisions of both structure and governance determined by the larger culture. But while religious institutions will follow the longer external reshaping of the landscape, there is also the immediate internal work that needs to be done to question current democratically shaped values and practices to ask whether those values and practices continue to support purpose and the public, not the private, mission of our institutions. In challenging tacit assumptions in search of quiet courage, there are three assumptions of a democratic nature that rise to the top: decision making, representation, and egalitarianism.

Decision Making

Overall, democratic practices have developed ways for individual voices to be heard in the process of decision making. Most commonly this has been done through the voting process and through the rules of engagement, such as Robert's Rules of Order. Robert's Rules, originally published in 1876 by U.S. Army Officer Henry Martin Robert, is a parliamentary process that gives space for every member's opinion and within a minimum of time both shapes proposals and provides a known path for decision making. Used widely and for a long period of time, practices such as Robert's Rules undergird the assumption that parliamentary processes and voting are the proper way for communal decision making.

What is missed in the long-held assumptions about such familiar practices is that cultural and contextual changes can minimize their effectiveness. Again, let us draw on the shift from the convergent values of the aberrant time in the first half of the twentieth century to the increasingly divergent postaberrant period beginning in the 1960s.

In a convergent time, values of uniformity and agreement are dominant. In such a convergent time individuals who differ from the majority position of any group (outliers) do not insist on standing against the majority but know to sublimate their differences in order to move toward the preference or position of the larger group. In convergent times, the desire of the group supersedes the desire of the individual, and the individual is expected to change to accommodate the group. At such a time parliamentary procedures and majority voting are helpful, efficient, and effective. Such processes measure the majority position in short order, and in a time of convergence those who are outliers to the majority position instinctively shift to align with the larger group's decision. The work is quick, efficient, and satisfying.

In a divergent time the experience is quite different. Again, recall that the postaberrant time has been marked by an increasing and legitimizing diversity that values individual uniqueness over group conformity. In such a divergent environment parliamentary processes and majority voting no longer set a path toward conformity but actually measure and confirm disagreements. Where in a convergent time a majority vote signals the path forward to fuller agreement as outliers align, in a divergent time it is more likely that a vote draws the lines of disagreement over which competing groups will then contest with one another. Old tools and practices of unity, in the shift of cultural values, become the new means of disagreement.

Quietly courageous leadership operates on the capacity to know what to fear. Changing well-established and familiar practices of decision making that seem so clearly linked to a sense of democracy that protects the equality of every voice will undoubtedly lead to critiques and complaints. No one likes for the rules of the game to be changed, especially after the rules have been mastered and can be used to one's advantage. However, straightforward practices such as debate, parliamentary procedure, and voting no longer lead us to agreements but to contest. Courageous leaders need to know to fear the absence of discernment and clear decisions more than they fear critique and criticism for changing familiar ways.

Increasingly leaders and decision-making groups are exploring means of consensual decision making. "Consensus is a state of mutual agreement among members of a group where all legitimate concerns of individuals have been addressed to the satisfaction of the group," write Steven Saint and James Lawson in their exploration of ways to reach consensus.[20] Parliamentary procedure is a process of *talking*—of persuading others through argument in order to gain votes and win majority support. Consensual procedure is a process of *listening*—of paying attention to legitimate concerns so that the group is able to move ahead in an informed way. A nonbinding show of hands may be used in consensus to gain a sense of the will of a group, and individuals have the opportunity to weigh in on agreement or disagreement. However, processes of consensus allow the group to move ahead, acknowledging but unblocked by the increasingly different opinions and differences that are now normative in all groups. Done well, consensus does not take appreciably more time than parliamentary procedures, particularly because parliamentary procedures now commonly lead to gridlock or a damaged sense of community in which people feel unheard. In his classic work on community Peter Block points out the importance of building community by paying attention to engagement rather than immediately moving to problem solving and the persuasion that comes from older forms of decision making.[21] Institutional leaders, particularly leaders who lead "in community," will need to learn much more about consensual decision making and how to provide direction and alignment for different voices by using the narrative, the story of the group, and the clarity of the group's purpose to move ahead. We currently live in a culture that does not move ahead by agreement. Instead leaders will need to learn to help others move ahead on the clarity of their story and purpose amid their differences. Familiar democratic practices will need to cede space to less familiar community practices in order for our congregations and denominations to live in the new cultural landscape.

Representation: A Redefinition

There are two essential reasons that congregations and denominations assiduously practice democratic representation in their decision-making bodies. The first is that within a democracy the value of egalitarianism, the principle that all people are equal and deserve equal rights and opportunities, is fundamental. However, from the very beginning it was understood that the ideal of egalitarianism could not functionally be met by having all people involved at all points of decision making, which then necessitated representation. Representation is intended to honor the equal rights and opportunities of many individuals by consolidating their voices in a representative whose responsibility is to advocate on their behalf, to represent. Representation has become increasingly important as diversity has become legitimized by a divergent culture. The second reason that representation is highly valued has to do with issues of social justice. There must be some way to bring all voices to the decision-making table where mission is developed, priorities are set, and resources are directed. Not to have a place at the decision-making table is to be barred from access to the power of determining mission, priorities, and the use of resources. The United States and its institutions continue to live out of a history shaped by race and colonialism. The reality is that congregations and denominations must still attend to representation bringing all people to the decision-making table where there is access to power. Leadership groups must be representative, or they cannot expect to be listened to by the wider church.

It is here, however, that further thought must be given to living in the new divergent culture that will consistently invite representative groups to contest over their differences rather than align with their shared purpose. The church is now in the curious position that any and every leadership group must be highly representative if it is to have any credibility in a culture that recognizes diversity. However, in order to be effective once constituted as a representative group, the members of any representative group must take care not to represent—at least not in assumed ways.

Historically, to be invited to represent meant to be invited to the table in order to represent the issues, needs, and preferences of the *subgroup* of which one is a part. By definition that means that people who are asked to represent are not expected to advance the purpose of the *whole*; instead they are expected to advance the agenda and preferred outcomes of the *part* of the whole that they represent.

Within the highest governing bodies of American denominations over past decades the various constituent voices of each denomination have been increasingly caught in gridlock because the multiple agendas and preferences of the competing, representative parts of the church could find no way ahead for the whole. These institutions are now at a point at which it is folly to gather, at great length and at great cost, representative groups and give them the task of finding a way forward by repeating the same contest with one another over the same differing agendas of the parts of the institution that have produced paralyzing gridlock in the past. Surely "representation" must mean something other than contesting over different expectations and outcomes and competing for shrinking resources.

To move ahead will require careful reexamination of what is expected from even the most familiar ideas and words that guide how we live together. For example, in the earlier time of great cultural consensus following World War II, the word "harmony" meant *agreement*. As described in that time of convergence, life was in harmony when individuals sublimated their differences, large and small, in order to participate in a consensus dominated by the specific gender roles, traditional family values and behaviors, and uniformity defined by employment and membership. Now, no longer in a time of cultural consensus, the meaning of words such as "harmony" has necessarily shifted. "Harmony is not everyone singing the same note," observed humorist Wally Armbruster. "That is monotony. Harmony is when everyone sings their own note and then listens closely enough to others to blend their note into a song." [22] Where once harmony meant being alike, harmony now means being respectfully different. In a similar way even the most familiar words, such as "connection" or "community," that have been used in the past to define life within institutions must be reexamined to see if past definitions are sufficient to current challenges or whether old definitions constrain new opportunities. "Representation" is one of those words.

Let us be clear that our common assumptions about representation—meaning contesting to advance the needs, preferences, and outcomes of one's own subgroup—have a rich and appropriate history in the church. In particular, the lineage of mainline denominations rests too steadily on the shoulders of older, white, North American males. It is a lineage that does not capture the richness of the full kingdom of God. Too many congregations still have hallways lined with portraits of white male pastors uninterrupted until only recent years, if at all, with portraits of women or people of color. As those denominations and congregations wrestled with their history, representation (that is, a place at the table) appropriately meant access to shared power—a share of the resources and a share of the decision making. As other races and distinct groups joined the larger body, a place at the table through representation and through caucus was both a tool of the community that people were seeking to build and of social justice that had previously been missing. Clearly, at that time, representation meant the opportunity to claim attention to the needs and preferences of one's subgroup and to negotiate to favor one's own perspective.

Representation *in the service of the whole body*, however, needs a different definition. In this case, the need is not limited to finding a place for missing voices at the table. That is work that gives necessary and ongoing attention to our competing *parts*. It is increasingly the case that congregations and denominations are trying to give attention to the *whole*. How does the whole body, given its divergence, *all* find a way forward together in an increasingly changing mission field? Representation that serves the whole needs to begin with different assumptions. Leaders now need to understand that each representative voice holds its own partial truth that is needed by the whole. One is invited to the table not to argue for one's own preferred outcomes but to bring one's own truth to the conversation in the service of the whole body. In this redefinition, representation calls more on a careful listening than on a forceful talking. If all who come to the table acknowledge that they hold only their own partial truth, then discerning next steps for the whole community requires careful listening and learning to complete the picture.

This new understanding of representation is captured by a meeting room used by the board of directors at Haverford College, a small liberal arts school outside of Philadelphia, Pennsylvania. In the middle of the board room in this Quaker institution is a non-weight-bearing pillar that partially blocks the view of trustees who are trying to listen to their colleagues seated directly across the room on the other side of the pillar. The pillar is not structurally needed but serves as the constant intentional reminder that in order to fully hear one's colleague it is necessary to shift out of one's own comfortable space to get the complete picture. It is the hard work of listening for what one can't understand from one's own comfortable position.

In national or global denominations, with multiple members and participants spread over a whole nation or even several continents, it is virtually impossible to invite all differences to the table. Even at the local congregational level the people are spread across generational, political, economic, racial, and ethnic divides. To expand the table to a size reflecting all nuanced differences would be to assemble a group too large to function.

The reality of the new cultural situation calls for new and different understandings. If representation is not a contest over outcomes but a shared discovery of truth, if listening is more critical than talking, then a representative body must also be willing to listen to voices not at the table. The work of a small representative group must go beyond its own borders of the people in the room to listen for the other partial truths still not present in the room. Processes of listening by engaging other groups not invited to the table, reading, individual conversations, prayer, and discernment expand the function of representation in a search for the fuller portion of partial truths that can lead to a new way forward for the whole body.

For those who remain passionately constant in their contest for their own preferred outcomes, it will remain difficult to understand that being "heard" is not the same as "being agreed with." Some will never be satisfied being heard until their preferred outcome is achieved. Such passion, undoubtedly, is a measure of the importance of the issues to those individuals. Such passion, though, makes it difficult for those so committed to a specific outcome to understand that even the clarity that drives them is only a partial truth. However, the task of a representative group is not to measure the greatest passions within the parts of the congregation, denomination, or institution but to discern the most faithful path ahead for the whole body. Such changed assumptions about representation require the quiet courage of listening and the hard work of weaving together discordant voices. Perhaps less satisfying than the louder debate of contesting representative voices, in a divergent mission field it is the only way ahead.

Egalitarianism

In the exploration of representation discussed earlier, egalitarianism was defined as the principle that all people are equal and deserve equal rights and opportunities. This critical American democratic value needs to be further explored because, over time, it has also taken on the notion of *equal treatment* most commonly expressed in terms of *fairness*. In the current cultural landscape leaders must look deeper than fairness. Fairness is an idea easier to fulfill at a time of abundant resources such as the rising tide of the recent aberrant time.

Consider a quite important functional difference among congregations. The current North American culture has five generations living side by side, from children all the way up to great-great-grandparents. The most effective of congregations are able to span all five of these generations with their ministry. The potential of such congregations to speak to the present generationally divergent mission field and therefore make disciples is considerable. Consider in contrast the congregations that have within their members and participants only the oldest two of the five possible generations. Such congregations have a clear ministry to people who already attend and participate. However, given the differences in values and behaviors among generational cohorts, the stretch that would allow the great- and great-great-grandparents in a two-generation congregation to be radically hospitable to children and their parents in their community is relatively unlikely. These congregations are cut off not only from their community but also from their future. Many of our oldest congregations are our smallest. The central issue here is not size. The smallest of our congregations may be vital and effective in missional purpose. But what is at heart here is that many of these small congregations, because of the age disparity and generational distance from the youngest generations, will not be able to make the leap into the new divergent mission field. In fact, many of these congregations will not live into the next two decades. In these congregations new missional purpose will not be addressed and ministry will be limited to the nurture and care of current members.

Consider then the report from the Study of Ministry Commission that was given to the 2008 General Conference of the United Methodist Church gathering in Fort Worth, Texas. This study, which was to bring clarity to the orders of ordained ministry, noted that the United Methodist Church has congregations in all but 138 of the 3,141 counties in the United States. The report then stated,

> Because of this range, The United Methodist Church is reluctant to leave any preaching post without a preacher. More than 10,000 of our 35,000 local churches have 35 or fewer people present for worship on a typical Sunday. The vast majority of these churches were built to serve the population as it was 100 years ago when 40 percent of Americans made their living by farming.[23]

Following the norm of egalitarianism interpreted as fairness, this report then went on to determine that the denomination must resource each and every one of these congregations, even though, as the report noted, more than 40 percent of the local churches had had no new members join by "profession of faith"—people entering the Christian life by decision as opposed to joining one local congregation by transfer from another. The report was equally inclusive of clergy as of congregations. Later in a section on preparing and supporting clergy for the work to be done, the commission suggested that "*every* deacon or elder" be part of a learning group, that "*every* pastor" moving to a new appointment of a different size be given training, and that "*all* full-time clergy under appointment" be assigned a mentor.[24] This report from a denominational study committee is not singled out as a rare instance of the dominance of this norm of egalitarianism. It is simply one example of a very wide array of initiatives based on the assumption of egalitarianism that continues to influence strategies, practices, and attitudes—each insisting that *all* parts of the system be included and treated/resourced the same.

The assumption is that all congregations must be given equal attention. All clergy must participate in learning groups and be mentored. All members must be satisfied before we can agree on a change in worship or programs. Yet not all congregations will be effective in making disciples, not all clergy are interested in or capable of learning new skills that will align with missional purpose, and not all members are willing to change their worship to make it hospitable to new participants. This is another of the conflicts between *our values* (what we claim to be important as our missional goal) and *our behavior* (how we distribute the resources of the church without regard to effectiveness in addressing mission). Egalitarianism practiced in this way leads to "the tyranny of the all." We cannot move ahead until *all* churches have the pastor they desire. We cannot move ahead until all clergy have received proper continuing education and are willing to go. Not moving until all are ready is a commitment not to move. "No church left behind" is a commitment not to move ahead.

Sometime at the beginning of the twentieth century, Italian sociologist and economist Vilfredo Pareto offered the concept of the Pareto principle, alternately known as the 80/20 rule, the law of the vital few, or the principle of factor sparsity. This principle pointed out that 80 percent of the effects in most situations come from 20 percent of the causes. It is a principle that seems to live out in many forms across all of our organizations and institutions: 80 percent of sales come from 20 percent of the salespeople, 80 percent of the giving to a local church comes from 20 percent of the givers, and 80 percent of the problems experienced in an organization come from 20 percent of the people. The Pareto principle is the more helpful guideline in the new cultural landscape than is an indiscriminant norm of egalitarianism. If the public mission of our congregations is to make an identified and intentional difference, we can expect 80 percent of the difference to be made by 20 percent of the congregations. If the goal is ministerial excellence, we can expect that 20 percent of the clergy will commit to new learning and deeper disciplines to effect 80 percent of the increase in excellence.

In their research based on in-depth interviews with eighty thousand managers in four hundred companies, Marcus Buckingham and Curt Coffman of the Gallup Organization identify a number of norms that need to change, rules that need to be broken in order to move a company toward excellence. One rule that must be broken, they contend, is equal attention to all employees, and they give reasons why the best managers "spend the most time with the best people."[25] The shift from assuming that the leader's task is to change and improve everyone to understanding that the leader's task is to support the gifts that the most productive people already have is an "insight we heard echoed by tens of thousands of great managers: people don't change that much. Don't waste time trying to put in what was left out. Try to draw out what was left in. That is hard enough."[26]

The deeply changed mission field requires a continued learning curve that remains steep and demanding and requires the innovation of new ideas and behaviors. If Pareto is helpful in recognizing that most of the change will come from a smaller section of the system, Everett Rogers's work on the "diffusion of innovations" is further evidence that the old norm of egalitarianism as fairness no longer serves mission.[27] Diffusion of innovations is the process by which a new learning or a changed practice is communicated and picked up by members throughout an organization over time—how innovations are spread throughout an organization. What Rogers's research points out is that there are different segments within any organization or institution that will react to innovations and change in different ways. There are early adapters— those within the system that ride the earliest wave of change, either because they see a possibility worth the risk or because they are of a personal temperament that makes something new too attractive not to try. Behind those early adapters is another much larger segment of people who may be more cautious but who will watch the early adapters closely and will follow behind if the results of the earlier efforts prove worthwhile. However, there is a third subset within any organization that will not adapt to innovation. What this subset of people has done in the past is what they will do in the future, out of preference or out of fear. Come what will, this subset of the organization will not follow others into change.

Egalitarianism, defined as the fairness of fully equal treatment, requires resources and attention to all segments and subsets of the organization, whether or not purpose is being addressed. Leaders in the current divergent landscape must be much more discerning to follow the actual definition of egalitarianism as an equality of rights and opportunities, not an equality of treatment. The practice of egalitarianism in which all must be treated equally and no one moves ahead until all are on board directs missional resources and attention toward weakness rather than strength. If 80 percent of the missional effectiveness will be accomplished by 20 percent of the system that is willing to learn new ways in the wilderness, *egalitarianism practiced as fairness paradoxically requires leaders to focus 80 percent of their time, attention, and resources on the 20 percent of the system that demonstrates recalcitrance, weakness, inability, and disinterest.* Asked for leadership that will produce the innovations and change that will allow the church to live in the new mission field, leaders are still most positively rewarded for caring for and directing resources to the 20 percent of the people and congregations who complain most about the changes needed or are unwilling or unable themselves to take the trip into the new wilderness. Holding to old assumptions of not moving ahead until all are ready to take the trip precludes living into the new world.

Strengths overused become weaknesses. Assumptions that once supported effectiveness, allowed to go for too long without challenge and redefinition, eventually become the constraints to that same effectiveness. Quietly courageous leaders do the hard work of being more afraid of not challenging old assumptions and known ways than of being afraid of change.

6

A WORD ABOUT LEARNING

Assumptions about How Leadership Is Formed

This chapter on the formation of leadership will focus specifically on clergy. In voluntary associations such as congregations, leadership is always shared and negotiated between the employed staff and the key volunteers. This shared, negotiated leadership is true in congregations as clergy and laity collaborate to lead. However, it is the pastoral leadership of the clergy that is credentialed and accountable, and it is pastoral leadership that has been given primary attention around issues of formation. It has long been held that congregations do not vision larger than their pastoral leaders. While clergy cannot do everything by themselves, congregations rarely do more than can be supported by the capacity and courage of their pastoral leaders. Clergy are understood to be a critical resource of leadership for healthy and vital congregations.

Again, however, there are assumptions that guide the preparation and certification of clergy. The dominant assumptions focus on content and process. Assumptions around *content* primarily focus on the role of the seminary, where it is assumed that clergy in formation learn the essentials of what is needed for their professional role with congregations. Assumptions around *process* focus on the denominational requirements and steps for certification and deployment to be followed from the earliest sense of call into ministry to the time of retirement. Retired United Methodist bishop Janice Huie describes this process as a "pipeline"—a linear, orderly, and regulated path that involves local congregations, denominational certification committees, colleges and seminaries, deployment processes, continuing education requirements, and retirement rules.[1] Importantly Huie identifies the pipeline as a closed system. It is not open to the environment or sensitive to the multiple cultures in which it operates. Once in the pipeline, it is the pipeline that directs and controls all steps and responses of the people seeking to serve as clergy.

Like the other assumptions identified in this book, the long-held assumptions about the content and process of clergy formation need to be brought to the surface to be examined and challenged because of the changing times in which we now live. What is already clear is that in the postaberrant time the previous learnings and practices of the church have lagged considerably behind the cultural changes. This lag has become more pronounced as the rate of change in the liquid culture allows less chance for institutional and organizational efforts of change to solidify before the continued cultural morphing requires the next phase of institutional and organizational adaptation. The assumptions that have been steady and stable for so long and that undergird the training and certification of clergy need to be tested.

A DESCRIPTIVE ASSESSMENT OF LEADERSHIP FORMATION

The appropriate place to begin the inquiry is with a descriptive assessment of basic clergy leadership formation. The primary place of clergy formation has historically been the theological seminary. In the case of the inquiry of this book, the type of formation that is under particular examination is *leadership formation*. Apart from theological, spiritual, or pastoral formation, the question at hand is how clergy learn and develop a practice that enables them to assume the role of leader within a congregation.

It is abundantly clear that leadership is expected of clergy. Having worked directly with a very large number of pastoral nominating committees, pastor-parish relations committees, personnel committees, and denominational deployment offices, I have had extensive firsthand experience of the stylized expectations that congregations express about clergy. There is a dominant pattern at the time of pastoral transition in which congregations identify their hopes and expectations for the next clergyperson who will serve them. The almost unfailing pattern is that congregations want their next pastor to (1) be a good preacher, (2) care for them as people, (3) help them to ____, and (4) be different from their departing pastor (in some described way). It is number 3 that is the statement about leadership. Number 3 is commonly a statement about change. A congregation wants their new pastor to help them increase their ministry to children and youth, help them reconnect with their community, help them grow in size as a congregation, or help them become more missional so that they extend their care beyond themselves, etc. In each of these cases congregations use the opportunity of self-assessment that comes with the time of pastoral transition to identify a part of themselves that is missing, is insufficiently developed, needs to be corrected, or is a hope of what they believe they are called to become. Stating their current situation as a problem that needs to be fixed or a hope that needs to be pursued, at the time of pastoral transition the congregation views the next clergyperson as the leadership resource that can help them reach their identified next step. "We want a pastor who can help us ____" is the expression of an expectation of leadership. Congregations invite and expect a pastor with the basic skills and courage to help them change or become more than they currently are.

Expectations about pastoral leadership are also endemic to church conflict. It is part of many, if not most, of the conflicts that disturb or disrupt pastoral relationships with congregations either because leadership has not been exercised or because it has been approached without the skills needed to manage the necessary relationships to see the changes through.

What is clear is that while leadership is an expectation, it is not a widely recognized discipline in seminaries, where it is assumed clergy receive formation sufficient to their role in congregations. In a very informal 2015 exploration of the websites of forty theological seminaries across six denominations, it was clear that almost none offered a basic master-level leadership track, very few had a department or full-time faculty dedicated to the area of leadership, and few offered full courses on the issues of organizational leadership. Seminaries, as the assumed locus of clergy formation, have not historically treated leadership as a discipline for inquiry in which those who are learners can develop theories and constructs that could inform their practice as it develops post-seminary. Doctor of Ministry programs, which are extensions of the foundational training offered by seminaries, are more likely to include leadership studies in their curriculum, which reflects the questions that people already engaged in ministry bring to that level of their educational development. Nonetheless, in not too many decades past, faculty in a theological seminary could all too commonly consider leadership as "a concept unbefitting Christian ministry."[2]

Research attention, however, has been given to leadership development of clergy. It is here that we are helped to gain an accurate and descriptive assessment of the current situation of clergy leadership. For over fifteen years David Gortner has been involved in research funded by the Lilly Endowment to explore the habits, skills, and capacities of clergy who are effective as agents or catalysts of transformational change in ministry. He reports finding notable examples of effective clergy with the capacity of such leadership and has developed markers of their leadership. However, he importantly also reports that the much more common "products" of seminary education are "placeholder" clergy and "talented but tenuous" clergy.[3]

Placeholder clergy have the basic skills in the core functions of preaching, pastoral care, and sacramental ministry but have not developed the capacities for effective leadership of congregations. Such clergy can be called by or assigned to a congregation and be expected to continue that congregation's familiar practices, but they will be unequipped to help the congregation shape its vision for the future or adapt to generational challenges, local demographic or community changes, or large-scale cultural value shifts. In a fast-changing culture in which competing generational preferences make the cultural waters even choppier, any institution, as organizational management professor Robert Quinn so notably framed it, that does not choose deep change is actually choosing slow death.[4] In a fast-changing culture, placeholder clergy are not leading; they are simply sustaining whatever life is left until time and resources run out. These are the clergy who try to hold the church steady while the death tsunami and generational shifts deplete their congregations of present and future participants.

Talented but tenuous clergy are those who are more creative and able to see beyond the basic maintenance of the practices and traditions of the congregation. Able to vision and come up with worthy ideas and goals for the future of their congregation, these clergy lack the self-confidence and capacity to help congregations bring ideas to substance. Conflict averse and unclear about the nature of human systems and organizations, talented but tenuous clergy wait for permission to lead. Given that leadership commonly disturbs very stable organizations, and that organizations do not routinely reward disturbances, permission giving is rare and such leaders are tenuous indeed.

Following Huie's image of a closed pipeline, Gortner notes that seminary and certification processes produce what they are designed to produce: a high percentage of placeholder and talented but tenuous clergy. Gortner's research further describes the influence, or lack of influence, on the development of clergy leadership by seminaries. His data were collected from 302 recently ordained mainline pastors and priests who also benefited from postseminary training and transition-into-ministry programs. In his research he asked his respondents to rate their own self-confidence in the following broad areas of ministry:

- preaching and proclamation
- being a role model
- sacramental and liturgical ministries
- communications
- self-development and self-management
- Christian education and formation
- pastoral care

- -

- supervising others and work
- setting objectives and program plans
- developing lay ministry and leadership
- congregational/group development
- organizational leadership
- community outreach and connection

These areas of ministry are, in fact, listed in the declining order of Gortner's results. Preaching and proclamation were identified as the area of greatest self-confidence. Each subsequent area reflected a decreasing self-confidence until community outreach and connection were identified as the area of least self-confidence. The dashed line, about halfway through the list of areas of ministry, is imposed by me to reflect that *the areas of greatest self-confidence above the line are the areas most directly correlated to the disciplines of the seminary.* Those areas of ministry below the dashed line are least connected to the disciplines of the seminary but are integral to leadership. A more studied and nuanced statement of conclusion to the results that Gortner offers in part is that

> the pattern in responses suggests that clergy are most confident in tasks that pull on their abilities to be kind, benevolent, understanding, steady, and religiously expressive, in settings that involve less risk. They are least confident in tasks that require more assertiveness and decisive direction, systemic thinking, formation of partnerships for leadership and engagement with people beyond the walls of the local church or denomination.[5]

In a closed system, a pipeline, in which the process and content are prescribed from the time a person enters the system until they leave, the results are systemically determined. As Gortner notes, "the whole system pulls toward maintenance, and toward a model of pastoral/priestly leadership that overemphasizes the pastoral, homiletic, and sacramental facets of ministry and de-emphasizes (and even seeks to avoid) the facets of ministry having to do with organizational leadership and the high art of community-building."[6]

It is also noteworthy that a byproduct of such closed systems is *dependency*. The message received by anyone entering such a system is that if you follow the process outlined you will be credentialed. The system takes responsibility for prescribing steps and for quality control. An anecdote from one of the mainline denominational offices responsible for clergy standards tells of their response to criticisms that the denominational process for ordination was too complicated, too long, and too regulated. To see how they could simplify and shorten the process the national staff methodically went through their polity procedures and put every required step toward ordination on newsprint so that they could follow all that a candidate would have to do to move from stating an intent for ministry, through education, through certification, to ordination. When they completed the task they stepped back and looked at the very complex process outlined on newsprint that was taped to every wall of the conference room. After careful consideration they concluded that the process could not be simplified and that each and every step was necessary to produce a clergyperson of the required standard. What is demonstrated in the anecdote is that the denomination held agency over the formation of their clergy. Control was with the denomination. Dependency was the appropriate response of the candidate. Candidates that followed every step and did not step outside the lines could fast-track their path into ministry. Such a system naturally produces placeholders and talented but tenuous leaders who follow rules and wait for permission. It also prepares leaders who will subvert their own initiative or instincts while leading "in community," in which the reward system is based on satisfaction of members, the absence of discomfort and complaints, and the absence of permission.

HOW DOES ONE LEARN A PROFESSION?

In order to test the current assumptions that shape the prevailing practice, it is often helpful to change the question that guides the inquiry. Rather than ask how one gains certification and ordination as a clergyperson or how one becomes a leader, for the present purpose the more helpful question will be: *How does one learn a profession?* Stepping back to a more generic question allows a different exploration of the content and process needed for the practice of a profession.

A Caution

However, before rushing off to a new exploration, one important caution must be offered. Because the postaberrant time has been difficult for religious institutions to thrive, much criticism has been heaped on clergy because of their central role in congregations that struggle in the cultural changes, and much blame has been heaped on seminaries for not producing clergy with the assertiveness and skills necessary to steer their institutions into the new postaberrant age. It is important to remember that the seminary curricula and practices, as well as the denominational polity and practices that continue today, have roots developed in the midst of the sweet spot of the aberrant age. It can also be said that those curricula and practices have been managed, up until recently, mostly by people for whom the aberrant time was still fresh in memory and a guiding orientation. Those earlier seminary and denominational standards and practices were right for their day. Seminaries were developed from and continually operated out of a European model of the academy in which particular disciplines and educational content were understood to be the standard of both education and training. Denominational and educational standards in a time of convergence in which all congregations and all clergy leaned toward being similar, if not the same, allowed for standards of certification and practice in which conformity over individual assertiveness was valued.

Seminaries and denominations may be liable for overpracticing strengths until they became weaknesses. However, blame is not helpful, as if a fixable problem went unaddressed. The argument in this book is that the change we are facing is deeper than simple problem solving and that new learning is required. Problem solving in this case would most likely lead to new or more requirements and regulations or to new or more diverse curricula—all of which would be more growth from the same roots that currently constrain. What is needed is not new or more but different. Stepping away from blame in order to frame a different question can invite changed insights. Stepping away from blame allows us to stop trying to fix what is, allowing us to ask where what we already know appropriately fits into what we must learn to do next.

Learning a Profession

The suggested question for this inquiry is: How does one learn a profession? A profession is a paid occupation that requires prolonged training and formal qualification. In a truly fascinating study of the development of the system of professions, Andrew Abbott describes professions as "exclusive occupational groups applying somewhat abstract knowledge to particular cases."[7] Professions develop by both setting up and protecting the boundaries for the practice of their occupation through the development of theories and a language that distinguishes their work from others and by learning to deal with the questions that live within the jurisdiction claimed by the profession. Mastering a profession requires a weaving together of information, language, experience, personal integration, risk, and a thirst for continued maturation. Because professions are practiced in continually changing environments, learning toward mastery does not end. And, as we will see, learning a profession also requires disorientation and challenge.

For our purpose, one of the most helpful approaches to investigate the learning of a profession is the Dreyfus model of skill acquisition. Stuart Dreyfus was a mathematician and system analyst, and his brother Hubert Dreyfus was a philosopher. Together they developed a model of skill acquisition based on the study of chess players and airline pilots. Although their own writing was exceptionally brief, their work has been picked up and has influenced practice across multiple professions. In particular it is worth noting the influence on the practice of clinical nursing. In an examination of the training of clinical nurses, Patricia Benner began with a description of training that I will argue applies to and still guides much current thinking about the training of clergy. She wrote, "Nursing educators were engaged in a competency-based education movement. This movement was designed to pre-specify learning outcomes in well-defined behavioral objectives. The assumption was that both learning and nursing practice could be reduced to a collection of techniques."[8] Among groups responsible for certifying clergy, identification of competencies and behavioral objectives continues to be the mythic solution for defining vital leadership. The dilemma, however, was that nursing practice was far more complex and situation specific than theory could project. Learning could not separate theory from practice. I would argue that in thinking about the leadership training of clergy, too much effort is focused on competencies as if they could be taught. I would also argue that, like clinical nursing, the practice of leadership in ministry is far too complex and situation specific to be addressed only by educational models. What is most helpful about the Dreyfus model of skill acquisition is that it moves past consideration of discrete competencies that assumes a toolbox for leadership. Instead, stages of development are identified, and movement through the stages depends on the agency of the practitioner—the investment of the learner—not the requirements of the training or the certifying institution. As in many professions, it is not particularly difficult to be certified as a nurse or a clergyperson. There is, however, a significant difference between being able to enter into the baseline practice of a profession and the mastery of that profession. The difference is a factor of one's willingness and passion to continually learn, which means being willing to learn beyond what the academy can teach. In particular, the discipline of leadership is an area that requires continued learning guided fully by the agency of the learner.

As a way of thinking about professional development, the Dreyfus model uses the following five stages:[9]

- Novice: Learning the Rules of the Game

    Key for the novice stage is the separation of theory from practice in learning. For the novice stage, theory is a lot of "context-free" information, both theory and rules of thumb, that can be understood at a basic level without experience in the area being learned.

- Advanced Beginner: Using Rules in Context

    The advanced beginner draws on accumulated facility in using a set of rules and also starts to attend to various situational factors. Competence develops out of the advanced beginner's experience of being overwhelmed. In order to control a multitude of variables, one chooses a plan that helps to focus and organize one's performance. In addition—and this is a key difference—one begins to feel ultimate responsibility for the outcome of one's acts and deep emotional investment in the choice of a course of actions.

- Competent to Proficient: The Intuitive Leap

    Proficiency describes a stage at which one acts intuitively "without thinking," drawing on "know-how" that is the result of many similar experiences that now provide the mental backdrop for an immediate cause of action in this current situation ("holistic similarity recognition"). The difference between the proficient performer and the expert is that the former does not yet have enough experience with the outcomes of a wide variety of possible responses to react automatically. The proficient performer must still decide what to do. Emotional involvement in decision making and the pain or elation related to various outcomes are essential to the development of the capacity for the transition to the stages beyond competency.

- Expertise

    Expertise emerges when the conscious decision also becomes intuitive. Experts do engage in deliberation when something quite important or novel is at stake, but this is not the calculative deliberation of the novice or competent beginner; rather, it is a critical reflection on one's intuition. What distinguishes expertise is fluid motion.

- Mastery

    Mastery posits that the highest expertise requires patterns of apprenticeship that allow one to train with various masters and to utilize multiple disciplines sequentially.

Utilizing the Model of Skill Acquisition

Using the generic developmental categòries of the Dreyfus model allows for observations about leadership development for clergy. It also helps find the appropriate place and role for the institutions, strategies, and models used for leadership development that the church has currently developed. Again, rather than argue about what the church thinks it got right or wrong, the rapid changes of the current cultural mission field are better addressed by asking how we can bend what we do know to the purpose of leaning into the changes of the postaberrant time.

Context-Free Learning

It is clear in the Dreyfus model that there is a role for the traditional academy (seminary or alternative educational track) in which the student is pulled out from and learns free from the context of the practice of a profession. As Abbott points out in his study of the development of professions, each profession has its specific jurisdiction, interior language, central disciplines, and history that must be mastered by the initiate in order to enter the practice. Theology, as the mother of all sciences, has a very long history, rich tradition, and specific disciplines, all of which shape and form the contemporary practitioner. Note that the Dreyfus model argues for a novice stage in which learning is "context free"—in which information, theory, and rules of thumb are to be understood at a basic level without being attached to experience. This is clearly the dominant role of the seminary and the alternative nonseminary basic training paths that denominations establish for those seeking certification. Hence one can argue that it is appropriate that seminaries do not focus heavily on leadership studies at the basic master level where students are learning context free.

Context-free learning, however, has its limit in the development of the practitioner, and that limit imposes more constraint on the importance and effectiveness of academic approaches to learning than once suspected. The limit is well identified by retired bishop Will Willimon. With the better part of his own ministry deeply embedded in the academy at Duke Seminary, Willimon sojourned in the mission field as a bishop, then retired to a position back in the seminary. His wandering back and forth across the boundaries and his service in the mission field both as a theologian and as an ecclesiastical officer give unique perspective to the appropriate gifts and necessary constraints to both sides of "the fence." He writes,

> I know not to ask seminaries to give training in the practical skills required to creatively lead a congregation. That's the job of the annual conference. I take the classical view of seminary education—a seminary's job is to teach the classical ministerial disciplines of biblical interpretation, sermon preparation, theological discernment, church history, Christian theology, liturgical theology, counseling protocol, and biblical languages. A seminary is literally a "seedbed" in which the seeds are planted to bear fruit in later ministry. The church ought to prepare the new minister for the leadership skills that are required to produce fruit in the church in the present age. [10]

Willimon's description of the limited capacity of the seminary aligns well with Gortner's assessment of what students actually gain from their seminary education. I will later argue that "the church" itself may not be the only or the best forum for teaching leadership and practical skills beyond the seminary. However, for the moment it is clear that as part of the development of a professional practice, learning that is experience based is beyond the reach of the seminary except in its most fundamental introduction. It is beyond the seminary's basic competency.

Being Overwhelmed and Willing to Own Responsibility

The next stage of professional development beyond the novice depends on using what was learned in the academy "in context," as part of the actual practice of the profession. The advanced beginner stage initially develops as the student moves out into the working field of the profession to use the rules and the disciplines learned in the academy. It is very helpful for the student to walk into this next stage when he or she is still connected to the seminary and can reflect with instructors as theory and practice come together. Student pastorates, field assignments, and practitioner years in which the student fills some professional role yet also has a connection to the seminary are invaluable half-steps in development.

However, for one who is still a student, moving into this next stage of practice is only a half-step because the seminary cannot fully project its work into this arena. Note that in the Dreyfus model, fully moving into the advanced beginner stage requires two additional factors: a *willingness to be overwhelmed* and an *acceptance of ultimate responsibility*. No doubt students learning any profession feel overwhelmed and responsible in taking the initial steps into the practice of that profession. However, the identity of being a student releases a significant portion of these burdens that are the drivers for the next stage of development. A parish that has a "student minister" is significantly less demanding and more forgiving of missteps or poor practice knowing that the relationship is time limited and aware of the early stage of development of the student. Being overwhelmed and knowing one is accountable are hooks that students certainly feel, but from which they can more easily extricate themselves because of their status, saying, "Oh well, I'm only learning." The practice of ministry develops not when the student practitioner is able to escape the discomfort of the hooks but when the discomfort and the sense of responsibility are felt by the fully employed practitioner and produce the next burning question that must be addressed in order to stay in the profession with any self-confidence.

Questions are invaluable in learning the practice of a profession. From the beginning of the practice of a profession the questions that the advanced beginner lives with drive the next steps of learning, not curricula or regulations. Tony Wagner is co-director of the Change Leadership Group at the Harvard Graduate School of Education. His critique of even the best schools centers on the difficulty of teaching what he identifies as "new survival skills" instead of teaching information or techniques.[11] Among the survival skills that undergird imagination is critical thinking, which is guided by questions. In a simple example Wagner notes the common practice of elementary-level teachers who use videos as part of their established curriculum. Videos are not uncommonly used by teachers as a break from active duty. They simply set up the classroom video system, push play, and settle back to enjoy the easier pace of watching the video with the classroom. At the conclusion of the video, the teacher then seeks to engage the class as to what they learned from the video by asking a series of questions, for which the responses are predictably few and the conversation halting. What was missing that would produce learning based on critical thinking were *guiding questions*. Wagner points out that effective teachers introduce the video prior to playing and then list the three to five questions that they want the class to answer for themselves as they watch the video. At the conclusion, when the teacher reengages the class, the conversation flows and multiple ideas bump into each other as the students share what they discovered. Questions prompt learning; information alone does not.

Further, in his work on innovation, Wagner distinguishes between the extrinsic and intrinsic motivation that comes with questions. Extrinsic questions and motivation come from outside the individual—from a teacher, an instructor, an employer. Intrinsic comes from within the individual her- or himself. Of the two, he is clear to note that "people will be most creative when they are motivated by the interest, satisfaction, and challenge of the work itself—and not by external pressure."[12] As practitioners learn their profession, the questions that will motivate and guide their development toward excellence are not questions assigned or imposed by teachers or institutional requirements but the questions that burn internally because on their answer depends self-confidence and the ability to stay in the field of practice.

The ability of practitioners to form their own questions and guide their own development is central to the difference between the very limited novice-level formation that can be done at the academic master level in the seminary and the further support of development that the seminary can support at the DMin (Doctor of Ministry) level. Because enrollment in a DMin requires some prior specified amount of full-time professional practice in the field, candidates for the degree come with questions already formed. In addition, the project orientation of the degree requires that at some point the work of the practitioner/student be formed around a central question of practice that is of high importance to the individual. Nonetheless, even here the relationship of the seminary to continued professional development is limited because the work remains a step removed from the field of engagement.

Note that in the Dreyfus model there is no safety net that supports ongoing development. As noted in the model, discussed earlier, "Emotional involvement in decision making, and the pain or elation related to various outcomes, is essential to the development of the capacity for the transition to the stages beyond competent." Institutional initiatives to eliminate, mitigate, or manage the risk or investment necessary from learners in developing a mature professional practice of leadership may hamper rather than support the development of the leadership needed. As Huie points out, "excessive caregiving" through denominational policies, seminary overextension, and overempathetic credentialing agencies provide comfort to the struggling or unsure individuals seeking a way into the practice of ministry at the expense of the mission field where leadership is deeply needed.[13]

Proficiency

The Dreyfus model clearly suggests the limits of institutional educational training for learning a profession. Willimon points to the line beyond which the seminary has limited competency and then suggests it is the role of the institutional church to pick up the slack by providing additional teaching and training in practical leadership. On the one hand, the middle judicatory of a denomination is better positioned than the seminary to provide leadership training because it operates in the field rather than in the academy. Beyond the level of beginner, professional development must maintain a close connection to the active practice of the profession. So it would seem that teaching done by people in the field with their own experience, and learning within the arena of practice, is a natural next step in which denominations and middle judicatories can take up the responsibility for required programs of leadership development.

On the other hand, there are significant institutional limits that apply to the denomination and middle judicatories as well. An institutional requirement such as a probationary/supervisory period for seminary graduates entering the field of ministry or requirements of additional continuing education courses or workshops in areas not addressed by the seminary is still part of a pipeline. These become the next steps to be fulfilled by the candidate, and as such they are steps required by the institution. They are not driven by the internal question or need of the individual who is developing her or his professional practice. Ed Friedman pointedly said that "the colossal misunderstanding of our time is the assumption that insight will work with people who are unmotivated to change."[14] The agency for growth and development remains external to the individual. While providing additional information in a context-appropriate way, such programs may also extend the invitation for dependency and create uniformity and the need for permission to lead.

The principle here is the same as that which operates in the formation of communities. It makes a difference whether the individual claims responsibility for helping to shape community or whether the individual wants to simply receive from the community. The difference is expressed by Peter Block in his work on community as the difference between being either a citizen or a consumer.[15] A consumer is one who believes that his or her own needs can best be satisfied by the actions of others, while a citizen is one who willingly takes responsibility and is willing to be accountable for the greater well-being of the whole. Citizens make communities, consumers don't. It makes a difference where agency, responsibility, and accountability lie. If the seminary takes responsibility for formation and training, and the denomination extends that responsibility beyond the limits of the seminary, the developing practitioner remains in the position of consumer waiting for his or her needs to be fulfilled by others and holding others responsible for problems encountered and disappointments experienced. In terms of professional development, the consuming recipient will not develop beyond what any profession would recognize as a basic journeyman and expertise will remain far beyond reach. The clergyperson will not advance beyond "place keeper" or "talented but tenuous." To move further, the questions driving development must come from within, the motivation to address those questions must come from within, and the purpose of the pursuit must be larger than the self.

Expert Intuition

In learning a profession the move from competency to proficiency is described in the Dreyfus model as a stage at which one acts intuitively, without thinking, and drawing on know-how that comes from the backlog of experiences in similar settings. Experience itself becomes the teacher. Acting intuitively, in this sense, would be described by William Duggan as a form of "expert intuition."[16] Duggan identifies different types of intuition. The most common form of intuition is "ordinary intuition," which is a form of emotion. It is a feeling, a hunch. One just knows—and it requires no thought; one just acts, knowing. Ordinary intuition is immediate, operating in a flash. "Expert intuition" is not a feeling; it is a form of rapid thinking. It depends on recognizing something that has been encountered before and relies on experience. The response to expert intuition is also very quick because one is operating in a known situation—or at least in a situation sufficiently similar to times and places previously encountered that can inform the response. Time and experience make the difference.

In his work on what makes people successful in their work or profession, reporter and author Malcolm Gladwell acknowledges that there are some people who have natural or innate gifts for what they do.[17] It is not uncommon to hear a person described as a natural leader. Gladwell, however, uncovers that the "natural born" successful people are much more rare than one might think and that it is much more likely that they have simply worked longer and harder than most others. They have more to draw on to direct their next steps. He notes that researchers have even put a number to what it takes for expertise—ten thousand hours. Yes, he argues, The Beatles came to the United States in 1964, setting off a British Invasion with music and performances that reset the bar on pop music. What was not given attention was that they had been playing as a group for seven years beginning in 1957, in unending gigs, for mercilessly long hours, in poor conditions, and had long surpassed their ten thousand hours, making whatever they encountered in the United States feel simply like more of what they already knew (except, perhaps, for the crowd's reactions).

So the first part of moving from simple competence to proficiency in learning a profession is simply time and experience. If you practice long enough, you get better. You also get quicker, needing less time to think about what is required and acting intuitively. Time and experience increase proficiency but are insufficient to move toward expertise. More learning is required for expertise. Time and experience must be met with disciplined inquiry of another form that requires understanding the difference between horizontal and vertical learning.

Vertical Learning

"There are two different forms of development—horizontal and vertical," writes Nick Petrie of the Center for Creative Leadership. "A great deal of time has been spent on 'horizontal' development (competencies), but very little on 'vertical' development (developmental stages). The methods for horizontal and vertical are very different. Horizontal development can be 'transmitted' (from an expert), but vertical development must be earned (for oneself!)."[18]

Horizontal learning happens—horizontally—between two people: the teacher and the student. What is learned is passed between the one and the other. This is reflected in the old saying that a lecture is an event in which the notes of the professor pass to the notebooks of the students without going through the brains of either. Perhaps an insensitive joke, it does not recognize the hard work of both teaching and learning or the value of information passed from one to the other. Nonetheless, horizontal learning and horizontal development operate between teacher and student, between the expert and the initiate, and are limited, as identified in the Dreyfus model. There are times and circumstances in which the horizontal information from experts must be limited and constrained because it does not deepen learning but instead discontinues critical thinking by providing answers when, in fact, questions are needed.

Beyond the limits of horizontal development is the work of *vertical development* in which the practitioner must bring ideas, critical thinking, and experience together with the purpose of resolving his or her own quandary. This is the work of going deeper (vertically) into one's need to learn, change, and improve. Petri notes four conditions necessary for vertical development:[19]

- an area of frustration;
- limits of current thinking;
- an area of importance; and
- available support.

To do the work of vertical development there may be experts used (for resource only), but the work fully belongs to and must be shaped by the learner, not by the instructor. Continuing education initiatives have long sought to address this need among clergy as they sought to develop their practice, postseminary while in the field. Leaders in the field like Bob Reber, Mark Rouch, and Bruce Roberts sought to honor the need to keep the work close to the field of practice and aligned with the specific questions of the learner.[20] However, the field of continuing education among clergy has been overpopulated by forms still dominated by the models of the academy: by teaching, short-term courses, workshops, or seminars.

The richer work of vertical learning is best done in "communities of practice." Communities of practice bring professionals out of the isolation of their own individual practice into communities of inquiry and accountability. Mike Schmoker is an author and consultant working on issues of education and schools. He has identified "isolation as the enemy of improvement."[21] He notes that public school teachers commonly think of their classroom as their own professional "turf" and that, as a whole, teachers and administrators tend to think that, left alone, good teaching happens when individual teachers operate out of sight. It is not unusual for principals to feel like intruders and for teachers to feel intruded on when principals must step into the teacher's classroom for mandatory supervisory review. The reality, Schmoker reflects, is that "isolation ensures that highly unprofessional practices are tolerated and thus proliferated in the name of . . . professionalism."[22] In isolation without accountability he notes that what "works" for a teacher can easily morph into no more than what the teacher feels comfortable doing.

Clergy operate in a very similar isolation in a congregation that they often protect for similar reasons identified by teachers. Clergy largely operate in an isolated congregational "turf" largely unobserved by other professional clergy and unsupervised in actual practice. The answer to this isolation is not for denominational executives to step into the congregation to provide supervision. In order to do the critical work of vertical development, clergy, like teachers, must themselves step out of the isolation into "communities of practice." Looking at the four conditions necessary for vertical development identified earlier by Petrie, it is in the community of practice where the support (support in terms of transparency, challenge, and accountability) is found. Communities of practice allow the professionals to see their own practice, to assess, to adjust, and to test new ways.

Etienne Wenger was a senior research scientist at the Institute for Research on Learning at Menlo Park when he published his research on communities of practice in 1998.[23] Communities of practice are based on learning as social participation. As a part of his research Wenger observed how new learning developed within the claims processing departments of the insurance industry. Claims processing is a difficult place to work, with a high level of employee turnover, because it is the intersecting point where the uniform rules and regulations of the insurance company meet the individual and unique (particularly in the eyes of the claim customer) situation of each claim. The claims processor is the staff person who must reconcile the claim with the rules, and vice versa. Wenger notes that in order to prepare the claims processor for his or her position, there is a time of training (horizontal learning) in which rules, processes, documents, and forms are all explained. It is a necessary level of learning. However, when mistakes and/or frustrations built up in the processing of claims, the typical response of the insurance company was to increase the amount of training, which frequently led to an increase in the number of mistakes, an increase in frustration, or an increase in employee turnover. Horizontal learning had its clear limits.

The question then became: How do the best claims processors actually learn how to do their work? On inquiry Wenger observed that the best of the processors, when they encountered a claim that they were unsure of, would not turn to their training or the company's rules. Instead a good claims processor would simply stand up in his or her cubicle, get the attention of two or three colleagues, and ask, "How would you treat this?" Learning as social participation makes a person's own work transparent to him- or herself. One must describe what the issue is and how one already is thinking about the situation in order to have a conversation with colleagues. It brings the work into direct contact with the standards and practices as known, searches for new ideas and information, explores alternatives, and tries new choices with both the support and the accountability of colleagues. The support and accountability often come a bit later as the consulted colleagues look back and ask how things worked out in the questioned claim. It taps into all four of the areas for vertical development that Petri identifies: an area of frustration, the limits of current thinking, an area of importance, and available support.

Clergy professional peer groups are perhaps the best example of communities of practice available to clergy. Consultants, mentors, coaches, and spiritual directors are all avenues that clergy can use to make their work and life transparent to themselves; hold their work up to current knowledge, standards, and peer review; and receive feedback with support and accountability. However, clergy professional peer groups (in which participants *intentionally choose* to participate, as opposed to *being required or assigned* by their denomination) appear to be the richest opportunity for vertical learning and continued development of professional mastery. They must, of course, meet the standards of vertical learning and communities of practice. However, at the conclusion of the initiative on "Sustaining Pastoral Excellence," in which the Lilly Endowment, Inc., supported a broad range of ongoing structured clergy peer learning groups, the endowment also funded a research project to evaluate the impact of the groups. The research was able to track and measure the importance of the groups and was able to identify characteristics and strategies of the more effective groups. But perhaps most significantly as a reflection of the importance of communities of practice in the vertical development of a profession, the researchers noted that even the worst of the clergy peer groups was better than the best of other forms of continuing education for clergy seeking to improve their ministry.[24]

Learning to be an effective leader in a congregation requires the practitioner to become vulnerable to him- or herself and with colleagues about the challenges and questions that are actually faced in the immediate moment. Such learning is managed best through communities of practice that function in the immediacy of the fast and continually changing mission field in which the learning must continually adapt. Importantly, communities of practice among clergy have demonstrated a capacity to generate not only new learning for participants but also new courage. Over the more than ten years that the Texas Methodist Foundation has provided communities of practice for clergy (facilitated clergy development groups), ongoing evaluation of the groups continually surface testimonials about courage along with learning. Participants speak about being more courageous in their leadership and willingly seeking to be effective with change because they have colleagues who both understand their situation and who, at the next gathering of the community of practice, will ask about what happened. Much more than the permission-giving that the talented but tenuous clergy are seeking, communities of practice offer transparency, new insights, challenges, courage, and accountability. More will be said about TMF's clergy development groups in chapter 10.

The Deep Generalist: Mastery of a Profession

In the Dreyfus model, mastery is identified as the highest level of professional performance. Critically, mastery of a profession needs to be understood apart from expertise. There is a significant difference between the professional who is exceptional at what she or he does because of the time and experience he or she has invested that makes all things familiar to him or her and the master of a profession who is able to use his or her knowledge, skill, and insight broadly beyond the confines of the particular place in which he or she practices his or her profession. As an example, Harrell Beck, Old Testament professor of wisdom literature at Boston University School of Theology, was such a master. When I attended his classes at seminary he began every lecture with a prayer. Commonly there were fifty or sixty students in the room for the opening prayer. At the conclusion of the prayer, all those who were not actually taking the course would get up and leave, and the fifteen or so students who were enrolled in the course would remain—at which time Harrell would begin to teach. His prayers were stunning and comprehensive. The prayers would include the people and events at the seminary but would quickly reach out to include the city of Boston, the nation, and the world. At the conclusion of the prayer the people in the room knew that they now saw things differently and found new things to consider. The prayers were transformative.

At one point in a private conversation I asked Harrell how he did it. I asked what books he had been reading, or what journals, that could give him such insight to inform prayers that would draw us into such community and help to explain the world. His thoughtful response was that he did not know more about the world than others did, and he did not read things that others didn't. But what he did know was wisdom literature, and when he looked out at the world he looked through the lens of the Old Testament and could see what others could not. Harrell was clearly an expert in wisdom literature. However, more than that expertise, he was functioning at the level of mastery at which he could use his expertise in arenas outside of his own practice to make clear for others what he could see but they could not.

Harrell was deeply embedded in his chosen field of expertise. He did not simply know his area of expertise; he lived through it. Importantly, he allowed his area of expertise to engage and inform the other parts of the world that he connected with. He was a clear example of what Jagdish Sheth and Andrew Sobel describe as a "deep generalist." They describe a deep generalist as a person who has a core expertise onto which he or she layers other knowledge of related or unrelated fields, giving him or her the capacity of new insight and helpfulness that can be broadly applied.[25]

There is a critical difference between an expert and a deep generalist. An expert is one who digs deeply into his or her own field of enquiry or practice to master the complexity of that particular field. It is a difficult piece of work for anyone to commit the time, effort, and passion necessary to be an expert in any field. However, after such discipline the inquirer finally becomes an expert—in the area in which he or she is expert. The old adage about a hammer applies: If the only thing you have is a hammer, everything looks like a nail. Experts are of little help unless one's question is specifically within the field in which the expert has schooled him- or herself. If you actually have a nail, the expert is the right tool to use to hit it.

The deep generalist is significantly different. The deep generalist has a core expertise, a mastery of a central discipline that forms the core of his or her work. In this sense the deep generalist is also an expert. However, the deep generalist then supplements that core expertise with information and experience from other disciplines so that, living deeply within his or her own core, he or she can look about across a wide plain to see things in a new and different way. The consulting firm McKinsey and Co. referred to this as a person who was "T-shaped" (deep and wide), "someone with deep knowledge of an industry or function, but who had sufficient experience in other fields to maintain a generalist approach to complex business problems."[26]

To develop as a deep generalist, one must first develop a core expertise. These are the initial four stages of the Dreyfus model. One then must add (simultaneously or sequentially) complementary knowledge from other related or unrelated fields. The Dreyfus model refers to training with various masters or utilizing multiple disciplines. It means reading and learning eclectically, not always sure of the application to one's core discipline.

To operate deeply from one's own core discipline allows one to wander widely as a generalist in many other areas and see what others cannot. The value of excellent theological training for a pastor is not to be able to replicate the seminary experience for parishioners through the pulpit or through pastoral teaching. The master-level pastoral practitioner uses his or her deep theological core to be able to wander across the questions and quandaries of the parishioners' breadth of relationships, work, community, and world and simply see what others cannot. It is not the pastor as "expert" arriving with the answer from sacred text or theological tradition. It is the pastor, schooled sufficiently in his or her own discipline and practice, able to add the biblical perspective or the framing of faith that can help change what others see in their own lives.

Experts can be dangerous when the only thing they bring is their own certainty, wanting others to understand their lives by looking into the world of the expert. The deep generalist/the master, however, is of value because she or he is able to look at the same world that others are living in and help them see new things for themselves. The expert has a few possibilities for others; the deep generalist has many. Deeply embedded in their own expertise, the deep generalist walks in the wider world as an equal. The great Zen master Shunryu Suzuki wrote, "In the beginner's mind there are many possibilities, but in the expert's mind there are few."[27] Mastery is much more than knowing more about what one already knows and becoming more proficient at what one already does well. Mastery requires moving much more broadly into other people's worlds and disciplines as a generalist, a beginner, to inform and be informed so that new possibilities exist for all.

CONCLUSION

The current assumptions about the content and process necessary to train clergy as leaders are insufficient to the task. As tradition-based institutions, congregations are difficult and slow to change. Yet they seek to thrive in a constantly and rapidly changing liquid culture. Clergy leaders will increasingly need to learn to be deeply formed in the standard traditions and disciplines of the faith, but they simultaneously need to learn to be agile and adaptive to the people and the mission field in which they will practice their ministry. Developing such leadership will depend less on the answers to be found in the seminaries and in the denominational requirements for certification. Developing such leadership will depend more on the individual inquiry and risk of the clergy practitioner. Quiet courage in this instance is not to be found in the bold clergy leader who claims to have the answers for others. Quiet courage is with the one who is deeply disciplined in the faith but then stands with the people helping to name the next questions that they will need to address together in order to be faithful.

How then should denominations form clergy leaders for a divergent, postaberrant, liquid culture? Clearly, a better pipeline is not the answer. Pipelines, as noted, are closed systems. Pipelines are constructed from rules and regulations, from academic standards and institutional requirements. Pipelines seek to control rather than to empower. As noted, the basic "products" of the current certification and training pipeline of our denominations are people who fit the profiles of Gortner's "placeholders" and "talented but tenuous."

Clearly there is a role for the traditional seminary as well as the alternative academies of training that are beginning to gather more shape alongside the seminaries. However, the seminary and the academies have a limited role in shaping clergy for leadership and should be appropriately constrained to that role. In a similar way there is a role for the denominational staff, boards, and committees responsible for the certification and continuing education of clergy. However, again appropriate constraints must be imposed so that these institutional points of contact maintain a relationship of support and accountability with individual clergy but do not become the standard bearer of conformity in the practice of ministry.

If the pipeline is the standard of control and conformity, then the necessary counterresponse in the postaberrant time is to lean further into releasing controls. In her paper on the formation of clergy, Huie notes that the opposite of a pipeline is an ecology.[28] An ecology is a natural environment, an open system, that balances its own growth and constraints through the harmonizing of need and opportunity. Control does not serve an ecology well—control, in fact, unbalances. Where forest rangers once fought to prevent fires from occurring, forests suf-

fered and died under the control. When fires were given their natural
freedom, burned-over areas were freed up from old growth and replenished to make room for new growth. Where wolves were hunted and
eliminated in order to control the land for ranchers, the landscape
changed and animals and vegetation suffered collateral damage. When
wolves were reintroduced and allowed their natural place, the ecology
returned to its full health. Elk overpopulation was controlled, which
allowed the willow trees that the elk fed on to replenish, which improved the habitat for beavers that used the willow trees, which provided more dams to slow the flow of water, which improved the conditions for fish spawning. The lesson for the postaberrant time is to loos-
en, not tighten, controls. Rather than increasing the standards and controls for clergy development, a more ecological approach might honor
natural selection.

To loosen control will initially make the work of denominational
executives more difficult. Without controls, wider variance occurs.
Clergy will begin to appear with different forms of preparation and
expectations for beginning their ministry. Square pegs are difficult to fit
into round holes, and so denominational leaders will struggle with how
to include and deploy differently shaped leaders. Their dilemma will be
compounded by the current clergy and congregations who continue to
operate with current institutional assumptions and who will feel a great
unfairness as rules seem to change. Denominational executives will
need to weather the pending discomfort of old forms of leadership no
longer working and of more assertive, more purposeful leaders needing
to be recognized and rewarded when they challenge congregations that
would prefer to be comforted. Clergy will need to take responsibility to
creatively learn their own practice of ministry by pursuing the internal
questions by which the movement of the Spirit will shape them rather
than continually pursuing the familiar interests of the academy that lead
to conformity.

The ecology of spiritual purposefulness is already rebounding, although largely not in the current forms of institutional religion. In their
latest work, friends and colleagues Angie Thurston and Casper ter Kuile
ask the question, "What is the project of being human in America in
2018, and how do we do it well?" Ministry Innovation Fellows at Harvard Divinity School, Thurston and ter Kuile are forming an impressive

network of people addressing such questions from an "unbundled" perspective. They write,

> Unbundling is the process of separating elements of value from a single collection of offerings. Think of a newspaper. Whereas fifty years ago it provided classified ads, personal matchmaking, letters to the editor from neighbors and fellow citizens, a puzzle for your commute, and of course the actual news—today its competitors have surpassed it in each of these, making the broadsheet a rare sight in public. Craigslist, Tinder, Facebook, HQ Trivia and cable news offer more personalized, deeper engagement and perfect immediacy. The newspaper has been unbundled and end-users mix together their own preferred set of services.
>
> The same is true for religion. No longer do we want a 360 degree set of services from one community or ordained leader. We rely on the Insight Meditation Time for peaceful reflection, a football game or outdoor hike for ecstatic experience, Instagram hashtags for membership in a tribe-like community, and Afro-flow Yoga to conjure and carry out ancestral practices. [29]

As Thurston and ter Kuile watch the newly forming spiritual landscape, they see new platforms, new leaders, and a new language emerging. In this next iteration of religious life they also see new roles of leadership emerging. At the moment, they see nine new roles developing, none of which conform easily within the teaching of the seminary or to institutionally formed roles of leadership:

The Gatherer: brings people together in the face of alienation and suffering.

The Elder: connects generation to generation and self to community.

The Steward: provides the necessary services that support spiritual community.

The Seer: helps people approach the ultimate.

The Venturer: delights in funding creative approaches to meaning making.

The Tracker: captures relevant data that illustrate hidden value.

The Healer: breaks cycles of violence.

The Anointer: recognizes spiritual leaders and sends them forth.

The Maker: reminds humans to be human. [30]

Such new roles will not supplant the more traditional forms of clergy leadership needed for congregations and denominations. These new roles, however, are an indication of forms of leadership that resonate with the larger religious landscape and are finding their place in the liquid culture. To thrive, institutional religion will not need to challenge these new forms of human meaning making but will need to learn from the agility and responsiveness of these new leaders and from the new roles that they are learning to play.

If pipelines are rigid and conforming, ecologies are supple and nurturing. In ecologies, that which works thrives. For the institutions of religion, old ways of forming leaders that are guided by the established assumptions of content and process are proving insufficient to the task. New forms of leadership are gathering response but are, as of yet, untested in important ways. It takes quiet courage to know to be more afraid of institutional control that makes the work easier but is not effective or fruitful. In the messiness of the postaberrant age, leaders in formation need to be more quietly afraid of conforming to institutional controls than of following the questions that the Spirit now puts before them.

Part III

The Temptations

Temptation (definition): a desire to do something, especially something wrong or unwise.

Temptations are most delicious because they feel as if they are quickly rewarded. However, the rewards eventually do us in, reducing us to a skeleton because we have actually been feasting off of ourselves—our own purpose, our own hope, our own future.

7

THE TEMPTATION OF PLAYING IT SAFE

Nostalgia

I know the names of the doo-wop bands of the late 1950s and early 1960s. I can instantly tell the difference between Chad and Jeremy and Herman's Hermits from the old days of the British Invasion. Bob Dylan's voice is unmistakable, and at times the lyrics flow effortlessly when I sing along. My personal preference for quiet music to accompany conversation with my wife or reading still comes from the Great American Songbook of the post–World War II era. I have my music. And so do you.

For most of us our favored period of music is from an earlier time in our lives. The music is accompanied by memories that can locate us in particular places, with particular individuals, and in particular activities. Most memories are fond, but not all memories are pleasant. They can include some unhappy times, some remembered naïveté, and some loss. However, for the most part such memories are fairly comfortable. They remind people of what seems now to be a younger and simpler time. If they are of a time of naïveté, they can now be remembered from the position of having figured out a lot more about life. If they are memories of loss or disappointment, they are losses and disappointments that have found their appropriate places in people's lives. The memories are enjoyable, instructive, comfortable, and important. At times the memories are wistful enough to make people wonder what it would be like to go back. Nostalgia is like that. Nostalgia takes people from what bothers them now to what was figured out from an earlier time and what is missed.

Nostalgia is a warmly remembered past. From the Latin, the word "nostalgia" means a return home from pain and suffering. First used in the seventeenth century, the word described the anxieties displayed by Swiss mercenaries fighting away from home. The notion of nostalgia has an early connection with medical conditions such as melancholia. It was understood as a natural coping mechanism. Often triggered by negative feelings, nostalgia has a number of benefits, such as an improved mood, increased social connectedness, and positive self-regard. At its heart, when facing an unpleasant or stressful present, nostalgia has always connected to the warmly remembered past that once was and was better than what now is. It is a longing to go home.

ASSUMPTIONS AND TEMPTATIONS

Nostalgia is also a temptation. So far this book has not dealt with *temptations* but with *assumptions*. The postaberrant time of a liquid culture makes difficult demands on leadership. In order to face into these new demands leaders must do the very hard work of unearthing old assumptions. This book has focused on assumptions about how change happens, about resources, about organizational structure and democracy, and about how the skills and practice of leadership are developed.

Dealing with assumptions is hard work because the assumptions are hidden from daily awareness. Assumptions are tacit and must be intentionally called up in order to be tested and challenged. As such, they can also quickly disappear from awareness and still exert their control. Like a New Year's resolution, leaders resolve to operate in new ways outside of the control of old assumptions. But like New Year's resolutions, the old familiar habits can easily reassert themselves simply through familiarity and tenacity. They are so embedded that they exert influence reactively, like all learned behavior. The old assumptions must continually and laboriously be brought to mind so that new habits can be formed to replace them. Think about the difficulty of breaking a smoking habit or changing your diet. Dealing with assumptions is hard and tedious work. It is tiring.

Not so temptations. Temptations are easy. They have a lure that can be comforting even when not healthy or helpful. Temptations fill the difficult gaps that we face with easy rewards. When things are hard, temptations are desires to engage in short-term enjoyment or relief that threaten long-term goals. Like looking at our to-do list for the day that is filled with tasks that will take our time, energy, and attention, temptation invites us to pick up our smartphone or electronic tablet and spend time with digital solitaire. It is not necessarily harmful; it is just easier. Temptations are always the easier way ahead.

As the title of this chapter suggests, nostalgia is playing it safe. The argument in this book is that this is a quite different time in which the social contract in the United States has shifted, the cultural connections with institutions have been frayed, and technology, consumerism, and a global reordering of power have changed the rules of the game. The challenge for leaders has been exponentially increased. Far beyond the simpler tasks of understanding the next trends or the upcoming generational shifts, the changes in the cultural mission field are systemic and deep. The territory is sufficiently unfamiliar so that leaders must be able to shape a vision and outcomes for the future without being sure of their own direction. When one is being asked to lead with quiet courage in a situation in which no one can provide assurance about the right direction, it is far easier to turn back and play it safe in the familiar turf of nostalgia. Further, as will be explored shortly, leading others into the familiar territory of nostalgia is rewarded in ways that leading them into the unknown will not be. Because nostalgia requires only what is already known, not what is not yet known, it offers a sense of certainty and a feeling of competence that the unknown can never provide.

THE THREE TEMPTATIONS OF NOSTALGIA

Like most temptations, there are particular releases and rewards that make nostalgia attractive and seem worth the cost. It is important to understand that nostalgia, for all of its comfort, invites us into the temptations of living a one-sided story, relying on past diagnoses and avoiding necessary but difficult questions. Each of these are worth exploration because unless leaders are clear about the costs, it is simply easier to head back into the remembered past than to forge ahead into an unsure future.

Nostalgia Invites Us into a One-Sided Story

Mark Lilla, professor of humanities at Columbia University, offers a study of the reactionary mind and explores significant examples of philosophical attempts to turn back to remembered pasts when the future is unsure.[1] In all of the situations involving the temptation of nostalgia there are two voices, two opposing stories, that form a contest over people's understanding of the current moment.

This nostalgic contest is seen in the Book of Ezra in the Hebrew Bible in the familiar story of the building of the new temple in Jerusalem following the Diaspora. King Cyrus of Persia issued a proclamation that allowed the Israelites to return to Jerusalem and to rebuild the temple. A bit more than a year after their return, the Israelites had completed the construction of the foundation of the new temple, a portion of the temple sufficient to allow for the religious practices of the people to begin. At that point in the construction a great celebration was planned, with priests clothed in all their vestments, trumpets and cymbals, and all the people gathered, young and old. The text reads, "All of the people shouted with praise to the Lord because the foundation of the Lord's house had been laid. But many of the older priests and Levites and heads of families, who had seen the first house, wept aloud when they saw the foundation of this house, although many others shouted loudly with joy" (Ezra 3:11–12). In other words, the people who gathered saw two different stories. Some saw the new temple and a promise of a new future, and they made loud sounds of joy. Others saw only a different temple, not the remembered temple of old, and saw a past that slipped away unfulfilled, and they made loud sounds of weeping. As the text says, "No one could distinguish the sound of the joyful shout from the sound of the people's weeping" (Ezra 3:13). Two stories in contest with one another.

Lilla notes that nostalgia represents one of the contesting stories and is the tool of the reactionary. It is an orientation that looks back on what is lost and seeks to reclaim and preserve it. The reactionary's story, writes Lilla, begins with a happy, well-ordered state where people know their place in harmony and submit to tradition and their God. Then alien ideas promoted by intellectuals—writers, journalists, professors— challenge this harmony and the will to maintain order weakens at the top. (The betrayal of elites is the linchpin of every reactionary story.) A false consciousness soon descends on the society as a whole as it willingly, even joyfully, heads for destruction. Only those who have preserved memories of the old ways see what is happening. Whether the society reverses direction or rushes to its doom depends entirely on their resistance.[2]

Lilla suggests the presence of two stories: that of the revolutionary and that of the reactionary. The revolutionary sees the ideological future that is splendid in all of its promise. The reactionary sees the past in all its splendor and resists the "lies" of the future. Further, Lilla suggests that the reactionary feels him- or herself to be in the "stronger position than his adversary because he believes he is guardian of what actually happened, not the prophet of what might be."[3]

One cannot be a leader in an established congregation and not run into this contest of stories between the uncertain future and the once secure past. As a consultant to congregations for many years, I long understood that these competing stories formed the platform on which the work of planning and conflict resolution needed to be addressed. For example, in one congregation the contest focused on music and the traditions of worship. The revolutionaries saw places where newer and younger people could be included because the culture was moving toward intergenerational involvement and the strict boundary between sacred and secular music was softening. The revolutionaries believed that youth and music were two pillars on which a stronger future could be built. They proposed that youth be involved in worship by distributing the elements of the Eucharist, and they proposed the inclusion of contemporary worship music. In response, the reactionaries insisted that if youth were involved in the distribution of bread and wine during the sacrament, they would first have to allow the congregational members to see them publicly use hand sanitizer because "everybody knows where their hands have been." Further, the reactionaries insisted that the music in the denominational hymnal (accompanied only by the organ) was more than sufficient for worship. One gentleman, in all sincerity, came to me saying, "Gil, I don't understand why we can't just sing from the twenty approved hymns of the church." His remembered story of the strength of the church was of days in which people sang the same hymns over and over because those hymns sufficiently reflected their understanding of faith.

This congregation was not unusual or exceptional in its two-storied contest over how to move ahead with younger and newer participants. Middle judicatory and denominations as a whole have their own versions of these competing stories in which some suggest change while others fight to protect and preserve whatever already is (whether it be institutional legislation that might be only fifty years old or institutional structures and practices that are well under one hundred years old but feel as if they are sacred). The revolutionary story revolves around what could be possible if changes were allowed. The reactionary story is centered in the assertion that "we were once strong and this is how we did it."

Nostalgia is often built on a remembered reality of strength and certainty. At the heart of the argument in this book is the shift from the aberrant to the postaberrant time. The aberrant time described in chapter 2 was such a time of strength and certainty that has a nostalgic lure. A convergent culture undergirded by a post–World War II people who understood how to sacrifice and collaborate around a shared national agenda drove people toward membership in institutions, including the church. Mainline denominations and local congregations steadily grew, and the resources of people and dollars were constantly replenished. Institutions, high among them the favored religious institutions, had a public voice that was listened to. Commerce gave way to the sacred with Sunday blue laws. Scouting aligned itself with the purpose of congregations in the formation of good and responsible youth. Examples, seemingly without end, can be recalled to give evidence of the strength of religious institutions and their alignment with the culture in that aberrant time. From that perspective, the nostalgic voice of "we were once strong, and this is how we did it" carries a good deal of weight in the eyes of many.

However, nostalgia is a one-sided story of a much more complex situation. If the nostalgic reactionary is one part of the story, the counterbalance comes from the revolutionary who provides the story of what lies ahead. The revolutionary, nonetheless, does not hold a truer story than the reactionary. If the reactionary looks nostalgically to the past, the revolutionary is the futurist who looks with a mix of hope and warning to the future. But the future path is not secure. It is only based on what can be seen and understood at the moment. Alan Roxburgh writes, "We are living right in the middle of these disruptions. We are, therefore, too much a part of them to see the shape of things to come."[4]

The past cannot be recaptured; it is an aberrant time that can no longer be supported because the conditions that nurtured the aberrant strength, clarity, and growth no longer apply. The future cannot be secured. Leaders do not yet see enough, do not yet understand enough, and now live in a liquid culture in which stasis will continuously be challenged with repetitive waves of change.

In such a situation two things can be said. The first is that quietly courageous leaders must learn how to stand with some confidence in the anxiety of the present moment—between the already insufficient past and the clearly uncertain future. More will be said later about this position of courageous leadership in the anxious present. The second thing to be said is that the unknown future, coupled with the anxiety of the present, makes the nostalgic past a grand temptation. For a leader to speak with great certainly about what is already known, what has already been done, and what has worked in the past is highly rewarding and highly rewarded by others. When all is insecure, people naturally seek out a confident voice. It is easy work to be confident about what has already happened. It is reassuring to assert that if we just keep doing what we've done before (or hold to the shape of our beliefs as we've understood them before, hold people accountable for what they once naturally did before, or remain faithful to the structures, process-es, practices, and rules that we've developed before), then we will re-claim what we feel we've lost. However, this is Lilla's "shipwrecked mind"—the nostalgia of the reactionary who stands in the river of time seeing the debris of paradise drifting past.[5]

Nostalgia Invites Us to Rely on Past Diagnoses

The second temptation is related to diagnosing our present situation. A diagnosis is the identification of a problem or a situation by examination of the symptoms that are evident. Diagnosis is important because it makes understanding actionable. We do what we do because of the way in which we understand the situation. Hence diagnosis is terribly important.

Indeed, there is considerable concern in both medicine and law about what drives diagnoses because of the way in which an improper or constrained diagnosis leads to faulty treatment. Physicians are concerned about insurance and hospital standards that continually pressure them to see an increasing number of patients daily in order to manage costs. Shorter visits give physicians less time for diagnosis. It is now estimated that a physician will form a diagnosis about treatment within the first fifteen seconds of greeting the patient. First impressions of the patient mixed with the initial complaint offered by the patient form a quick pathway to treatment that might have been quite different and more effective if time had allowed more conversation and symptom checking. As medical records are digitized, diagnosis is standardized and physicians spend time dialoguing with the software protocol on their computer that has decision trees of questions to answer that will lead to standard diagnoses. Standard diagnoses lead to standard treatments that might easily be inaccurate without the unique information carried by the stories of the patient describing what she or he is experiencing. Similarly, judges are increasingly constrained by legally prescribed categories of criminal judgments, which, once a defendant is found guilty, require a pre-established punishment. Without being able to factor in the circumstances and stories of why the individual was involved in the crime, the punishment might clearly not fit the crime. Insufficient time, software protocols, and prescribed treatments for patients or sentences for lawbreakers all pressure inadequate diagnoses that, given time and the inclusion of better information, would lead to much healthier and compassionate action. Diagnosis is important.

An additional condition affecting accurate diagnoses might be described as the influence of "leftover" or past diagnoses in which people see what they do because they have trained or acclimated themselves to see it. This is where the temptation of nostalgia again gives us an easy and seemingly secure path to describe what the problem is—which, because of our familiarity with the problem, will then prescribe our action, which will be as familiar to us as is the diagnosis.

This temptation to settle for the ease of a familiar diagnosis is at the heart of our current national political gridlock. Yuval Levin's argument that the first half of the twentieth century was marked by *consolidation* and *cohesion* was noted in chapter 2. It was a time of massive growth of economic industrialization and centralization of government. He described the second half of the twentieth century as a time of growing *deconsolidation* and *decentralization* in which our economy diversified and deregulated in energizing ways. There was a sustained pushback against uniformity and cohesion followed by an upsurge of individualism and the need for personal identity. Levin captures the mid-century moment (that is described in this book as the aberrant time), saying, "Keeping one foot in each of these two distinguishable eras, midcentury America combined cohesion and dynamism to an exceptional degree."[6] This unique combination of cohesion and dynamism prompted the strength and growth over which we are currently so nostalgic.

Given the strength and vibrancy of the past, a part of the focus of Levin's work is to understand the current debilitating American political impasse in which neither party can develop an agenda for the future. The impasse, the gridlock, is the product of leftover nostalgic diagnoses of the situation that we face. Levin writes,

> Liberals look back to the postwar golden age of midcentury America, which they believe embodied the formula for cultural liberalization amid economic security and progress until some market fanatics threw it all away. Conservatives look fondly to the late century boom of the Reagan era, which they say rescued the country from economic malaise while recapturing some of the magic of the confident, united America of that earlier midcentury Golden age, but was abandoned by misguided statists.[7]

Action follows diagnosis, and old (nostalgic) diagnoses lead to old (nostalgic) solutions. Levin notes, "Democrats talk about public policy as though it were always 1965 and the model of the Great Society welfare state will answer our every concern. And Republicans talk as though it were always 1981 and a repetition of the Reagan Revolution is the cure for what ails us."[8] The current gridlock is the product of two different and competing solutions based on two different and nostalgic diagnoses. This is not the dialectic between the revolutionary who looks to the future and the reactionary who looks to the past. This is a contest of two different diagnoses, both looking to the familiarity of the past as a solution to the problems of the present. A failure of diagnosis, he notes, leads to a failure of self-understanding. "As a result, they [the political parties] are focused less on how we can build economic, cultural and social capital in the 21st century than on how we can recover the capital we have used up. That distinction makes an awfully big difference."[9] It is a distinction that courageous church leaders need to clearly understand.

Nostalgia carries the temptation to work harder at what we already know how to do in order to recapture a time and strength that no longer exist. This temptation carries the rewards of feeling certain and secure in our efforts and the satisfaction of getting tired from work that is familiar to our hands. Nostalgia does not ask us how to be different for the future, which is much harder work.

If American political progress is stymied by competing nostalgic diagnoses, American religious institutions have fallen to the same easy temptation. Playing off known and familiar diagnoses of liberal versus conservative politics, there has been much argument over the importance of conservative theology in contrast to liberal theology. Playing off known and familiar diagnoses of generational differences and preferences, there has been much argument over the importance of contemporary music and worship compared to traditional music and worship. Playing off known and familiar institutional biases, there has been much argument over the importance of a nondenominational or independent identity as opposed to a denominational connection. Playing off known and familiar cultural pressure points, there has been much argument in institutions of faith over the place of issues of social justice, issues of human sexuality, and the importance of particular forms of marriage and family. These are the biases and influences of known and nostalgic past diagnoses.

In each of these cases it is implicitly important for a congregation or a denomination to understand themselves accurately in terms of their theology and purpose. In each of these cases it is implicitly important for a congregation or a denomination to understand the context and the neighborhood in which they are called to mission. However, none of the issues found in these common nostalgic diagnoses are causal to either the thriving or the demise of a congregation or a denomination. Work done by the Hartford Institute for Religion Research and supported by the work and observation of the consultants of the Alban Institute continually demonstrated that vitality and growth did not depend on having one "correct" identity or position on any issue.[10] Theologically liberal and theologically conservative congregations both thrived as long as the congregation was clear about its own theological identity and was able to operate and communicate clearly with others about its identity and purpose. Congregations committed to evangelism and congregations committed to social justice both thrived as long as the congregation was clear about its identity and was able to operate and communicate clearly with others about its identity and purpose.

Easy and tempting past diagnoses about what is wrong and about who is wrong are often rewarded by those who agree with the diagnosis. However, seeking to reclaim an aberrant past by reasserting former strengths of any persuasion is playing it safe. If old, easy, safe answers are shown to be shallow for the demands of the current moment, then leaders will find looking ahead with much more accurate diagnoses to be much harder work framed with much anxiety that requires risk instead of providing safety.

Nostalgia Invites Us to Avoid Difficult Questions

The third temptation of nostalgia's allure is the opportunity to avoid difficult questions. There is an old joke (with multiple variants in its telling) about the man who was seen searching under a bright streetlight for something lost. When asked what he was searching for the man replied that he was looking for his car keys, which he dropped somewhere over by his garage. When further asked why, then, he was searching in the street under the streetlight instead of over by his garage, he responded that it was so much easier to see there. The temptation to do the easier thing is powerful, even when we know it won't help.

Chris Argyris, noted Harvard University organizational development expert, has long helped leaders understand organizational defensive routines. He identified these routines as "actions or policies that prevent individuals or segments of the organization from experiencing embarrassment or threat. Simultaneously, they prevent people from identifying and getting rid of the causes of the potential embarrassment or threat. Organizational defensive routines are antilearning, overprotective, and self-sealing."[11]

In other words, organizations and their leaders will collude to give attention to those things that won't embarrass them. It is embarrassing to stumble about in the dark of not knowing. It therefore becomes much more tempting to go to those places where the "light" of familiar questions and known answers offers a sense of progress even when, intuitively, people know that they are searching in the wrong spot. So leaders encourage people to double down on efforts that have lost their effectiveness. This is an encouragement to work harder, a temptation that will be picked up in chapter 9. Working harder at what is no longer effective is a nostalgic reflex. It comes from looking back at what once worked and satisfying oneself with action and activity that is familiar. While ineffective, such nostalgic reflexes protect leaders and organizations from embarrassment.

Consider the difference between planning and learning. There is less anxiety and more comfort for a leader to gather people together for *planning*. Planning suggests action and gives a sense of direction. Planning infers understanding. If we know where we are and know where we want to go, planning means we only need to put steps in place to get from here to there. This is problem solving at its most familiar. Leaders who pull teams together for planning are rewarded for their sense of direction and action. However, in a fully postaberrant time when the "known" has been eclipsed by deeply changed cultural, technological, and global conditions, action-oriented planning may be a tempting streetlight-luring activity that will provide nostalgic comfort when the real hope actually lies in darker corners.

Less rewarded and potentially embarrassed will be a leader who calls a team together not for planning but for *learning*. Learning does lead to action but often not directly or immediately. In fact, learning can first lead to further embarrassment by uncovering even more questions. Learning begins with questions that do not necessarily have easy, known answers, such as: How do unchurched people in the postaberrant culture actually form community and search for meaning if they don't trust institutions? Such a question is actually quite large and very difficult. Such a large question can only, at first, lead to more difficult questions—an embarrassment when what people hope for from their leader is clarity and answers.

There are, however, more modest and more easily workable questions that leaders can help their organization walk into that might also produce embarrassment. Questions such as: Does the organization actually accomplish what people say it does? Consider the congregation that developed a program of evening dinners in the homes of members, designed for small groups of participants to gather in order to get to know each other better. The purpose of the program was to broaden and deepen relationships within the congregation so that people would feel more connected and have a community to call on when needed. Calling a team together to plan the program of home meals is familiar and known work. It is conventional committee planning work. However, to call the team together after the dinners to learn if, in fact, community was broadened and deepened is closer to having to search in the dark. It is a task of learning, not planning. If the team discovers that over 90 percent of the people who participated in the home meals were the core leadership group of the congregation who already knew each other well, already cared for and called on one another, then additional and more difficult questions would be raised about how to actually build community and extend care in the broader congregation. It is tempting to go back to old ways and old questions and just keep planning without doing additional learning. However, the old adage applies—if the same people have the same conversations about the same questions, it will produce the same results.

Nostalgia, the reactive, reflexive mind of going back to the actions and activities that the people best know, is tempting because it allows us to avoid much more difficult and disturbing questions. Honestly raising questions about purpose and the intentional outcomes of work are both difficult and potentially embarrassing in a moment of changed culture when so much is unknown. Nostalgia allows work avoidance. It is a way of not acknowledging what is difficult to address. As Argyris notes, "Organizational defensive routines make it highly likely that individuals, groups, intergroups, and organizations will not detect and correct the errors that are embarrassing and threatening because the fundamental rules are to (1) bypass the errors and act as if they were not being done, (2) make the bypass undiscussable, and (3) make its undiscussability undiscussable."[12] Staying connected to a nostalgic past allows leaders and their organizations to sidestep difficult current questions that are embarrassing, so they don't even have to talk about them. However, staying connected to a nostalgic past also precludes learning new ways to move into the future.

USING NOSTALGIA TO START THE NEXT CYCLE

Nostalgia itself is a symptom that the time of strength is over. As a symptom, it provides evidence and reason for informed corrective action that enables and empowers the next steps toward health and new strength. Consider an early, well-known model of a lifecycle of a congregation that identifies the generic stages of development of a congregation. The lifecycle stages of a congregation are visioning, structure, ministry, nostalgia, polarity, and death.

Visioning: The first stage of the lifecycle shapes the purpose of the congregation. This stage forms agreement on the *why* of the congregation. It may be the very first vision of a group of people who looked about and concluded there was a need for a new congregation on the corner of Third and Spruce Streets in their community, where there was no congregation. Such a vision responded to what was missing in the community and the difference a congregation could make. Or it may be a subsequent vision of an established congregation in which members of the congregation look about their neighborhood and see new home construction, expanding schools, and an increasing number of children on the street. They begin to talk about a new purpose for their established congregation in serving children and families. The visioning stage of both new and established congregations is full of energy because it has purpose and direction, although it also has a lot of questions and work that lie ahead.

Structure: The second stage in the development of the congregation is the time of bringing structure to the vision. In this stage of the lifecycle the question shifts from *why* to *how*. It is no longer a conversation about why we need a new congregation or why we need to focus our ministry on children. The conversations begin to focus on strategies and resources—how people will do it. Problem solving along with the structuring and alignment of effort now take center stage. If it is a new congregation at Third and Spruce, a building committee needs to be formed, money raised and loans arranged, denominational requirements negotiated, and community awareness and support sought. If it is a ministry to serve children and their families, it might require new programs, perhaps additional staff, even the construction of a new family life center to provide needed space for what could be done. Again, the energy is high and people tend to align and collaborate easily, especially if the vision is both clear and passionate. People with a good, clear *why* tend to work well around their *how*.

Ministry: The third stage in the lifecycle of the congregation is the stage of ministry, the stage at which the congregation actually lives out its vision. Ministry is the stage in which the new congregation constructed at Third and Spruce begins regular worship services, receives new members, begins religious education programs, and makes a difference in the community. Ministry is the stage at which the established congregation in the community with a growing number of children hires an additional staff person who begins to make contact with the new families in the area and begins to develop a team of volunteers to plan and manage new programs for the children and their parents.

This third stage of ministry also starts with a high level of energy. After all, the congregation has finally reached the place where their vision is a reality and the intended difference is being addressed. However, this stage of ministry is a long-haul project. It has taken a good deal of work to get to this stage in the lifecycle and much energy has already been expended, yet the work is not actually accomplished—it has just begun. Commonly, energy and resources begin to diminish and, over time, even the purpose of the congregation begins to shift. Over time a new congregation becomes an established congregation with very different needs to address and questions to ask. Over time new communities with young children grow into communities from which those children move away, or become communities in which the current homes become the new housing stock for a new group, perhaps a very different group, of people. Congregations that reach this stage of ministry cannot stay there for an overextended time because the world about them changes. Yet many congregations, remembering the good years of the early high-energy stages of vision and structure, cling to the stories and memories of what once was but now has changed. Enter the next stage: nostalgia.

Nostalgia: In this next stage of the lifecycle of a congregation, all that has been described in this chapter about nostalgia begins to happen. People look to the past for comfort to deal with the anxiety of the present and the uncertainty of the future. Notably, in the stage of nostalgia, people begin to raise questions formed by memories of the past. They ask why they no longer have to set up extra chairs in the sanctuary for worship during the high holy days of the year like they once did.

They ask why there are more deaths in the congregation than baptisms like the good old days. They ask why the youth staff person is being paid so much more when there are so many fewer children in the programs. The questions are framed by their discomforting diagnoses of what they see and their wish to go back to higher-energy, remembered days.

Polarity: In the next stage of the lifecyle, people begin to answer their questions based on their memories of the past and their diagnosis of the present. "If the preacher preached better sermons," they might answer, "then we'd be setting up more chairs on the high holy days." "If the youth director had regular office hours and spent more time where we could see what she's doing, then there would be more children around here." Present answers based on past memories (whether the memories are accurate or not) become the basis on which the congregation polarizes internally between those who agree with the answers to the questions and those who do not. As this stage develops, the energy may increase around the contest over the questions being asked, but overall the energy for mission and ministry is significantly depleted.

Death: If the stage of polarity is not addressed or interrupted, the congregation will move toward its final stage of death. No one likes to go to the home of friends when they are actively engaged in an argument, so in a polarized congregation the flow of visitors and less active members begins to come to an end in this stage of the lifecycle. People simply begin to stay away. Without clear purpose around which energy can build, without alignment of efforts, and without any stream of new people coming in, the congregation ages in place, experiencing a steady decline of resources and people until it can no longer go on.

Such a lifecycle of a congregation is certainly simplified and stylized, but can be easily pictured, as shown in figure 7.1.

It is very helpful for leaders to know at what stage in this very normal lifecycle their congregation is currently living. Diagnosing where the congregation is in its lifecycle offers indications of what needs to be done next. As this chapter has been describing, the normative response in the stage of nostalgia is to look back and wonder how to recapture a higher-energy and a purposeful past. Leaders in nostalgia ask how to get back to the remembered stage of ministry. This is the reactionary mind based on an oversimplified diagnosis of the issues of the present. It is the hope that recapturing the past will address the discomfort of the present.

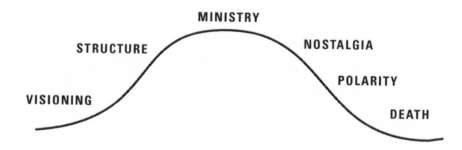

Figure 7.1. The Lifecycle of a Congregation

It is somewhat counterintuitive, but instead of asking questions about the past stage of ministry at the point of nostalgia, quietly courageous leaders need to start a conversation about the next full cycle of the life of the congregation that begins with the *why* of the next vision. When energy begins to fade, quietly courageous leaders do not look back and mourn the loss of once abundant energy; they look ahead to a bolder vision that will require (and stimulate) the natural production of a new flow of energy.

The issue for leaders and their organizations is no longer why they are not who they once were. The issue that a quietly courageous leader must raise in a time of nostalgia builds on a much more current and accurate diagnosis of identity, purpose, and context: Who are we now? What does God call us to make different now? Who is our neighbor now?[13] What is needed is the quiet courage of inquiry. The asking of new, unanswered questions (that require new learning) is not an effort to go back but a willingness to risk starting new. The graph of development that can begin in the stage of nostalgia most helpfully looks like figure 7.2.

Playing it safe means looking back to what is already known and asking how to get back to what was lost (or asking whose fault it is that the organization has slipped away from that remembered time). In comparison it is a risk, not quickly rewarding or rewarded, for leaders to look ahead and to ask what's next. In a time of liquid culture no one knows a lot about what's next, so people naturally and intuitively remember what once was.

There is always laughter in the room when I am working with a group of leaders and ask how many think of themselves as younger than

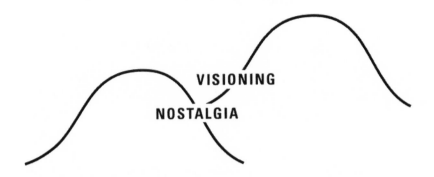

Figure 7.2.   Nostalgia as the Time to Begin Again

they actually are. Hands go up and people smile. Then I commonly point out that thinking of ourselves as younger than we are reflects the fact that we actually know a lot more about who we once were than we know about who we currently are. Smiles break into laughter of self-recognition. Nostalgia is tempting because it can be pleasant and reassuring. Quiet courage resists temptation and asks questions about new purpose based on a realistic diagnosis of the way things actually are—questions not about who we once were or who we are now but questions of who we have been called to be.

8

THE TEMPTATION OF CHRISTIAN EMPATHY

Healthy leadership is always framed from a clear sense of purpose. Daniel Goleman reflects that need for purpose in a concise organizational description of leadership when he writes, "Visionary leaders state a mission, set standards, and let people know whether their work is furthering the group goals."[1] Direction is determined, standards are set, and people are expected to align their efforts. Leaders give the people feedback, both positive and negative, to help them work together toward common ends.

If the frame of reference shifts from organizational to spiritual leadership, the deep sense of purpose is not diminished. Drawing from the writings of the early Church Fathers, Christopher Beeley (reflecting on the image of the shepherd as a dominant image of leadership in the church) writes, "Like actual shepherds, Christian pastors exercise a clear and necessary authority over their flocks, by which they are able to guide the members of the church toward God."[2] Again, direction is determined, standards are set, people are expected to move, and feedback (both positive and negative) is to be given—all necessary actions of a good shepherd. Both organizational and spiritual leadership are meant to indicate direction and shape steps to help move people to a new place and help them be in a way that they don't yet know.

In chapter 5 the work of sociologist Peter Takayama helped to frame the essential dual nature of leadership in which the leader must attend to both of two poles on which all vital organizations must live—both purpose and relationship. Leaders must be able to articulate a clear purpose that is meaningful to the people and then help people shape themselves and their relationships to align with that purpose. We will look deeper at this essential polarity between purpose and relationship later in this chapter. For the moment it is sufficient to name the two poles because of the temptation of Christian empathy to heavily skew the necessary polarity away from purpose because of an oversensitivity to relationships.

Congregational and denominational leaders are constantly tempted to focus on relationships because such attention is rewarded. In an earlier chapter the issue of leading "in community" identified the way in which leaders of voluntary association organizations are called to lead the very same people who hold their contract for leadership. Leaders in all organizations are careful to attend to the people who hold their contract because both their leadership and their livelihood depend on satisfying those who set the terms of the contract and will evaluate their performance. In for-profit organizations those who set the terms of the leader's contract and do the evaluation (the owner, the board, the supervisor) are more clearly identified and more easily managed. In for-profit organizations owners, governing boards, and supervisors are not usually discomforted by the actions of the leader that might require change by others in the organization.

In the nonprofit organization, like a congregation, the terms of the leadership contract are set by a much more diffuse group of people, and the lines of authority lack focus. The ones who evaluate the leadership are the same ones who are subject to the leadership. And leaders who set directions that require change in such organizations end up discomforting the very people who will evaluate their leadership. No one looks forward to being evaluated by someone who is upset. So if leadership is to attend to both purpose and relationship, the reality is that in nonprofit voluntary association organizations the sensitivity to relationships can more easily eclipse purpose. Satisfying the members (the positive goal) and avoiding complaints (the negative goal) consume the leader's attention, often to the detriment of purpose. Leaders who give time and attention to relationships in such a system are positively rewarded with appreciation while escaping the "negative rewards" associated with complaints. It is in such a situation that empathy becomes a real temptation.

EMPATHY IS A CHRISTIAN GOOD

However, before marshaling an argument about the limitations of empathy, it is critical to recognize the importance of a religious discipline that takes us outside of ourselves. All of the major world religions have some variant of a Golden Rule in which others are to be valued equal to the self. The Christian New Testament Law of Love is the fundamental discipline of caring for the other. Empathy is a Christian good, shared in some form with all religions.

Empathy is the capacity to understand and feel what another human being is experiencing. Stemming from the Greek *pathos* (passion or suffering), empathy is what leads us to the common good. In a visit to Emory and Henry College in Virginia, I was part of a group in conversation with Tal Stanley, director of the Appalachian Center for Civic Life. Emory and Henry College lies deep in the liberal arts tradition in which the purpose of education is not just to prepare the student for the workforce but to form the student as a person. Stanley spoke about citizenship and the college's commitment to form persons connected to others in their place, their community, through *imagination* (a picture of what does not exist) and through *empathy* (the ability to see beyond themselves and be mutually connected to others). Empathy makes us part of community. If reflected in education, empathy is equally at the heart of the Christian experience and the fundamental concern for "the least, the last, and the lost." It is reflected in the mission outreach, the concern for nurturing Christian community, and the pastoral care of one another in times of need. Empathy connects people to one another. As such, empathy takes on an even more important role if the culture moves away from the more cohesive, convergent values that held people together as they once did in the aberrant time.

In the current cultural American moment that is driven by individualism, as noted in chapter 2, Hugh Heclo argued that our national social contract is now understood as the right of every person to pursue his or her own happiness as long as his or her pursuit does not infringe on the right of other individuals to do likewise.[3] Empathy, as embodied in churches, schools, and families, is deeply needed as a corrector to this individual pursuit of happiness gone awry. It is easy to argue that individualism, unchecked, leads to a consumerism that produces emptiness, that it leads to greed that robs us of meaning, and that it leads to personal security that endangers others. Empathy reminds people that they are more than individuals; they are also community and are responsible for the establishment and care of a common good. It is the difference that Peter Block pointed to between being a *consumer* and being a *citizen*. The consumer waits for others to address his or her sense of happiness; the citizen addresses the pursuit of happiness on behalf of the common community. Empathy motivates people and moves people from the focus on their own desires to the needs of the common good of the fuller community.

Empathy Overused

To understand the temptation of empathy it is important to note that, at its heart, empathy is sensitive to and engaged by suffering, by pain. Empathy connects people to others and quite rightly leads them to want to reduce the suffering and to relieve the pain of others. However, the argument to be made in this exploration of quiet courage is that, despite empathy living at the heart of faith, in the current situation *unconstrained* empathy can lead us away from our purpose. Individualism unchecked leads to emptiness. Empathy unchecked, I will argue, can lead to paralysis. Unchecked empathy for the pain that is seen in strained denominational systems and communities can easily become a Christian strength practiced to the point that it becomes a missional weakness. As noted in chapter 5, strengths overused become weaknesses. Empathy overused, while continually rewarded, will lead to a weakness in mission.

Empathy, in leadership, was never meant to be a deterrent to action. Being a caring pastor or denominational executive does not preclude the other actions of determining direction, setting standards, and giving feedback to others. As Beeley notes in his study of pastoral leadership, "Contrary to what many think, the mark of humility in a Christian pastor is not low self-esteem or a weak personality. Effective pastoral leadership requires much confidence and a comfort with exercising authority in people's lives."[4] If empathy is the dominant or singular Christian discipline that influences the leader, the pastor easily becomes Lischer's "quivering mass of availability" or Gorton's "place holder clergy" who can manage to continue failing practices of the institution but does not have the strength or skill to set missional direction that may discomfort or require change.

From the very beginning pastoral leadership was a much bolder enterprise than simply comforting people. In his study of the early church Beeley drew on the writings of early Church Fathers such as St. Gregory of Nazianzus, St. Ambrose, Augustine, St. John Chrysostom, St. John Cassian, and Pope Gregory. The writings span the time from the early fourth century through the sixth century—a time of formation for the church and congregations. Pastoral care, from those earliest moments, was purpose centered. Beeley notes that Gregory Nazianzen (329–90) described pastoral ministry as the "cure of souls." "Soul" referred to the center of a person's life, including their values, commitments, choices, thoughts, feelings, memories, and hopes for the future. Such pastoral care required a "full range of spiritual treatments" providing direct individualized feedback that went far beyond a singular dependence on empathy. Beeley wrote,

> Gregory gives a representative list. Some need frank and direct instruction, while others are better taught by example. Certain people need to be encouraged, while others need to be actively restrained from what they are doing. The sluggish will need to be stirred up by being "smitten by the word," while the overzealous need to be cooled and restrained. Some need praise, others blame. Again, some people need to be rebuked publicly, but others should be approached privately. In some cases we should give direct and obvious attention, yet in others we should make people feel that they're being left alone (even though they really aren't). There are even situations where the good pastor must show anger or despair (without being overcome by them), whereas in others we must not be angry or despondent or it would hurt the person terribly. In order to be effective leaders, we must be able to provide whatever treatment is actually needed, adapting our ministry to the conditions of our flock.[5]

Such a full range of leadership behaviors requires both a capacity to diagnose the condition of the people leaders work with and the capacity to manage pain—both one's own and the other's. In a postaberrant time, pain is a constant for those who remember the earlier period of strength and the cultural comfort of being a key institution that participated in the earlier social contract of belonging and being responsible for the common good. The pain comes from living in a time in which such favorable conditions no longer undergird the institution.

If, indeed, congregations and denominations were constructed as large, strong, bureaucratic denominational institutions in that aberrant era that thrived on institutions that were large, strong, and bureaucratic, then it is not possible to sustain what was created when those earlier aberrant conditions changed. Leaders are now in a place where they are living off the increased giving of a smaller and smaller number of people who are getting older and older—an unsustainable formula. Denominations have thousands of congregations once appropriately located for easy access to the travel patterns and distances of an earlier age but that no longer relate to the demographic shifts and transportation patterns of the current time. The average worship attendance needed to support the salary and benefits of a full-time ordained clergyperson is 150. The current average worship attendance across all congregations in the United States is seventy-five.[6] It now requires that a congregation be twice the size of the average just to satisfy the basic institutional economic model. Denominations continue to have vital congregations, most of which tend to be larger. However, projections of the survivability of the small congregations within the United Methodist denomination indicate that over a period of a few decades as many as a third— over ten thousand—may close.[7] The bottom line of the current situation is that, denominationally, we cannot avoid internal pain and suffering.

Such internal pain marks a distinction between periods of growth and periods of decline. While it takes hard work and can be exhausting, growth is not necessarily painful. Recall that in the chapter addressing assumptions about resources Thomas Friedman and Michael Mandelbaum pointed out that it does not take a plan to grow.[8] In a time when all is growing around you, when consensus breeds agreement, and when resources are both available and constantly increasing, "a rising tide raises all ships." When only decades ago a culture of consensus and cohesion pushed people toward congregations in search of membership, when an expanding economy made resources both available and cheap, earlier generations of leaders were tireless, effective, and efficient. Denominations grew, new churches were started, new buildings were built, and institutions became complex and were managed through a centralized structure. Tiring, yes. But it was not painful work. It was highly rewarded.

However, as Friedman further notes, when conditions change, leaders *do* need a plan to shrink. Shrinking is harder work than growing. Resources (people, dollars, time) become limited and restricted. All agendas can no longer be satisfied, all preferences cannot be honored, all traditions cannot be continued, and all expectations cannot be met. In other words, leaders must make decisions. Priorities must be set and acknowledged so that people will understand that resources must be directed in the most purposeful and strategic manner. Leaders must be able to say that "this" is more important than "that" and direct attention and resources accordingly. At such times some congregations will feel discounted, some clergy will feel uncared for, some constituent wishes will not be satisfied, and some issues of ministry will not be funded or supported.

When a system shrinks from an earlier large size, when resources once dependable become restricted, the result is felt as pain. As noted, pain engages empathy. Every year as local churches get smaller the aggregate dollars available to pay clergy salaries can shrink by as much as $250,000 or more in a single denominational middle judicatory. Yet the expectation that lingers from a time of growth is that clergy, throughout their career, will with every appointment or call be sent to a larger congregation with a larger salary. When reality intrudes and a pastor is appointed or called to a smaller congregation, receives a reduction in salary, or can find ministry only in a community that is not preferred, it is often received by the clergy as being misunderstood, underappreciated, or disregarded. Pain is felt and empathy is invited. When a congregation shrinks to a size at which annual giving can no longer support the pastor's salary, leaders may wish that the denominational executive find dollars from the general church to allow them to continue as they have been. The congregation might argue that they have been in place in that community for multiple generations, even hundreds of years. To not be subsidized by the denomination to which they have sent their missionally apportioned dollars year after year can be felt as callous, as part of a system in which the larger church always takes but never gives. Pain is felt and empathy is invited. When a member of the denominational middle judicatory seeks the continuation or increase in funding once directed to a place of personal importance (the church camp where he or she met his or her spouse, the college where he or she felt his or her call to ministry, the caucus or ethnic group to which he or she belongs, the specialty of ministry for which he or she has great passion) and the funding cannot be provided, pain is felt and empathy is invited.

Quiet courage, being steadfast in the face of empathy, requires that leaders practice the Christian disciplines of caring, mercy, and justice in their personal lives and not be swayed by all expressions of pain or dissatisfaction in the church where they are called to be missional and strategic leaders. Unconstrained empathy in the face of necessary institutional restructuring and redeployment can lead to paralysis. When the difficult but necessary decisions of leaders lead to expressions of pain, and when empathy calls forth a reflexive response to reduce pain, people will naturally sanction their leaders to make difficult decisions—leaders will choose comfort over purpose, and they will choose to forgo mission rather than to appear callous to colleagues or feel guilty about unaddressed suffering. Unchecked empathy in a stressed system paralyzes in at least three ways.

Unchecked Empathy Favors Relationship over Purpose

Let us now go deeper into the polarity of purpose and relationship noted by Takayama. Religious institutions are composed of these two separate but essential parts. Congregations and denominations are *purposive* organizations. Expressed missionally, in my own denomination this is the United Methodist Church claiming its purpose to make disciples and to transform the world. However, congregations and denominations are also *communal* organizations. People give great attention to socializing, to attending to one another within the organization. At their best, people care and are cared for.

Each of these two sides calls forth different responses and each is rewarded differently. The purposive side is rewarded when progress is made on intentional outcomes. The communal side is rewarded when people feel cared for and when relationships are not disrupted.

As early as 1980 Takayama noted that *denominational agencies and seminaries commonly give preference to the purposive side* of the church while *congregations, quite naturally, give preference to the communal side.*[9] These two sides of a denominational system function in a pendular relationship, each expressing its own truth but moving in opposition to the other (figure 8.1). Purpose demands discipline and sacrifice in order to address outcomes, which commonly intrudes on personal satisfaction and comfort to make gains. Attention to personal satisfaction and unstrained relationships to avoid disagreement or disappointment commonly intrudes on missional strategies constraining decisions that favor priorities over other preferences.

Denominational executives work more freely in the purposive side of the system because they are somewhat less fettered by closeness to the staunchly communal side of the congregation. Local church clergy, accountable to the denomination for purposive gains but also accountable to the congregation for smoothly managed relationships, commonly find themselves caught between the different reward systems of the two pendular expressions of the same institution.

Nostalgia for the highly cohesive, consensual, mid-twentieth-century, resource-rich institutional church *favors the communal side* of the healthy tension between purpose and relationship. People remember a time of agreement and rewards. Simply by tenure, clergy could expect successive calls to ever larger congregations with ever larger salaries over the years of their career. People remember a time when resources were plentiful and could support a very wide range of "good work" simply because it was good work for a Christian people to do, not because it was missionally strategic. Nostalgia, as noted earlier, makes

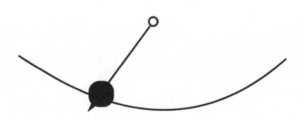

PURPOSE	RELATIONSHIP
PURPOSIVE ATTENTION	COMMUNAL ATTENTION
TO OUTCOMES	TO RELATIONSHIPS
(THE NATURAL DOMAIN	(THE NATURAL DOMAIN
OF THE DENOMINATION)	OF THE CONGREGATION)

Figure 8.1. The Pendular Tension

people long for such a time of abundant resources, high rewards, and secure relationships, and they long for the leaders who can take them back to that time.

The more recent history of membership decline, aging populations, and shrinking congregations has *required the church to be more purposive*. Resources are shrinking, which forces leaders to make decisions, which means that some things must be identified as more important than others. Caught in this postaberrant time, the church is not, by any stretch of the imagination, uncaring. But all things can no longer be cared for. So leaders are now confronted by those about them who are disappointed, discouraged, or even angry. The natural expression of empathy, a cultivated emotion of discipleship, will want to bend leaders toward the communal, relational side of the polarity. The temptation to want to relieve internal suffering will paralyze the purposeful, missional side that is now needed to be dominant as the means by which religious institutions will live in this new cultural mission field.

Unchecked Empathy Favors Weakness over Strength

At its worst, overattention to stress and discomfort invites leaders to align their decisions and resources to favor weakness, not strength. When threatened, denominations and congregations (like all organizations, families, or individuals) are driven by anxiety. Ed Friedman has given a lot of attention to this normative response in his work with family systems theory and speaks of people now living in a culture of "free-floating anxiety." People now live in the stress of economies that are shifting from local to global, of industries shifting from production to information, of decisions and directions shifting from macro power centers to micropower centers. People are generally uncertain of what to expect in most areas of their lives.

Such anxiety, Friedman contends, invites people to become reactive, to herd together for safety, to blame others for their anxiousness, to seek quick fixes, and to sabotage leaders.[10] Friedman writes about the "fallacy of empathy" under these pervasive conditions of anxiety:

> As lofty and noble as the concept of empathy may sound, and as well-intentioned as those may be who make it the linchpin idea of their theories of healing, education, or management, social regression has

too often perverted the use of empathy into a disguise for anxiety, a rationalization for the failure to define a position, and a power tool in the hands of the "sensitive." It has generally been my experience that in any community or family discussion, those who are the first to introduce concern for empathy feel powerless, and are trying to use the togetherness force of a regressive society to get those whom they perceive to have power to adapt to them. [11]

"A power tool in the hands of the 'sensitive'" may feel like an overstatement in many cases within the institutional church. But anxious people too often call on empathy, either wanting to express it or receive it. And because empathy is a response to pain and suffering, it can be used as a "tool" to ease the pain of the suffering and assuage the feelings of the disappointed by interrupting (sabotaging) leaders whose decisions are seen as the cause of the pain.

Quiet courage, in the face of empathy, is the act of leadership keeping attention and resources on those people, and that part of the system, with the most potential to align with purpose and to move toward identified outcomes. Quiet courage is to choose missional strategy over relational comfort—and to resource the strategy as needed. Quiet courage is to choose not to be redirected by empathy when choices cannot missionally be avoided.

The Pareto principle, introduced in chapter 5, states that roughly 80 percent of the effects in any system come from 20 percent of the causes. Phenomena in nature as well as in organizations roughly seem to follow this distribution of causes and effects. The Pareto principle suggests that 20 percent of an organization (its vital few) will produce 80 percent of its intended outcome. If we were to consider a very simple example of a shoe store with ten salespeople, general management strategy would be to resource and support the top two salespeople at all costs (the 20 percent vital few). These two most productive salespeople would be scheduled during the most productive business hours on the busiest days, they would be highlighted in ways to encourage customers to form relationships with them, and attention to their sales numbers would let them know their managers were aware of their efforts, and they would feel motivated to do even more. This 20 percent, this vital few, carry the purpose of the shoe store and make it thrive. Wise managers would simultaneously direct few resources and little attention to the two weakest salespeople. Managers would not assume that additional training for unproductive people would improve performance by teaching what the poor performers seem unmotivated to learn or incapable of learning. By focusing on the strongest part of the organization, resources and attention are directed appropriately to accomplish purpose. Partly because a shoe store is not a communal organization, but also because it is clearly purposeful, empathy for those not receiving substantial resources and attention does not redirect or misdirect the organization from its purpose or the managers from their leadership.

Precisely because religious organizations are so communal, and precisely because empathy is an emotion connected with Christian discipleship, religious institutions over the second half of the twentieth century have been tempted and trapped into an inverted organizational strategy. Denominations have routinely directed 80 percent of their attention and resources to the congregations and clergy least capable of fulfilling the denominational mission. Denominations have routinely subsidized dying congregations. They have required continuing education of clergy uninterested in learning new ways. They have promoted and required attention to programs of congregational redevelopment for congregations unwilling to change.

I do not wish to make an argument of blame. Some congregations have simply slipped below the threshold of vitality and purpose because the conditions surrounding them or within them have naturally changed. Some clergy have passions, capacities, or motivations that no longer correspond to the deeper needs of the current challenges to the church. There is no part of the conversation that needs to be directed to separating the positive and negative—congregations or people. Rather, the quietly courageous leadership question is more clearly one of strategic deployment of limited resources: How does a missional leader identify and steward the potential that is within individuals and congregations to make disciples and change communities? Despite our empathetic impulses, leaders must attend to strength. They cannot be paralyzed by empathy.

Giving attention to strength in congregational and denominational systems that are now aligned to weakness is a personal challenge for quietly courageous leaders. Friedman goes on to note that systems that favor weakness over strength quickly resort to sabotage of their leaders. In such chronically anxious systems, he writes that "a good rule of thumb for leaders who are trying to pull any institution out of its regression is that when people start calling you 'cruel,' 'autocratic,' 'heartless,' 'hardheaded,' 'unfeeling,'. . . . there is a good chance you are going in the right direction."[12] Personal courage intentionally developed by leaders, along with clarity of institutional purpose, is necessary to break a debilitating focus on empathy that weakens a focus on responsibility.

Empathy Holds Leaders Hostage to the "Client in the Room"

There are additional characteristics of empathy that make quiet courage in the face of discomfort and pain difficult. One characteristic is "empathy distress," which is experienced by professionals who work with people in pain and find themselves joining in the pain rather than being able to help people manage their own pain. The example used by Daniel Goleman in his work on emotional intelligence is a pediatric nurse who requests a transfer to a different service at a medical clinic because she feels that she cannot hold another child who is dying from cancer.[13] Pain, like anxiety, is transferable. Any leader in a discomforted system is subject not only to sabotage from others but to empathy distress from within as well. To deal with empathy distress requires self-management and an ongoing awareness by the leader of his or her own feelings while leading. However, it is clear that "too much" pain in a system invites leaders to their own personal distress.

Coupled with too much pain, additional characteristics such as locality and singularity are also aspects of empathy that tempt leaders to subvert purpose to relationship. In their work on understanding the practical use of wisdom and the way in which leaders make right decisions, Schwartz and Sharpe note that large-scale suffering can be grasped intellectually but is close to unfathomable emotionally. However, individual suffering that can be localized engages our emotions without a necessary balance from our intellect. Write Schwartz and Sharpe,

> We read an article in the newspaper about a famine that is starving three million children in sub-Saharan Africa. We shake our head and turn the page. Then we see a TV documentary that explores the life of one such child and his family. Our check is in the mail. Why is it that a matter-of-fact account of suffering of many spurs little while a vivid account of the suffering of one immediately gets us to do something? Psychologist Paul Slovic suggests that we are driven in situa-

tions like this by our own emotional reactions to suffering . . . it is our
empathy and compassion—our emotions—that compels us to act.[14]

It is easier to identify with the plight of one individual than with the
plight of three million. It is easier for people to imagine themselves in
the story of one individual than to imagine themselves in the story of
three million people. Scale and location influence empathic responses,
and the more local and the more singular the pain or discomfort borne
by the other person, the more leaders are tempted to empathic responses that can subvert purpose. Yet the most common encounter of
distress by congregational and denominational leaders is both singular
and local.

In a very telling example, I had a contract to work with one of the
mainline denominations to review and revise their system for recruiting
and certifying candidates for ordination. The denominational leaders
were concerned about the "quality" of the candidates who were being
produced to serve as clergy in their local congregations. As part of the
work I asked the leaders to categorize the candidates who came through
their certification system. Interestingly, they identified three categories
of almost equal size. The first category was young adults who came
through college, moved directly to seminary for their graduate study,
and then appeared before the denominational committees for certification for ordination after all requirements were satisfied. The denominational executives were encouraged by this group of candidates, recognizing the potential, if not experience, that they brought. The second
category was older adults, most commonly second-career persons, who
had met the necessary educational and institutional requirements but
who also presented themselves with life experience that would be valuable to them as clergy in local congregations. Again, the denominational
executives were encouraged by this group. The third category, about
equal in size to each of the other two, was described as "damaged
people." These were individuals who may have fulfilled educational and
institutional requirements but who came to the denominational committees with evidence of life issues that made it hard for the denomination to ordain them for leadership. Many of them were living with
trauma in their lives or were seeking safe sanctuary hoping that a congregation was a place where people would care for them as opposed to a
place where they would be pastor and leader to the people.

My work with the denominational executives got very interesting when I asked which of the three groups of candidates demanded the most time, attention, and resources from them. Overwhelmingly, the energetic and frustrated response was "the damaged people," with the executives saying that their certification committees spent two to three times the attention and resources on this group with lowest potential. The executives recounted stories that would be familiar with most if not all certification committees of sister denominations in which people being interviewed for ordination would be asked to take another course, take remedial training, seek emotional resources and support, etc., before being invited back to be reinterviewed with the next cycle of candidates. Commonly, denominational dollars would be provided to help the candidate address the additional requirements, and commonly an individual or two from the committee would be assigned as contact and support persons to help the unacceptable candidate wrestle with trying to rise to the level of bare acceptability before the next interview. Time, money, and personnel were all being expended to try to raise the candidate to the lowest level of potential leadership to be called by a congregation for pastoral leadership—a level well below the standard needed by the congregation.

With the data and the stories before us, I then asked the executives why. Why would they spend most of their time, attention, and resources on the very group of people who had evidence of least potential to provide what was needed in vital local congregations? It was a full afternoon's conversation that was brought to conclusion by the person who said that the real reason they were caught in such a quandary was because "it was the candidate that was in the room." In other words, the denominational executives and the certification committees were fully aware that they were screening candidates for ordination that would place the people in local congregations as leaders. In that sense, the real "client" of their work in certifying candidates was the local congregations—and one could argue that beyond that congregational client was the client of the mission field in which the local church was located. Clergy are trained and deployed to serve the congregations and the communities where they will be placed.

However, the local congregation and the community were not in the room when the "damaged person" candidate was being interviewed. The pain or discomfort of the local congregation trying to operate without healthy clergy leadership was hidden from the committee, but the pain and disappointment of the candidate who was sitting in the room with them and was so obviously distressed from being turned down for ordination was palpable. The location, singularity, and transferability of the discomfort they felt had the capacity to engage empathy fueled by the "pastoral hearts" of the committees, subverting their own purpose of providing healthy leadership to congregations in order to care for the immediacy of relationships.

The purpose of an institution is rarely "in the room." The real client of the mission was out of sight, while the pain of the disappointed candidate was overpoweringly local and specific. Empathy overused was tempting leaders away from purposeful mission.

WHEN BEING NICE ISN'T ENOUGH: MANAGING THE SELF

Being nice is regularly rewarded. Being nice is being thoughtful, considerate, accommodating, and caring. In systems that are stressed, being nice can be an empathetic posture of leadership. Niceness routinely honors the pole of relationship. But as I have been arguing, empathic niceness must be balanced by purpose. This is the quietly courageous act of leaders who seek to be purposive without being uncaring. Leaders must constantly recognize that the rewards for niceness can tempt them and their systems away from what is both needful and mission. Ed Friedman notes that the original concept of empathy came into the English language only in 1922.[15] If that is the case, the period since 1922 is a very short tenure for a temptation to gain such power.

The primary way in which a leader needs to address the temptation of empathy is in the management of self. It is not realistic to imagine that leaders can talk others out of their self-concern or their discomfort stemming from the changed conditions around them. It is natural for people to begin first with their own perceived needs. In my conversations with him, my colleague Ian Evison would regularly remind me at my most idealistic moments that I could not count on people voting against their own self-interests, no matter how lofty or noble my goals for them might be. He, of course, was right. People will not put aside their own needs unless the leader can point to a purpose that makes risking self-interest a perceptibly higher value. However, pointing to a greater purpose requires more than vision and oratory.

People cannot be talked out of their pain. The leader must manage him- or herself in order to give visible preference to purpose, even when—especially when—the discomfort is palpable within the leader and within the system. It is an issue of mirroring. The people will mirror the leader and give attention to what most draws the attention of the leader.

The more that the leader can verbalize and demonstrate purpose in a stressed system, the more the people will mirror the attention of the leader. People over time increase their attention to that which the leader gives his or her primary attention. In their work on emotional intelligence, Daniel Goleman and others offer an explanation:

> The reason a leader's manner—not just what he does, but how he does it—matters so much lies in the design of the human brain; what scientists have begun to call the open-loop nature of the limbic system, our emotional centers. A closed-loop system such as the circulatory system is self-regulating; what's happening in the circulatory system of others around us does not impact our own system. An open-loop system depends largely on external sources to manage itself.[16]

A leader, by organizational position, is an external source to people that helps them manage themselves in an open-loop system. What the leader looks at is what the people will look at. It is a part of the natural alignment of organizational systems.

Although theatrical, a wonderful example of a fully aligned system can be found in the Blue Thunder high-tech urban surveillance and attack helicopter from the 1983 movie of the same name. Designed to function in the midst of the chaos of large-scale urban civil disobedience, the pilot could (hypothetically) hover over the confusion of the chaos and shoot at bad people and not at good people. The premise of the movie was a bit strained, as entertainment often is. But the systems mechanics of the Blue Thunder helicopter are a significant example of a fully aligned system. The pilot could react with immediacy and accuracy (hypothetically, again, because the pilot would need to be able to distinguish between good and bad while hovering over chaos) because there was no need to aim any of the helicopter's armaments. All of the guns of the helicopter were keyed into the sensors on the pilot's helmet. Wherever the pilot looked, the guns were aimed. The pilot simply needed to look and then make a judgment to shoot or not shoot, depending on what he or she thought about what was seen. Theatrical drama aside, Blue Thunder is a clear example of an aligned system in which the full system naturally moved to what captured the leader's attention. People will begin to, and will continually, align with purpose if a quietly courageous leader will continually focus on purpose, even when empathy is most clearly invited.

The quietly courageous missional leader needs to maintain focus on purpose while managing his or her own tension between reason and emotion. Again, this is leadership by self-management. The organizational polarity explored in this chapter is the tension between purpose and relationship. Yet within the leader (and the people) is another powerful and related polarity between reason and emotion. Academics and authors Chip Heath and Dan Heath note the two systems of planner and doer that reside in everyone:

> The conventional wisdom in psychology, in fact, is that the brain has two independent systems at work at all times. First, there is what we called the emotional side. It's the part of you that is instinctive, that feels pain and pleasure. Second, there's the rational side, also known as the reflective or conscious system. It's the part of you that deliberates and analyzes and looks into the future. [17]

Then, using an analogy from the writings of University of Virginia psychologist Jonathan Heidt, the Heaths identified the emotional side as an elephant and the rational side as its rider. The metaphor allows the reader to think of the rational side, the rider, as being in control—hands on the reins. What is significant is that the metaphor puts the elephant-sized emotional self in contrast to the human size of the rider, whose control is always precarious in any disagreement that the rider and elephant might have about intended direction. The rider may have the intellect and the ability to think long term and purposefully. However, the elephant has a hunger for instant gratification—especially if discomforted. If reduced to a tug-of-war between elephant and rider, it is simply too exhausting for the rider to keep the elephant on a rational, purposeful path. As the Heaths note, "self-control is an exhaustible resource." [18]

So the temptation to empathy demands a considerable and tiring response from quietly courageous leaders. Empathy is highly rewarded, and to resist it is demanding and exhausting. The counterbalance for pain and distress in a system depends less on relieving pain than on directing the attention of the system to a purpose that is more valuable than the cost of the pain. Because the people will follow the attention of the leader, quietly courageous leaders need to focus on purpose and outcomes above rewards. They must attend to strengths and potential over weakness and problems. Leaders need to keep their real clients (the mission and the outcomes) in mind, even when they are not in the room, visibly present. Leaders need to manage themselves first because organizations are rarely healthier or more focused than their leaders. The way through the temptation of empathy is a clear, missional, caring focus on purpose. It can be exhausting. However, if the quietly courageous leader can model it, the people can mirror it. The discomfort of the postaberrant time can be eclipsed by a mission future.

9

THE TEMPTATION OF TIREDNESS

And grant us grace to count our more complicated blessings: our failures, which teach us so much more than success; our lack of money, which points to the only truly renewable resources, the resources of the spirit." The prayer by Bill Coffin from chapter 1 is a good starting point to explore the temptation of tiredness. Failure does teach what success cannot. And the resources of the spirit are ever renewable. However, failure without learning and a depleted resource of the human self are not complicated blessings—they are only complications. Effective leadership is not measured by effort or hours expended or by how nobly one tilts at the challenges of a fast-changing culture. To fail without learning, to exhaust oneself without making a difference, does not make one a better leader; it only makes one tired.

Nonetheless, tiredness is tempting because it is another of those aspects of leadership that is highly rewarded. Being able to log eighty or more hours a week laboring at leadership is often perceived as heroic and as a demonstrable sacrifice in the eyes of many. Attending *every* meeting seems to show a leader's intentionality and commitment. Being considered indispensable so that no steps ahead can be taken unless directed by the leader is flattering and provides a feeling of self-worth.

One high-profile local church pastor of an urban church was widely known for his exhausting schedule. He was also suffering physical side effects from his work schedule that came to the attention of his congregation's personnel committee, who challenged him (restricted him) to work less than fifty hours a week, not attend more than two evening meetings per week, and take a full day off each week. I asked how he was doing with the restrictions, and he smilingly told me about the personnel committee meeting that he attended the evening just before our conversation. He said the committee members asked if he was able to restrict his work. He reported that he had somewhat reduced his hours and was trying to limit the church meetings, but that he had not taken a full day off that week. When the committee chairperson asked why not, the pastor replied that he couldn't take the day off because he had to attend their personnel committee meeting, which they had called on his day off. Then the pastor laughed. He felt fully rewarded by the attention, by people's awareness of how long he labored for them, and by his own sense of faithfulness to his calling as a pastor. His debilitating tiredness was not a problem for him to solve; it was a reward to be relished.

However, being tired and being effective are far from the same thing. Leading in the postaberrant time of deeply changing cultural values can guarantee tiredness. And tiredness can appear noble to anxious people who are comforted knowing that someone is working tirelessly on their behalf. However, being tired is not evidence of being a good leader. Tiredness is not evidence of the learning necessary to leading in new cultural conditions. Tiredness is not necessarily evidence of wisely using limited human resources for purpose rather than for comfort.

However, tiredness can be the product of not knowing, not wanting to be embarrassed, and not wanting to be undervalued. If the resources of the Spirit are ever renewable, the resources of the self are not. As a caveat to the earlier chapter on assumptions about resources, leaders need to understand that they and those they work with are by definition, as human beings, one of the truly *limited* forms of resources. We are all limited human resources. Given the limitation, it is more important to use the limited human resource of the leader and the people for missional outcomes than it is to simply exhaust efforts on missional aspirations, and less still to exhaust efforts on institutional activities, no matter how familiar and comforting they may be. Quietly courageous leaders do not succumb to the temptation of rewarded tiredness; instead, they use themselves and the other limited human resources around them purposefully.

THE RED QUEEN EFFECT: RUNNING HARDER TO STAY IN THE SAME PLACE

In her adventures in Lewis Carroll's classic book *Through the Looking Glass*, Alice encounters the Red Queen, one of a number of living chess pieces. Seeking to move ahead in her adventures (and away from the Red Queen), Alice runs without getting anywhere. "'Well, in our country,' said Alice still panting a little, 'you'd generally get to somewhere else—if you ran for a long time as we've been doing.' 'A slow sort of country!' said the Queen. 'Now, here, you see, it takes all the running you can do, to keep in the same place.'"[1]

Like Alice, it is dispiriting and confusing to many leaders to labor long, run hard, and seemingly get no place. Yet that does not dissuade leaders from working longer and working harder at what has already proved to make no appreciable difference. Running in place without making any headway, the Red Queen effect, is a natural enough experience to suggest several explanations.

One explanation is that we are at that time in which we are actually too close to, too much a part of, the deep cultural changes that require letting go of old assumptions. Being too close and too much a part of the cultural changes makes it difficult to see the bigger picture of our situation. Being too close to deep change invites one to respond to confusion as if it is caused by not trying hard enough—so running faster, taking more steps, seems a reasonable response, even if it does not produce any progress.

So, too, the lack of known alternatives invites us to run faster and work harder and longer without making appreciable differences. There is an old adage that when people don't know what to do, they do what they know. I have often recounted the story of the very first governing board meeting that I attended after arriving as the new pastor to my first parish in Philadelphia. It was September and the question was raised if we had enough candles for the December Christmas Eve candlelight service. After lengthy discussion someone was tasked with counting the candles. That prompted the lengthy October discussion about where to buy candles. Someone was tasked with finding out where the church usually purchased candles. After the report and lengthy discussion at the November meeting, another person was then tasked with actually making a purchase of additional candles. The backdrop to this three-month discussion was the reality that the city, and our immediate neighborhood, were in the midst of actively racist housing and real estate practices that were deeply unsettling. As pastor I could not seem to get any conversations going about what was happening in the neighborhood—especially not at the board meetings. It took me quite some time to understand that the board and I had no idea what to do about the racist community practices, but we did know how to have a committee meeting about candles and candlelight services. Had we simply, and reasonably, just asked someone in September to count and order candles as needed, it would have allowed board time in October and November for other discussions that might have led us to issues such as racism for which we didn't really have a good idea of what to do. When people don't know what to do, they do what they know. It creates more work and makes little progress. But at least it's familiar, using the space and time that protect from having to confront what is not known.

Which leads us to the third possible explanation of work avoidance: the real work of the church, such as addressing racism. In chapter 7 concerning the temptation of nostalgia, Argyris's work on organizational defensive routines was noted. Argyris points out how organizations and leaders follow actions or policies to avoid embarrassment or threat. He noted that people naturally collude to give attention to things that won't embarrass them or their organization. Few things embarrass leaders and organizations more than ignorance—the need to say, "I don't know." The seemingly reasonable response to not knowing is to avoid the real work of learning by doing the old and familiar work of the known, even when the familiar, known work doesn't help. Argyris points out that such organizational defensive routines are antilearning, overprotective, and self-sealing. Not only does running in place not produce results, it also precludes learning new things and new ways that could produce results.

CAUGHT BETWEEN SCYLLA AND CHARYBDIS

In particular, in the postaberrant time the leader's temptation to give in to the so readily rewarded tiredness of familiar activity leads to two forms of work avoidance: aspirations and activities. Aspirations and activities are very much like the mythical sea monsters in Homer's epic poem *The Odyssey*, in which he recounts the hero Odysseus's ten-year journey home after the fall of Troy. Part of the peril of the journey was steering the ship's passage between Scylla and Charybdis, which were the mythical "monsters" representing the perils on the opposite sides of the Strait of Messina between Sicily and the Italian mainland. Scylla, the six-headed monster, represented the mountainous rocks on the Italian side; Charybdis represented the whirlpool off the coast of Sicily. Scylla and Charybdis—mountains and whirlpools—lofty aspirations that defeat and swirling activities that deplete. To deal with the temptation of tiredness, quietly courageous leaders must do more than be purposeful with a constant eye on the outcomes of making intentional differences. Quietly courageous leaders must also navigate between the dual hazards of mountainous aspirations and swirling activities.

The Scylla of Mountainous Aspirations

Religious people are aspirational, with lofty goals on which they can be shipwrecked. An aspiration is a hope—a future goal or alternative reality. Like world peace, aspirations can be mountainous indeed. Aspirations can also be diffuse and difficult to define, which comes naturally to efforts of meaning making.

I have long been helped by the distinction between faith and science made by philosopher Ken Wilber. He notes that faith and science have never been in contest with one another; they simply serve different purposes. The pursuit of science is *truth*. The pursuit of faith is *meaning*.[2] As such, the two do not contradict one another and, in fact, demand different tools and strategies appropriate to their pursuits. Science, especially the hard sciences, can be quantitative and concise in a search for the certainty of truth. Faith, on the other hand, pursues meaning that is much more diffuse, nonquantifiable, and changes character contextually depending on the seeker. Faith puts its hand to understanding suffering, death, forgiveness, compassion, human development, work, and the importance of the other and of community. These are tall tasks—mountainous aspirations. As hoped-for goals, they are often difficult to bring to definition.

Meaning is often expressed in transformational ways such as spiritual fulfillment, personal development or actualization, connection with others, and caring communities. The intention always involves some transformation of what currently is and can be communicated, but the specifics are always initially unclear. It is the kind of transformation found in the wonderful biblical expression in the book of Philippians of "the mind of Christ."

> That the same mind be in you that was in Christ Jesus,
>   who though he was in the form of God,
>   did not regard equality with God
>   as something to be exploited,
> but emptied himself
>   taking the form of the slave,
>   being born in human likeness.
>   (Philippians 2:5–7 [NRSV])

This passage in Philippians picks up the lyric of an ancient Vedic hymn and uses it metaphorically to describe the servitude of Christ and the intended servanthood of the followers of Christ. As powerful as the metaphor is, the intent is much clearer than the specifics. Nonetheless the aspiration is that the followers of Jesus will empty themselves of self-attention and self-serving in order to pick up the role of servant, choosing humbleness to serve others. The aspiration of transforming from self-serving to serving others is clear. The path for getting from one form of serving to the other is not certain and cannot be generalized for all people.

Picking up the mission statement of my own United Methodist denomination, here again the intent is transformational and aspirational. The United Methodist Church states its mission as "making disciples of Jesus Christ for the transformation of the world." The aspiration of the denomination is to transform people to be disciples—to be people who follow the disciplines of a life of faith as modeled by Jesus. Through these transformed people—disciples—the United Methodist Church seeks to transform communities and the world.

To many, the intent is very clear. The mission statement is *aspirational*. However, it is not *directional*. As a mission statement it offers no definition of discipleship or even specificity of the disciplines to be followed. Similarly, there is an aspiration for a different—a transformed—world. Again, however, as a mission statement it offers no definition for specificity to the alternate reality of that transformed world.

The point here is not to critique mission statements or aspirations but only to note that by themselves they can be mountainous in their demands, with no clear path indicated. In his work on understanding organizations, Jim Collins notes that nonprofit organizations routinely don't know what they are trying to produce.[3] Participants and congregations know that they are to be better disciples, but in what way? Clergy know that they are to help lead their congregations to an increase of vitality and ministry, but in what way? Denominational leaders know that they have to prepare and provide better leaders for their congregations, but in what way?

Until aspirational goals acquire the specifics of actual, intentional outcomes (which will be explored later in this chapter), the aspiration invites tiredness to the point of exhaustion. One never comes to the end of being a better disciple, a more vital congregation, or a better leader. So without the time-specific definition of a clear difference of an intended outcome that describes the actual next steps to be taken, leaders are free to, are invited to, and are rewarded for throwing themselves into the fray and doing anything and all things that might (or might not) be helpful.

Because of the importance of the work of meaning making, the effort of the work, by itself, gets valued as much for being aspirational as it does for actually being productive and making a real difference. Leaders who deplete themselves in the pursuit of ill-formed aspirations still appear heroic, a self-portrait or an attribution from others that is highly rewarding and measured more by the energy expended than by the difference achieved. Consider the descriptions that have a history of use within religious institutions: that leaders "labor in the Lord's vineyard," "sow that others might reap," or "do good for the sake of the good." What is being honored here under the flag of aspirations is the effort given, the energy expended, without necessarily showing any product for the expense. For a limited human resource such recognition is a depleting reward, as tempting as it is. In the postaberrant time it is an empty form of leadership.

Surplus Powerlessness

Before leaving the temptation of mountainous aspirations it is important to recognize the potential that aspirations hold for actually inviting leaders to fail. Here again, as with the discussion of empathy, the careful place to begin is with acknowledging the central importance of aspirations to religious people and their institutions. Without the conviction that the aspirations of the Kingdom of God, the Holy City, or the family of God in all their fullness are worthy of pursuit, there is little purpose in any quest for change or in a pilgrimage toward holiness. However, the full expression of such aspirations, while certainly not the current reality, is ultimately beyond the reach of only human effort. Ultimately, the truly worthy aspirations in all their fullness lie beyond our reach.

New world orders that lie beyond our reach invite noble pursuit that is as rewarded in failure as it might be in success. Don Quixote is a literary figure that seems compatible with the martyred apostles of the early church for good reason. Sensing the rewards of failure, leaders are tempted to develop strategies that will exhaust them for efforts they know will not succeed. These are the rewards attached to any noble pursuit mounted in the face of impossible odds.

Michael Lerner has been a social theorist and practicing psychotherapist. However, in an earlier part of his life in the 1960s he was also a national leader in the antiwar and social justice movements and an editor of *Ramparts* magazine. As a young adult without institutional credentials or substantive supporting resources, he learned much about throwing himself into grand aspirations against overwhelming opposition. Because of this experience, later, as a psychotherapist working with labor unions, he recognized a repeating pattern among people he identified as *surplus powerlessness*. Of his own experience he wrote,

> I first developed the idea of surplus powerlessness to explain my own experiences in the social change movements of the 1960s. Although that movement was filled with a bravado about making revolutionary changes, I found that many of the people involved had a deep emotional commitment to losing, to being isolated, and to remaining powerless. Tactics and strategies often were shaped by an underlying assumption that no one would ever really listen or take them seriously.[4]

Surplus powerlessness is "the set of feelings and beliefs that make people think of themselves as even more powerless than the actual power situation requires, and then leaves them to act in ways that actually confirm them in their powerlessness."[5] Surplus powerlessness invites people to expect failure, in fact to plan for it, and then feel rewarded for failing. Surplus powerlessness certainly constrains clergy from pursuing accountability for practices of discipleship (at times even the practices of civility) in the lives of the individuals connected to their congregations. It constrains congregations from developing credible strategies for making their communities healthier or less assaulted by drugs, violence, or the breakdown of family structures. Surplus powerlessness constrains denominational executives and middle judicatories from experimenting with culturally relevant faith communities instead of nursing recalcitrant congregations that survive without evidence of missional expressions of the gospel. Grand, ultimate aspirations can so overwhelm that leaders will plan modest and meager (perhaps naïve) efforts that will quite naturally fail, knowing that failure will just affirm again how important and difficult their aspiration is and how noble it was for them to have tried. Like eighteenth- and nineteenth-century American literature that used images of the "noble savage" to describe North American Indians, losses (failures) at the hands of noble savages were also seen as noble in a commensurate way—and proof of their own nobility. In all noble aspirational pursuits exhaustion will be rewarded, and if leaders are bruised or wounded in the effort, so much the better.

Quietly courageous leaders do not fall prey to mountainous rocky aspirations of their institutional Scylla. They fully understand that aspirations are both vital and central to the narrative of the life that their institution and their people are seeking to live. Within the aspiration is purpose and energizing motivation. The temptation, however, is to expend oneself to the point of rewardable tiredness through the telling of and loyalty to the aspiration. But to actually thrive, aspirations need proximate goals that are realistically achievable rather than remain as ultimate expressions that can mobilize energy toward change that cannot be realistically accomplished. Quietly courageous leaders learn to tire themselves from the hard but often hidden work of learning that can lead to actions and strategies that actually make a difference. There is nothing wrong with tiredness. However, quietly courageous leaders understand the difference between the lesser rewards offered for strategic, proximate steps that actually advance missional purpose and the grand rewards for aspirational exhaustion, failure, and woundedness.

Lerner notes that escaping surplus powerlessness requires forgiveness and freedom.[6] Leaders must be able to forgive themselves—to release themselves from self-blame—for failing to be all that their aspiration describes that they should be or from failing to achieve all that their institution aspires to accomplish. And because proximate strategies that actually move a next step toward an aspiration are often constrained by the established rules and practices that protect the status quo, quietly courageous leaders must give themselves freedom from their own rules. Once again, quietly courageous leadership requires exceeding the level of authority that the system is willing to allow.

The Charybdis of Swirling Activities

Like tiredness, activity is also easily mistaken for leadership. American values honor movement and progress, with a preference for doing "something" rather than "nothing." Somewhere along the way I remember hearing a distinction between Japanese and American work cultures. In Japan, if an employee walked into a colleague's office and saw that the colleague was simply sitting there without moving or speaking, the employee would quietly back out of the office noiselessly. The assumption in Japanese culture is that the motionless colleague is thinking and that such work should not be interrupted. Not so in America. Here an employee walking into a colleague's office, seeing no movement and hearing no speaking, would simply begin to talk to the colleague assuming nothing was going on to be interrupted. Activity seems to be an American cultural default. If you are not moving, you're not doing anything.

Recently I spoke with the person who had been hired to fill a new position in a middle judicatory in the area of congregational revitalization. This work to resource congregations in efforts of renewal was a new commitment for the judicatory, requiring significant dollars to provide support for both the work and the new director's salary. When I asked how the work was progressing, the new director described nine different projects or programs that he would have online and active before the end of his first year in the new role. He and I both knew that nine simultaneously mounted initiatives would overwhelm the congregations he was to work with. And we both knew that several of the programs of redevelopment did not have particularly productive track records when used by other judicatories. When I mentioned my concerns he simply acknowledged that he felt the same. But then he went on to explain that his position was new, that the judicatory was risking significant resources on this work, and that by the time the finance folks were setting the budget for the next year, he wanted them to feel that they were getting something for their money. He understood that, as a new employee, his performance would be evaluated more on the activities he stirred up than on any actual increase in the vitality of the congregations. Stirring up activity can create a significant whirlpool that can disrupt navigation or even sink the ship. The Charybdis of swirling activity can exhaust—and, like aspirations, not produce much change—but the swirling will appear to be leadership, and it will be rewarded.

The Desperate Need for Intentional Outcomes

In order to understand the powerful temptation of swirling activities, we need to pick up the conversation about W. Edwards Deming's simple systems model begun in chapter 4 about resources. Recall that the model included three component parts: the input (that which goes into the system), the throughput (what the system does to or the way the system uses the inputs), and the output (or outcome—the difference that the system is trying to make) (figure 9.1).

Recall that in the earlier discussion about resources, several points were introduced that can be further fleshed out here:

1. Because the purpose of nonprofit organizations (like congregations and denominations) is shaped by their aspirations, they rou-

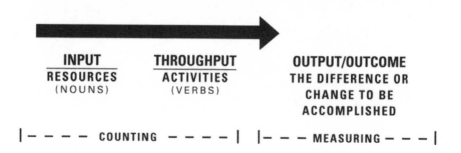

Figure 9.1. Counting and Measuring in the Deming Model

tinely don't know what they are specifically trying to produce or what clear proximate difference they are trying to make. Because nonprofit outcomes are difficult to determine, leaders commonly use aspirations as if they were outcomes. Tempting and highly rewarding aspirations provide motivation but not direction for efforts of change. Aspirations invite activity without being connected to outcomes.

2. For-profit organizations have very clear outcomes that can be quantifiably measured (the amount of profit at year end; the number of automobiles or toasters produced). Because nonprofits do not commonly have such clear outcomes identified (and routinely replace outcomes with aspirations) they cannot measure their outcomes.

3. When organizations are not able to measure their outcomes, they usually measure their *resources* and their *activities*, which are always easily quantifiable. Resources are nouns: how many dollars, people, books, buildings. Activities are verbs that people can participate in: how many programs, projects, initiatives, encounters, meetings. Nouns and verbs are easily counted—leading to McNeil's assessment noted in chapter 4 that the primary dashboard metrics that congregations and denominations use most commonly focus on how many, how often, and how much.

4. Resources and activities that are unaligned with clear and intentional outcomes lead routinely to scarcity and tiredness. Goodhearted and deeply committed people find themselves throwing as much time, energy, dollars, and programs at what they identify as problems *in the hope that* something will be different. With such diffuse attempts it is common that little changes, which then leads to wishing for more resources to make the difference (scarcity: "if only we had more money, time, or . . .") or wishing for more energy (tiredness: "if only we could have tried harder. . .").

In the earlier convergent aberrant time of constantly expanding dollars and people, resources and energy were not limited. "More" could always be directed at problems, and progress could be measured, especially if the metrics for progress were resources and activities, nouns and verbs.

In the postaberrant time the context and conditions have dramatically changed and leaders cannot lead without clear outcomes. Beginning in the 1970s, when denominations became both aware and anxious about negative trends of membership and vitality, new efforts of congregational redevelopment began in earnest and continued over decades.[7] Resources and activities were mounted and expended with little clarity of progress made or change achieved. Because the efforts of congregations and denominations are difficult to quantify beyond resources and activities, the dominant assumption by the beginning of the new century was that church systems needed better metrics—better ways to measure whatever difficult-to-quantify differences they were accomplishing. By 2009 efforts in our own Leadership Ministries initiative at the Texas Methodist Foundation (TMF) focused on the issue of metrics with the assumption that strategies and tools from the social sciences could help. Strategies and tools were already available from other disciplines and other institutions that could help measure less quantifiable changes that could not easily be counted. Gatherings were hosted by TMF, monographs prepared, resources developed, and case studies catalogued. The learning from that work is captured in the book *Doing the Math of Mission: Fruits, Faithfulness, and Metrics.*[8]

This earlier work helped to develop the distinction between counting and measuring (see figure 9.1).[9] *Counting* gives attention to numbers and seeks to answer the quantifiable questions of how many, how often, and how much. Counting is what one does with resources and activities. Distinct from counting, however, is measuring, which gives attention to change. *Measuring* seeks to answer the question of "how far"—as in, "How far have we come in the past year toward accomplishing our intended outcome?" There are tools from the social sciences, such as Likert scales and logic models, that can be used by congregations and denominations to quantify measures of such change.

The key learning of the metrics project at TMF is that the most difficult part of this postaberrant time of addressing change has not been the question of metrics but the more essential question of outcomes. Of all the work that leaders of congregations and denominations do, the most difficult task may be moving from aspirations and activities to actual outcomes. Yet all that we have learned about living and leading in the postaberrant time is that choices have to be made and that the available resources must be carefully aligned to address the priorities determined by the necessary choices. To make choices and to align resources and activities in service to those choices all depends on clear and intentional outcomes.

An outcome for the church is (1) the intentional difference that (2) one believes God has called him or her to make (3) in the next chapter of life or work.[10] That is to say that an outcome is (1) a measurable/describable difference formed by an intentional commitment to making a change. More than an aspiration or hope that things might be other than they are, an outcome is a clear naming of an intended change that is related (2) to God's purpose, as opposed to one's own preference or pleasure. Outcomes do require a connection to aspirations of faith, even as leaders wrestle those aspirations down to proximate realities. They reflect God's dream for the world, not one's own preference for what would be most liked or comfortable. Finally, outcomes are time limited (3) to be accomplished in a clearly defined and relatively brief time. Outcomes are about what we need to learn how to do, how to live, next.

Curiously, and frustratingly, leaders found the forming of actual outcomes to be the most difficult part of the work on the metrics project. The familiarity with our hopes and activities made the work of naming outcomes difficult. In fact, when pushed to develop outcomes that were clear, leaders repeatedly just used more adjectives to further describe or explain their aspirations. Aspirations and activities are very difficult to escape. But they are rewarded with tiredness. It is difficult to learn to be purposeful in aspirational and busy systems.

Activity, especially the swirling activity of what we've always done, is usually the repetition of what we already know—and what we already know how to do. When people don't know what to do, they do what they know. Outcomes, in contrast, are about change. In naming an intentional outcome, leaders in the postaberrant time commonly find that they name that which they and their organization do not know how to do. The necessary alternative to tempting but fruitless and tiring activity is learning. Friedman notes, "Conceptually stuck systems cannot become unstuck by trying harder. For a fundamental reorientation to occur, the spirit of adventure which optimizes serendipity and which enables new perceptions beyond the control of our thinking processes must happen first."[11]

Spirit of adventure and serendipity—perhaps the metaphor of *The Odyssey* serves well. In the Homeric voyage there were temptations on all sides in the form of lofty aspirations and exhausting activity. To navigate without being wrecked on lofty rocks or without succumbing to swirling exhaustion requires the quietly relentless leadership of attention to the purpose described by the intentional outcomes of change, a willingness to follow the spirit of adventure and discovery, and being open to what is not yet known. Learning and change is difficult work, which makes it even more tempting to become shipwrecked on aspirations and exhaustion, where less demanding noble attempts will appear heroic. It takes a quiet mind and a steady hand to be courageous and focused on purpose.

DOING BOTH/AND: REVISITING THE RED QUEEN

When cultures shift, the changes are deep enough to tire any and all leaders. To realistically address the temptation of tiredness, the appropriate response to a time of cultural change may well be fatigue—but to be tired for the right reason, of pursuing purpose and outcomes. This is an exhausting time in which we live in the midst of a historic shift of values, behaviors, organizational structures, and institutional purposes. What once was no longer is; what will be is not yet fully formed. At such a time fatigue may not be easily escaped. However, to better understand how leaders should be *more appropriately* tired, it will be helpful to revisit and extend the conversation of chapter 3 about how change occurs. The earlier aberrant time thrived on linear (progressive) change. In fact, change now occurs in a much more discontinuous and liquid way. As significant cultural change unfolds, leaders are not just challenged to stop earlier linear ways in order to pick up discontinuous new ways but to do both/and.

Alpesh Bhatt, in a marvelous little book that hints at the deep changes to be faced, draws the distinction between "gradual progression" in change (a linear form) and "punctuated equilibrium" (a discontinuous form).[12] The difference can be understood by considering how evolution proceeds. Bhatt points out that most people think of evolution as a process that is a gradual progression over a long period of time through which, for example, an early species of ape was formed into modern man. If thought of as a linear, gradual progression, evolution might look like figure 9.2.

However, evolution (like human development, technological shifts, and many forms of nonlinear change) is not progressive but is a series of *punctuated equilibria.* The current status of what is known experiences long periods of virtual standstill punctuated by the swift introduction of new change. The new change forms a new equilibrium that feels like its own virtual standstill, only to be itself, punctuated by new forms that eventually come along later. These moments of great change are *paradigm shifts* in which even the most basic assumptions are challenged and must be changed. Unlike gradual progression, the assumption of punctuated equilibrium in human evolution might look more like figure 9.3.

One plateau of steady sameness in which a species can acclimate and thrive is progressively interrupted (punctuated) with change deep enough to privilege another different and newly developed species. Every stage of steady state, when punctuated, becomes the ecology in which the new change thrives and in which the old ways die away or are subverted.

There are a number of implications in understanding change as punctuated equilibrium. Consider:

- There is actually a lot of change going on in the long periods of virtual standstill. However, the purpose of change, in times of standstill, is to constantly reestablish a balanced state. Bhatt likens this change to "the Red Queen effect," described earlier, in which leaders necessarily work harder, or in new ways, to achieve the same results. As noted, the hard work of running in place to escape moving backward can quite easily be mistaken as making progress.

Figure 9.2. Evolution as a Gradual Progression

Figure 9.3. Evolution as Punctuated Equilibrium

- In episodes of very fast punctuated change, species die off, incapable of surviving in the new ecosystem. Not all will make it into or thrive in the next ecology.
- During periods of punctuation, what once worked in the past is *actually a threat*. As Bhatt put it, "everything you know for certain is a source of massive risk because what you know is relative to a reality that no longer exists."

The birthing of a new paradigm is a disruptive moment.

However, most importantly, the introduction of a new paradigm is not a simple stepping out of the old into the new. More than fifty years ago, as historians of science were watching dramatic shifts in the paradigms of science (from mechanical to quantum physics, for example), Thomas Kuhn made the critical observation that when the new paradigm is birthed, the old does not go away.[13] The discovery of quantum physics did not invalidate the observations of mechanical physics. The laws of energy still applied because they were explaining the mechanical world. Quantum physics was, in fact, explaining a different kind of world, an ecology beyond mechanics. So when paradigms shift, both paradigms continue on, at least for a period of time. Going back to human evolution, the graphic might more accurately look like figure 9.4, in which each preceding species *coexists* with the new form as it is being birthed.

The stages in the development of the human species were not discrete. Evidence suggests that, at least for overlapping periods of time, multiple human species coexisted in a shared ecology. New ways and old ways do, for a period of time, live together.

Applying the construct of punctuated equilibria to the current experience of religious institutions offers a new way to describe our current situation and the challenge to leaders. Punctuated equilibria invites us

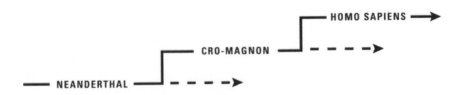

Figure 9.4.   Coexisting Equilibria in Evolution

to a new perspective of the current postaberrant deep cultural change as a moment in which leaders are challenged to do "both/and," that is, to work effectively with both the old and new paradigm expressions of their institutions. Leaders must do both what they know—and also learn what they do not know. Much has been written about postmodernism, post-Christendom, and postdenominationalism as if they are completed shifts. Using linear models of change, one is either modern or postmodern, one lives either in Christendom and denominationalism or in post-Christendom and postdenominationalism. In the terms used in this book, one either lives with the institutions birthed by the aberrant time or helps to build the new forms that will thrive in the postaberrant time. Nonlinear, punctuated equilibrium brings us much closer to our reality of both/and. The more realistic description of the present moment might be pictured as in figure 9.5, in which the institutions of the prior aberrant time still continue (under stress) while the new "species" of religious communities and structures are shaping.

Because we are in a punctuated equilibrium that dually experiences both what is familiar and what is new, the current reality is that leaders are now tasked with making decisions and directing resources in two quite different ecologies at the same time. One is the known work of congregational life and redevelopment. The other is in a more foreign and unfamiliar mission field beyond the natural draw of the established congregation. Both are needed because in the deep cultural paradigm shift what has not changed are people's questions of meaning, of faithfulness, of community, and of justice.

On the one hand, doing both/and requires constant adaptation and improvement of what is. It means giving attention to those things that will make a difference under the rules and assumptions of the earlier aberrant time. The institutions of that earlier time are obviously under stress, and a good number of the earlier "species" of congregations and

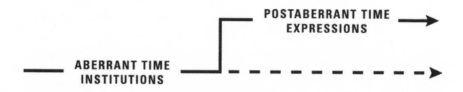

Figure 9.5. The "Both/And" Work of Leadership

denominational structures will not live into the new, reshaping ecology. However, that older "species" and the people who depend on it to shape their lives are far from lost. Leaders need to give continual attention to improving those essential practices that will allow the known forms of congregations to continue to thrive. For example, Bishop Robert Schnase has highlighted five essential practices of vital congregations:[14]

- radical hospitality;
- passionate worship;
- intentional faith development;
- risk-taking mission and service; and
- extravagant generosity.

To thrive in the postaberrant time, congregations will have to focus on practices such as these that have a demonstrated consensus on making a difference—and learn how to make improvements toward excellence. This is the legitimate work of the Red Queen.

On the other hand, and simultaneously, the discontinuous change of the postaberrant time requires attention to new learning and to serendipity about living outside of the norms and practices of the very institutions that leaders seek to improve. Doing both/and requires continuous improvement of what is known, along with simultaneous inquiry into what is not known. It is the improved application of old answers while also asking new, not yet fully formed questions. It is satisfying the expectations of the people who already come to institutions while simultaneously being willing to be changed by the people who are no longer attracted to them. Doing both/and is, itself, a formula for fatigue.

Whether tiredness is a tempting distraction or a necessary price for moving ahead depends on the type of work one is doing. Folk singer

Harry Chapin, who died in an automobile crash in his thirties in 1981, both sang story-songs and told additional stories along with the songs. In one story he told of his grandfather's distinction between two kinds of tired. The first kind of tired was one in which he would go to bed tired from doing a hard day's work that someone else told him to do. With that kind of tired he woke up the next day still tired, finding it hard to go on. But his grandfather described the other type of tired that came from doing what was important and meaningful to him. He might be so tired from this kind of work that he would find it difficult to make it to bed for rest at the end of the day. But with the second tired he woke in the morning fresh and eager to expend himself again. It depended on the kind of work and the type of tired. The tempting tiredness that comes from chasing unformed aspirations and repeating distracting activities is much like the empty calories of artificial sugar. It is rewardingly sweet to the taste but leaves one hungry. This is tiredness that produces only fatigue. Tiredness shaped by clear purpose, proximate outcomes, and learning from new and good questions is quite another thing. Such tiredness is not nearly so rewarded but is the pursuit of quietly courageous leaders.

Part IV

Where Do We Start?

The biblical text functions among us as a "second thought," coming after the initial description of our life in the world according to the dominant metanarrative of our society. One function of redescription is to protest against that initial description and to insist that the initial presentation of reality is not an adequate or trustworthy account.
—Walter Brueggemann, *The Word That Redescribes the World: The Bible and Discipleship*

Wilderness (definition): an uncultivated, uninhabited, and inhospitable region.

The postaberrant time in the church, as in so many other institutions, can be likened to a wilderness. The wilderness is disorienting and deeply unfamiliar territory that, assuredly, must make it a favored place for God to change the hearts, minds, and purposes of chosen people. In the wilderness leaders must lead with courage—without being sure where they are going. Such leaders must find the alternative narrative that redescribes the purpose and the place of the people. What, then, are the first steps?

10

TELLING THE STORY THAT WILL GET US THROUGH THE WILDERNESS

A primary goal of this book is to shift the orientation of leaders from problem solving to exploration. The productivity of problem solving has diminished because so many of the situations that leaders now face are no longer problems. Problems, by definition, have solutions. The distinction made by Ron Heifetz between problems and conditions was noted earlier in chapter 2. In order to address a problem there must be a solution. Using a medical example, Heifetz pointed to a broken bone, a clear problem that has an equally clear solution. The person with a broken bone simply takes him- or herself to the physician who has the solution. This is technical work—applying a known answer to a known problem. However, there are few "problems" that leaders can now face that have such clear solutions.

Also described in chapter 2 are the deep changes that require the quiet courage of learning new directions instead of trying to solve old problems. The shift to the postaberrant time has been driven by changes in cultural values and by technology that alters the speed, access to, and boundaries of information to the point that people no longer think, behave, or form community in the ways once known and managed. Where we were once on solid footing, we now live in a liquid culture. Such deep change does not favor problem solving because the primary focus of problem solving is to return to the earlier pre-problem state—to return to the time before the bone was broken. But there is no going back, which is why nostalgia has become so tempting in its diversion. Nostalgia invites leaders to go back to the time when they had problems that could be solved.

The opposite of a problem is a condition. Again, using medical examples, Heifetz distinguishes between a broken bone (a technical problem) and a chronic disease such as type 2 diabetes or heart disease (an adaptive situation). Chronic diseases, by definition, do not have solutions. A chronic disease is not a problem to be solved; it is a condition that one must learn how to live with. It does not require a technical solution; it requires adaptive learning through which one changes assumptions, values, and behaviors to find a new way to thrive under the changed conditions. When one cannot go back to pre-problem times, it is appropriate to stop problem solving in order to move ahead. So much of leadership now requires the shift from problem solving to exploration—from fixing and improving things to learning new directions that can be seen with a changed mindset.

A first step in loosening a leader's grip on problem solving is to address the assumptions and temptations that continue to provide the orientation that limits the leader's response to the new, deeply changed conditions. Assumptions, like well-established behavioral habits, reassert themselves without thinking because they are so familiar. In earlier chapters the dominant assumptions about change, resources, structure, process, and leadership formation were uncovered. Assumptions, like habits, operate at a tacit level and derive their power from being hidden from plain sight. If what drives behavior is hidden, then leaders are constrained from changing their behavior. What is tactic must first be brought to the light of full consciousness. Even then the power of learned and practiced behavior requires significant, intentional effort and energy to change from old ways. Assumptions require hard work to change.

Temptations behave in a different way. Temptations are easy, with a comforting lure that provides some relief from the difficult work of leadership. Temptations may not be particularly harmful and, in fact, can have an important role to play when approached appropriately and with moderation. Temptations such as the nostalgia, empathy, and tiredness explored in earlier chapters can seem to hold the promise of a way ahead, but the promise turns out to be empty when the temptation is a means of avoiding the hard work of quietly courageous leadership. Both the limitations of assumptions and the lure of temptations need to be brought to the fullness of light in order to break their constraints and allow for the exploration and learning that is needed to thrive in the changed mission field.

The difference between problem solving and exploration is the difference between single-loop and double-loop learning as defined by Chris Argyris. Single-loop learning detects and corrects errors. Double-loop learning questions underlying organizational assumptions, policies, and practices. Argyris describes the difference as follows:

> When the process enables the organization to carry on its present policies or achieve its objectives, the process may be called single loop learning. Single loop learning can be compared with a thermostat that learns when it is too hot or too cold and then turns the heat on or off. The thermostat is able to perform this task because it can receive information (the temperature of the room) and therefore take corrective action.
>
> If the thermostat could question itself about whether it should be set at 68 degrees, it would be capable not only of detecting error but of questioning the underlying policies and goals as well as its own program. That is a second and more comprehensive inquiry; hence it might be called double loop learning. [1]

Questioning what lies beneath our problem solving, our aspirations, and our activities is the necessary work of moving ahead. This is a necessary double-loop moment.

As noted, living in the very midst of a paradigm shift means that we are too close and too much a part of the changes to fully understand what is influencing the shift and too close to be able to accommodate the changes with any real certainty for the future. The Pauline metaphor of the mirror rings true: "For now we see in a mirror dimly, but then face to face. Now I know in part; then I shall understand fully, even as I have been fully understood" (I Corinthians 13:12, RSV). More time will be needed, more experience gained, more trust in God's hand in all of this, and more understanding gathered in order for leaders to find real confidence in their way forward. In the meantime what is most required is quiet courage to take the next steps.

WHAT CAN BE SAID ABOUT
COURAGEOUS LEADERSHIP?

Without a clear and secure path ahead what is left is to describe what can be understood so far, and there is much, even if not conclusive. Once again biblical stories provide sustenance to move ahead. The dominant biblical story that has shaped my own work for decades, and to a large degree shaped my life, is the tale of the Exodus. The Israelites moved from a limited and punishing life toward the promise of life rich with milk and honey, but they needed to find their way through the wilderness to get there. Sure of what they were leaving behind, trusting in their aspirational but not quite clear future, Moses and Aaron needed to shape each day's journey with the courage that they would be moving in a right and helpful direction. Any quick glance at a map of the Exodus and the conquest of Canaan at the back of a Bible provides evidence that it was the work of exploration and discovery. On some days the journey was as clear as following a pillar of fire. On other days the quandary about direction was so heavily clouded that all that could be done was to pitch a tent and wait. The journey was by no means a straight and continuous path.

Knowing *about* the destination can be enough when there is courage to take a next step. Quietly courageous leadership is about taking the next steps even when the final destination remains hidden. A story that I have depended on for years that has encouraged the next steps of many denominational executives, clergy, and their leadership groups is about a very young boy living on a farm who was instructed by his mother to go out on a pitch-dark night to check if the barn door was closed and locked. The young boy left through the kitchen door and returned in less than a minute. When asked what was wrong, the boy replied that it was too dark to see where the barn was and he was afraid to walk out where he could not see. His mother handed him a flashlight and told him to try again. But once again he returned in less than a minute, explaining that the flashlight was too weak and he still couldn't see the barn. "You don't need to see the barn," responded his mother. "Just walk to the end of the light." The insight in the story is that by walking to the end of the light, more of the path ahead is exposed. It is sufficient to have a basic sense of direction—a clear purpose, intention-al outcomes, and a willingness to calmly begin the journey in order to learn the steps that are not yet apparent. It takes courage to walk to the end of the light.

When complete answers from leaders are not available, Heifetz notes that what people look for in their leaders is direction, protection, and order.

> Direction may take the form of vision, goals, strategy, and technique, but on some preconscious level, it may simply mean "finding the next feeding site." Protection may take the form of negotiating a favorable and mutually beneficial agreement with a competitor, but basically it connotes scanning the environment for threats and mobilizing the response. Order . . . consists of three things: orienting people to their places and roles, controlling internal conflict, and establishing and maintaining norms.[2]

The flashlight that we have so far allows leaders to provide such basics. We now have better definitions of the changed role of leadership and a conviction to focus on proximate outcomes that bring real shape and next steps to our driving aspirations.

The Substance and Style of the New Leadership

A distinction between the *substance* of this new leadership and the *style* of leadership is somewhat arbitrary. However, such a distinction does offer a means to differentiate between *the what* and *the how* of what we are learning about courageous leadership: what a leader must focus on and accept, and how a leader can mobilize others to align with the new work. At the very heart of the new leadership is the capacity of telling a new story that will get us through the wilderness—a story of hope and promise that does not relieve our anxiety but mobilizes it for purpose.

Issues of substance (*the what* of leadership) include:

- beginning with a new narrative;
- the power of proximate purpose;
- leading without knowing; and
- the spiritual leadership of accepting mystery.

Issues of style (*the how* of leadership) include:

- the critical role of conversation;
- working slowly in a fast time;
- getting loose from a tight past; and
- working from the edge, not the center.

The institutional church has now been in the wilderness of a liquid culture long enough to begin to describe what we are learning about substance and style—the task of the remainder of this chapter and the next.

THE SUBSTANCE OF QUIETLY COURAGEOUS LEADERSHIP

Beginning with a New Narrative

More than all else, organized religion now holds the alternative story for people that offers meaning and purpose to the current experience in a liquid culture. As Brueggemann has powerfully written, "the biblical text functions among us as a 'second thought,' coming after the initial description of our life in the world according to the dominant metanarrative of our society. One function of redescription is to protest against that initial description and to insist that the initial presentation of reality is not an adequate or trustworthy account."[3]

There is no more powerful and necessary place for quietly courageous leaders to begin than by offering a new narrative, a second thought, that both captures the current reality and provides a better future. A world that is simultaneously furiously changing and stuck by breakdown, gridlock, and the absence of consensus on truth is ripe for a second thought. Philosopher Ken Wilber points out that in the contrast between value-free science and value-laden religion, what the disciplines of the soul have to offer is "wisdom."[4] Wisdom is the meaning that can be brought to bear on one's life experience that does not make sense otherwise. It is truly second thought. However, the meaning carried by faith cannot be delivered by a weak story of loss and decline. An honest picture of the current reality along with a real hope for a better future are the two sides of the most critical aspect of leadership in the postaberrant time: the building of a new and better narrative for people to live. These are the two sides of the most powerful lever that leaders can use to find a way forward while they are still learning their changed circumstances.

The quietly courageous leader must first tell the honest story of the present reality. The honest story is that the earlier aberrant time of growth, strong resources, and cultural compatibility is over. It is not someone's fault or failure that we must now live in a changed world. After a hundred years of a compatible climate, the Anasazi Indians had to face the reality that the rains had stopped and that they could not continue with the same assumptions and realities of their former life. In the midst of such deep change, old ways had to be dismantled. For us, the current consequences of changing information, technology, com- munications, and mobility are proving to be as forceful as the earlier Anasazi consequences of climate change, separating us from an aber- rant past and introducing a new normal. The honest story of the current reality is that we cannot go back to what no longer exists.

At the same time, the quietly courageous leader must offer a better story for people to live as they move ahead. It is a story clearly explain- ing that the fact that we are no longer who we were, or as we were, is not a loss to be mourned. It is the gateway to who we are becoming and how we are now learning to be. Shaping the better story that people can live into is the primary task of the new leadership now needed.

Using the notion of Walter Brueggemann, the dominant metanarra- tive of the culture has been that power lies in size, resources, and authority; that freedom lies in satisfying the consumer-based prefer- ences of the individual; and that morality is a personal judgment. In this dominant cultural story there is less room for the institution of the church because the church holds a story counter to the prevalent meta- narrative. The church is losing the size, resources, and authority so important to the metanarrative; it (at its best) constrains what is as- sumed to be freedom by bending people away from consumer-driven preferences toward deeper purposes, and it insists on a principle-driven morality that serves both the purpose of life and the common good that reach far beyond personal judgment and comfort. Out of step with the culture, the church no longer has a comfortable institutional place in the dominant metanarrative.

For many, the story of the church is told from a position of weakness because it is not aligned with the dominant story. However, even in this current moment, seeing the church as weak is a choice. Leaders can tell a weak story if they want to. There is data available about membership losses, financial trends, and generational differences that can be used to describe what is "wrong" and how the church has suffered losses. And, indeed, the membership losses, financial trends, and generational differences are part of the present honest reality that will, as surely as the disappearing Anasazi rains, reshape the landscape. However, it is a choice to tell this story either as a loss that leads to debilitating weakness or as changed circumstances that offer a new way to live with a vibrant purpose. The quietly courageous leader is the one who holds and uses anxiety to tell the new story of how a changed landscape is a renewed opportunity to live ancient truth in a new form. All about us the world is going through a demolition of the structure of power that is reshaping the locus of power from a very small circle of very large nations, corporations, armies, and institutions to a rapidly expanding number of consortiums of mini powers constructed of networks and value-based relationships.[5] This unstoppable shift in the reshaping of power can be told as an institutional loss—or it can be told as the story of a new, purposeful future that will provide the space to shape new forms to live out ancient truths at a higher level.

A primary task of the quietly courageous leader is to remain aligned with the alternative story of the biblical text. Bill Coffin's earlier prayer pointed out that our lack of resources is the reminder that the only truly renewable resources are the resources of the Spirit. It is easy to feel poor in a consumer society until faith prods us to understand that we already have what we need. Understanding life to be already sufficient is not naïve. R. Buckminster Fuller was able to give palpable evidence and clear thinking to global sufficiency as early as the 1960s.[6] The fact that so many continue to suffer from lack of basic food, health, and security is the more direct product of politics, corporate short-sightedness, nationalism, and original sin (not so very inconsequential sources of suffering). Nonetheless, it is the quietly courageous leader's task to help the people choose which story they wish to live as a first step toward making their story a reality.

If anyone, the biblical people—the people of God's story—are the truly alternative story people. Over centuries the biblical people carried the stories of Moses and the Israelites, who learned that God had the greater power of the water of the Red Sea when the world thought that

Pharaoh held all of the power in his army, land, and wealth. Moses and the Israelites learned that the desert, with all of its constrictions on food and comfort, was far from a place of suffering and would make them strong, reforming them as a new people. Brueggeman's essential point is that the biblical text functions as a redescription of reality—a reality that we don't need to control but one in which we can live in harmony and can be changed by a power greater than our own.

Starting with a new narrative is the primary leverage point of a quietly courageous leader in the postaberrant time. To live in the new normal, people need a new story. It cannot be a story of loss. It must be a story of purpose. It need not be a story that provides clear answers. However, it must be a story with better questions that open up spaces for new possibilities.

For example, in December 2015 the Texas Methodist Foundation hosted a forum "on Wesleyan potential." It was a United Methodist gathering to be sure, but it included a number of people from other experiences and other faith traditions under the assumption that if the same people always gather to talk about the same things, the answers will always come out the same as well. The experiment of the Wesleyan Potential Forum attempted to change both the conversation and the conversation partners. People were invited to a "non-problem-solving" gathering with the assumption that a search for problem-based "solutions" would take them back into known problems instead of inviting them to explore new ways ahead. The stated purpose of the gathering was to "gather thoughtful leaders from different fields of experience and different ages for a non-problem-solving conversation about the future of Methodism so that their leadership is less constrained by what is and more encouraged by what could be." More than one hundred exceptional leaders from across the United States gathered for a three-day conversation—clergy, laity, men, and women, from different traditions, experiences, roles, geographies, races, and generational cohorts. Episcopalians, Presbyterians, Unitarians, Jews, independents, and nones-and-dones were all willing and eager to talk to the Methodists about a future that would be different for everyone.

At the end of three days not everyone who left was happy. Problem solving dies a difficult death, and there were those who walked away frustrated, not quite knowing what to *do* next. However, now, more than two years later, it is possible to trace ongoing energized conversations, new relationships, and continuing networks that took early root in that conversation based on a story that affirmed a Wesleyan potential rather than a story that tried to solve a Methodist problem.

Methodist problems (as in other established institutions of religion) are deeply embedded in their established congregations, institutional structure, struggle over resources and polity, and questions about what to require concerning theological agreement. *The Wesleyan potential* for United Methodists may depend on established congregations, institutional structure, resources, polity, and theological agreement—or it may not. What is clear is that positing potential that is not defined by solving problems is a narrative that energizes exploration and frees up possibilities that did not exist before. Quietly courageous leaders need to help others decide which conversations are more important to have and which stories are more purposeful to live.

What is needed from quietly courageous leaders is a story that breaks captivity. Will Willimon writes, "All God gives us Christian leaders to move forward is nonviolent words. Transformative leaders help people live toward a new world by telling a story that is counter to the ones that hold them captive. Jesus came preaching. Just as God said, 'Let there be light' and there was (Gen.1), so Jesus dismantles an old world and brings a new with nothing but words."[7] Old worlds get dismantled and new worlds get built starting with words—with stories. Whether directly or indirectly, Howard Gardner notes in his research on leadership that leaders use words to fashion stories—principally stories of identity.[8] Identity carries with it not just the story of *who* people are but *why* a people are as well.

Larger purposes require larger stories, especially in challenging, postaberrant times. Gardner describes different kinds of leaders: ordinary, innovative, and visionary.[9] *Ordinary leaders*, he notes, simply relate the traditional story of their groups as effectively as possible. Given what was argued about clergy formation in chapter 6, based on Gortner's research, these ordinary leaders may well be the "placeholder" and the "talented-but-tenuous" clergy who serve congregations without transforming them. *Innovative leaders*, Gardner notes, take the story that the people already have and bring fresh attention or a new twist to it so that the story connects and prospers in a new way. Beyond the placeholder and talented-but-tenuous leaders, all denominations have that innovative subset of clergy, laity, and congregations who "get it"—

who see how their purpose connects with the changed culture and their immediate neighborhood. Such congregations and people are thriving with increased energy and outcomes. They have learned to tell their story in a new and fresh way that connects them with the questions people actually live. However, the rarest leaders, Gardner continues, are the *visionary leaders*. "Not content to relate a current story or to reactivate a story drawn from a remote or recent past, this individual actually creates a new story, one not known to most individuals before, and achieves at least a measure of success in conveying this story effectively to others."[10] Perhaps most needed in the moment of deep change is such a new story from visionary leaders.

Innovative, postaberrant times require innovative, postaberrant leaders. Such leaders carry stories large enough to free the people from the captivity of loss, nostalgia, empathy, tiredness, and old ways and limited assumptions. However, beyond breaking free from captivity, what are now needed are innovative leaders and new stories large enough to face into a dramatically changed future—a future marked by change deeper than first suspected. Phyllis Tickle, founding editor of the religion department at Publisher's Weekly, offered a hypothesis of the seismic depth of the religious change in her 2008 book *The Great Emergence: How Christianity Is Changing and Why*. She wrote, "About every five hundred years the empowered structures of institutional Christianity, whatever they may be at that time, become an intolerable carapace that must be shattered in order that renewal and new growth may occur."[11] Following her hypothesis of five-hundred-year seismic cycles, it is possible to go back five hundred years from the current twenty-first century to the Great Reformation of the sixteenth century; back an additional five hundred years to the Great Schism of the eleventh century; back an additional five hundred years to the Fall of the Roman Empire and the early Church Fathers of the sixth century; back another five hundred years to the first century and the turmoil of the councils that would struggle to define Christianity as either an ethnic or a global faith. More than mere change requiring adjustments, these are seismic shifts requiring full reorientation. If, indeed, the change that we now face in a liquid, postaberrant culture is such a semi-millennial shift, then problem solving will not do. Shaping the new story that will carry the church and the people into the future is the first and most important step ahead that leaders can offer.

The Five Lessons about Narrative Leadership

There are, at this stage, five things that can be said with conviction of what is being learned about the narrative leadership now needed. The first is that the quietly courageous leader must begin by telling the honest story of the current reality—as noted earlier. For all of the reasons uncovered in the assessments of the assumptions and temptations in the earlier chapters of this book, such an honest telling is a very anxious situation for both leader and people. If the honest telling precludes being able to go back, then people will need to move forward. If the honest telling cannot depend on what is currently known, then moving ahead will depend on what is yet to be learned. Telling the honest story of the current reality at times of deep change removes security and introduces anxiety so that a healthy anxiety can provide the engine and energy for inquiry.

The second is that it is not enough to tell the honest story of the current reality; the quietly courageous leader must also break down or deconstruct the old story that held everything in place. In his work on dialogue, William Isaacs charts the flow of how people teach each other new things through the shared inquiry of conversation. [12] Most conversation begins with polite monologues—stories told without challenge, politely received in ways that allow people to stay connected but without the change that comes from real engagement. These polite monologues are stories of how people understand themselves and how they choose to have others understand them. Polite monologues do not invite "impolite" engagement that might challenge or question. They are stories saying "let me tell you who I am," but stories that do not entertain the notion that the "I" might be different from the polite description offered. Polite monologues are the "social conversation" of life in which people disclose themselves without being fully honest or transparent. Much about the current institutional church is still told through such polite monologues in which people rehearse their own memories of the earlier aberrant time as if it still describes the church—or should describe the church. Keeping the narrative of polite monologues alive allows the church to hide from itself, its purpose, and its need to change and adapt in order to address that purpose.

Significantly, Isaacs identifies a second stage of breakdown following the first stage of polite monologues that must occur before the reflective dialogue of real inquiry can begin. The polite monologues must be challenged and broken. This stage of breakdown or deconstruction of the old story is necessary to clear the field for the search for a new narrative. Leaders must help others intuit that it is no longer sufficient to explain themselves in established, polite, institutional, but limited ways. In the hands of capable leaders the breakdown is managed as a controlled discussion or a skillful conversation that can be contained in processes like strategic planning, scenario building, or establishing clear outcomes; or the breakdown may need to come from the more chaotic source of conflict. In all cases, and by whatever method, what is needed is the sense that what once worked has broken down and that politeness (work avoidance) must give way to inquiry and discovery. Old polite stories that are left unchallenged and in place relieve anxiety—the very anxiety needed to move ahead.

The third is that the new narrative leadership that is needed must make sense. In other words, it is the beginning of a new formulation of meaning making, of helping people make sense of their own experience. "Making sense is the process of arranging our understanding of experience so that we can know what has happened and what is happening and so that we can predict what will happen; it is constructing knowledge of our self and the world."[13] The definition of leadership as an *activity* or *action* presupposes the role of leadership in *making meaning*. The new narrative needed must name, interpret, and categorize things in ways that offer explanations for why things have happened and what might be expected in moving ahead. A story without coherence, without meaning, is just a tale—easily told but lacking in reason or purpose for the change necessary to move ahead.

The fourth is that leaders must help others find themselves in the story. Finding oneself in a story requires that the story be both understandable and "livable." The story need not be complex and, in fact, functions better at an elemental level—understandable by what Howard Gardner calls the untutored or the unschooled mind.[14] However, the leader must also embody the story so that people can see that it is livable and can see themselves living it along with the leader. Gardner points to two tools that leaders use: the stories they tell and the lives that they lead.[15] There cannot be dissonance between the story that the leader tells and the life that others observe the leader living. To invite another into a new life-giving but anxiety-producing story, the leader must demonstrate that there is a place for others to join him or her in the new narrative.

Finally, the new narrative leadership must be able to connect the next identifiable steps to the larger story of meaning, purpose, and possibility. The argument in this book has been that the path ahead is not secure; leaders cannot yet see far beyond the end of the flashlight that exposes only part of the way. So leaders must learn how to construct new narratives that carry the hope of a redefined future but also point with the same conviction to the next proximate steps in the wilderness that are worth the journey because of the advance that can be made or because of the new learning that will be provided. New narratives cannot be based on repackaged and certainly not fanciful aspirations. They cannot be "spin"—stories told because they advantage some people or some constituencies in some way. New narratives must carry hope with enough substance, enough reality, that people can put their hands to them even before the story is complete. Aligning the new narrative that redescribes reality with purpose and with proximate outcomes is the next thing that will be addressed in this description of the substantive work of new leadership.

The Power of Proximate Purpose

For well over a decade the Texas Methodist Foundation has been hosting and facilitating clergy development groups (CDGs). CDGs are intentionally formed vertical learning groups made up of clergy who have been identified because of their potential and are invited to participate in a group of clergy peers who all share a similar question about their ministry. Clergy who participate in CDGs commit to ongoing three-day learning retreats over a period of several years led by a trained facilitator who will guide them into shared learning and help each participant put their own questions and their own work in front of their colleagues for peer review. Invitation to participate in a CDG has been described by many participants as both a game changer and a lifesaver in their ministry.

The change begins to happen in the very first gathering when participants (who tend not to know one another because they come from different geographic areas and different denominational systems) introduce themselves by telling their "call stories." A call story is a person's story of how they were called to ministry—the events and people leading them to consider ministry as a focus for their life, their hope in the difference they wanted to make in their own lives and in the world by entering ministry. They are stories of purpose. At their core, call stories recall the *why* of a person's ministry—the need they felt and the hope they held to make a particular difference in the world that would reflect God's promise and presence. They are not *problem* stories.

What became very clear very quickly was that sharing call stories was a foundational piece of the formation of each CDG. Leaders are too often gathered, formally and informally, to solve problems and address what seems wrong. When problem solving is the dominant agenda, energy and hope leave the room. Given the argument in this book that so much of what faces leaders is, in fact, not a "problem" because the deep changes faced are without "solution," the futility of solving problems in order to return to a time that no longer exists exhausts and depletes leaders. Sitting in yet one more problem-solving group deflates leaders.

However, remembering and staying connected to purpose energizes leaders, and subsequently hope grows. With hope, and with the companionship and challenge of other purposeful colleagues, courage grows. A part of the consistent feedback facilitators of the TMF CDGs receive is that participation in a CDG provides courage for leaders to try what they might not have considered on their own.

As earlier noted, over time established institutions develop a private mission that overshadows the public mission of what the institution claims to do. The private mission serves the needs and preferences of the strongest constituencies within the institution. The needs and preferences of any constituency commonly address issues of security and comfort that relieve the anxiety of the constituency, giving it an identity and a place of importance. Private missions provide rewards, and people do not normally or reasonably vote against rewards and their own self-interest—unless they have a purpose that is larger than their own security and comfort. Shaping a powerful proximate purpose is an act of leadership essential to moving forward.

The power of purpose is that it connects us to our *why* that lies well beyond security and comfort. If the postaberrant time is both confusing and daunting, then leaders need (and need to be able to offer to others) the *why* of moving ahead. One's purpose is often the missing but essen-

tial intermediary piece of life in between aspiration and activities. Aspirations are necessary and provide motivation for a spiritual people. But
they are also diffuse, often without obvious direction, and not actionable—targets "too big" to hit with any significant impact. Activities, on
the other hand, are the day-to-day actions that run directly off our own
energy. Activities, in their worst Red Queen way, can keep us running
in place without getting anywhere. What is needed in a time requiring
exploration is a clear and proximate purpose that resides between aspirations and activities, a purpose that is clearly connected to and an
extension of a new, redefining narrative but that brings shape and outcomes to our activities.

The shaping of proximate purpose is a significant part of the direction that Heifetz wrote about as one of the three key things people want
from their leaders when complete answers are not available. Proximate
purpose: the next "feeding site," the next appropriate piece of work, the
next necessary difference that a person or people believe God seeks in
their lives or in their community.

Shaping the next step in the wilderness is a key component in the
substantive work of leadership for the postaberrant time. What is increasingly clear is that proximate purpose is the "next step" that encourages people to walk to the end of the light in order to see more. The
purpose that is now the appropriate work of quietly courageous leaders
to do is a *proximate* purpose, not the ultimate purpose for all time.

For example, *proximate* steps are a necessary and more recent part
of learning for people trained in strategic planning. In the earlier aberrant time of growth, leaders followed linear models of strategic planning in which they measured or described where they currently were
(the actual outcome of point A), then measured or described where
they wished to be (the desired outcome of point B). Through methods
of strategic analysis, leaders could then determine the action steps
needed to move the organization from point A to point B. The primary
tool in the strategic gap analysis was a SWOT analysis, a scan of the
various (S)trengths, (W)eaknesses, (O)pportunities, and (T)hreats that
were held by or that faced the organization. Factoring in the SWOT
analysis provided a path of action steps to get from A to B. In that
earlier time of cohesion and convergence a SWOT could get you from A
to B because change was slow and linear and institutional trust could
depend on agreement for organizational steps to move ahead.

In the postaberrant liquid culture in which conditions and challenges will continually morph and reshape before new goals can be fully accomplished or new structures solidified, linear problem solving alone cannot move an organization between A and B. What is needed is the competent next step, the proximate purpose, that is fully aligned with the end in mind but is an actual actionable difference that will take people *toward* point B and allow them to learn how to adjust their journey along the way.

It is the appropriate and necessary work of a quietly courageous leader to shape a real next step, driven by the why of the people, but designed to teach what additional steps must then follow.

Confident Failure

In linear times planning felt solid, and the move from point A to point B was a series of steps that proceeded with confidence. Proximate steps that produce learning in order to continue progress toward point B do not happen with that sense of confidence but now must be approached with a spirit of exploration. And explorers must learn what paths *not* to take, as well as which proximate steps are most promising. Confident failure is a central part of setting direction, of forming a powerful proximate purpose. For example, pharmaceutical research companies know that their own business model for moving ahead is very uncertain and that only about one out of ten potential new drugs that they work to discover and develop will ever make it to the marketplace. At the same time, drug research is as exceedingly expensive as it is uncertain. The common proximate strategy of such companies is to have at least ten research experiments up and running at all times—and then to work to make the experiments *fail as quickly as possible*. A friend refers to this as "fail fast, fail cheap," a marketing term associated with new product development. When the problems that leaders once faced have morphed into conditions that they must learn, the proximate steps of a powerful purpose will include learning what not to do as well as which next steps to take. The way ahead must be measured in full alignment with purpose but only taken in proximate steps continually adjusted by learning what works and determining quickly what fails.

Leading without Knowing

A spirit of exploration requires both a firm conviction about the purpose and destination of the expedition and an equal awareness of what is not known about the territory to be explored. "Ignoramus," from the Latin, means "we do not know." Ignorance, in the sense of ignoramus, has become pejoratively connected with stupidity, a lack of good judgment—not a good place from which to lead. However, the healthier understanding of ignorance suggests that it is the source of inquiry—the place from which all learning begins because "we do not know." It is a significant part of the substantive work of new leadership to protect ignorance, to eschew flimsy certainty, to avoid casting partial answers as if they are final solutions, and to insist on the hard work of learning.

To live in a state of not knowing is anxiety producing. People want direction, protection, and order from their leaders, especially in the most uncertain times. As noted earlier, *proximate* direction, protection, and order can be offered. However, the counterpoint of leadership necessary to this present stage of the postaberrant time is the need for leaders to preserve ignorance and to keep people in the appropriate and necessary state of anxiety that will provide new learning for the way ahead. I commonly find myself coaching leaders that they must be willing to lead without knowing where they are going or convincingly set outcomes and steps ahead knowing that they will prove themselves wrong. People generally respond with nervous laughter to such ideas, but few deny the reality of living in the ambiguity between certainty and ignorance. A function of leadership is to appropriately keep people in the uncertainty and anxiety of such an ambiguous position until the inquiry of ignorance produces the next steady step ahead.

The critical importance of leading people into such an uncertain and anxious position is undergirded by the work of William Bridges and his study of transitions. Bridges identified three essential stages to all transitions, whether they are life transitions (marriage, births, deaths), situational transitions (graduations, employment changes, relocations), or cultural transitions (shifts in technology, communication, political mandates). The three stages, in order, are (1) endings (letting go), (2) the neutral zone (the confusion of the in-between time), and (3) making a beginning (starting over).[16] Importantly, the three stages are epigenetic; that is, the negotiation of each stage is dependent on the successful negotiation of the preceding stage. One must deal with endings first, in order to enter into the neutral zone where one reorients, in order to make a good new beginning.

Such an orderly progression makes perfect sense as we go through transitions. However, the real helpfulness of Bridge's work is that he demonstrates the natural preference and tendency to try to deal with transitions by *beginning at stage three*. Normally people would prefer to skip the first two stages.

Bridges points out that the endings involved in stage one are hard work that people would choose to avoid if they could. Consider a clergyperson going through a transition in appointment or call from one parish to another. In order to leave the first parish a lot of things must be put in order: reports must be developed for the denomination and the next pastor, meetings must occur with committees to make sure that work continues during the transition, shut-ins and people who have been under care must be visited and prepared to receive the new pastor, people who have been supportive must be visited with a word of thanks and a word about transferring support to the incoming pastor, people who have been difficult to work with must be visited in order to bring the relationship to a close so that lingering feelings don't travel with the pastor to the new assignment, books must be packed, movers must be arranged, etc. The work of stage one is substantial, hard, and can be painful. Yet unless it is done the clergyperson in transition will not be able to let go of what once was in order to pick up the new that, in good time, will need to be addressed. This work of the first stage is hard enough that people commonly wish to simply move ahead as if stage one does not need to be addressed. The problem with skipping stage one is that what is not let go follows the clergyperson into the new parish.

If stage one is hard, stage two—the neutral zone, the in-between time—is disorienting. The neutral zone begins as the clergyperson moves into the new parish, where everything and everyone has to be learned anew. People have to be met and all voices listened to in order to determine what messages and which people will be most helpful to and most distracting from ministry. New daily routines must be developed to accommodate and collaborate with the others in the parish and community who will be a part of the new work. New stories about the new parish have to be invited and uncovered in order to understand the character and the potential of the parish . . . again, on and on. Here again the work is significant and tiring, but it is also chaotic and disorienting. When everything is new there is little context to indicate what is urgent, what is important, and what can be dismissed. There is little rest in the neutral zone as the new pastor is in the full mode of learning new information, new relationships, and new patterns of work. Bridges points out that if people wish to skip stage one because it is hard and tiring work, people also wish to deny that they have to address stage two because it is disorienting. One can't easily rest when disoriented, and anxiety can easily overwhelm. It is much easier to simply pretend to be at stage three and dig in as if one knows what to do.

A favorite example comes from a transition in which I tracked the process followed by both the outgoing and the incoming pastor in one parish. The outgoing pastor did a good job of gathering information and planning a full day's orientation for the incoming pastor. The outgoing pastor hosted his successor to a day that included a tour of the community, a complete tour of the church, the passing on of a considerable amount of data and reports, the introduction to a few key select lay leaders, and a time of storytelling so that the incoming pastor would have a sense of the style and leadership of the pastor he would be following. At the end of the day the outgoing pastor offered, multiple times, to respond to any follow-up questions or conversations that the incoming pastor might have. After two weeks of silence the outgoing pastor received a single phone call from the incoming pastor with only one question: "Where is the best place to get a haircut in the neighborhood?"

There were no other questions asked because stages one and two were being denied and the incoming pastor was already mentally functioning at stage three. The incoming pastor was already—in his own mind, even before he had arrived—preaching from the new pulpit, setting goals and priorities for the new committees, and living in the new community with only a few details of convenience to be figured out. By starting at stage three, by avoiding the pain and hard work of stage one, and by denying the chaos and confusion of stage two, the incoming pastor set a volatile path of misunderstandings and miscalculations that undermined his ministry in the new parish for the first two years that he was there.

Leading without knowing is a critical form of leadership in which quietly courageous leaders do not assume that they know more than they do, do not jump out with rewardable answers, but do willingly accept the confusion and disorientation of the neutral zone in order to protect and provide for the learning needed for a new beginning. Ignorance is not bliss—it does not provide an escape from work or responsibility. Ignorance is necessary as an attribute of quietly courageous leadership that holds people in the learning context of stage two transitions.

Such leadership without knowing is enhanced when there is at least one solid place on which the leader and the people can stand. One of the images that I have used as a consultant for many years as I worked with conflicted congregations is the "one-footed rock." The question prompted by this image is: What would it be like if everyone in a congregation had to keep one foot steadily anchored on the rock-hard center of the purpose of the congregation but were free to dance with their other foot to follow the passions and discipleship of their own lives? The image of a one-footed rock was often a healthy and faithful image for people because it invited them to simultaneously pursue at least two necessary conversations:

- *What makes up our central rock?* What are the essential beliefs, convictions, or priorities that everyone, no matter whom, must steadily support and connect to in order to share identity and be one of "us"? One-footed rocks are best only when kept small. They do not hold long laundry lists of beliefs, behaviors, and priorities or they cease being central and become constraining. Room must be left for the other foot to dance or else we have lost our connection to the environment.

- *How far can we dance?* If a church (or a denomination) can clearly define the rock-hard center of purpose and identity on which all must anchor their one foot, then it can begin to measure the distance to the outer edge of their boundary—the dancing distance that would allow people to faithfully place the other foot in disparate places even if there are those in the community who disagree. The dancing foot becomes available for learning and for experimentation and does not depend on the agreement of everyone. Healthy community is not defined by agreement. Healthy community is defined by shared purpose and identity and a willingness to explore.

If there is one steady foot on a shared rock, the other dancing foot is where the learning takes place, where a permeable boundary is maintained with the surrounding culture. All living organisms (plants, animals, and organizations) must have permeable boundaries in order to exist. Nothing living is fully self-sufficient unto itself or can escape a vibrant, ongoing interchange with the very environment that sustains it. Plants need constant connection with their environment so that sun, soil, and water can provide nutrients across the plant's boundaries—and so that oxygen can be respired and seeds can be thrown back across the same boundary. Similar statements can be made about people and organizations. Local congregations have to be able to allow new people and ideas into their fellowship and to release them to leave, back and forth across a permeable barrier. As the environment shifts, living organizations change and adapt. In order to remain vital, plants learn to absorb water from the air when there is too little in the soil. In order to remain vital, congregations learn to invite and include new generations of people and to accommodate cultural and demographic shifts—always seeking to bring new people, energy, and ideas in, while knowingly releasing the old and outlived. A permeable boundary is more than a strategy for vitality; it is a prerequisite for life. Without a permeable boundary, all living things—plants, people, and organizations—quickly shrivel and die. Leading without knowing maintains a permeable boundary. Leaders stand securely on what they actually do know, particularly when it is related to their purpose and their identity. The willingness to lead without knowing, the willingness to lead while being wrong (in a state of ignorance), keeps the boundary between the institution and the culture permeable.

Permeable boundaries do not feel secure. Leadership that protects ignorance does not exude confidence. However, both are essential to life and are part of the substantive work of the new leadership.

The Spiritual Leadership of Accepting Mystery

I must now come back to the hubris of functional atheism. In a long-treasured insight into mystery, Frederick Buechner pointed to three different kinds of mysteries. The first kind of mystery is the one that can be thought out. These are the murder mysteries that we read and watch on TV in which clues are present and the insightful mind can track them to solution. The second kind of mystery is not to be solved; it is to be lived. This is the mystery of our lives, which we can't think out in advance and are not meant to be fully brought under control and to resolution, apart from being experienced. Our lives are mysteries to be lived. And then there is God, the third kind of mystery. Buechner wrote, "To say that God is a mystery is to say that you can never nail him down. Even on Christ the nails proved ultimately ineffective."[17]

The mystery that is currently afoot in the culture is connected to the mystery of God, one that we will not ultimately think our way through but can only experience as surprise as it happens. In a postaberrant, liquid culture in which power is being reshaped, the questions that people face have less to do with structure, security, and growth and more to do with meaning. This is a moment in which a significant part of the substantive leadership of quietly courageous people is to stay connected to a mystery that lies beyond the capacity of problem solving, control, and determination but can help people connect with that meaning. This is the appropriate cultural moment of the cartoon mathematician who does all of the hard work of the long, complex formula only to point to the empty box at the end and say, "And then something happens here." The hard up-front work of understanding and thought is necessary, but only to be connected to (not to control) the mystery of what will happen next.

For too long the leadership model in religious institutions has too closely mirrored the cultural model of an organizational leader that has focused on certainty and control. For example, the United Methodist denomination was identified as a "managerial episcopacy" by Edward Leroy Long in his 2001 study of the polities of a range of denominations and expressions of the Christian faith. Long looks at three denominations with episcopal heritage in which the biblical principle of oversight (*episkope*) is located in leadership persons and is a means of system organization. Long distinguishes United Methodism as a managerial episcopacy, as distinct from the Roman Catholic "monarchical episcopacy" and the Episcopal "pastoral episcopacy." Each of these episcopal systems defines different roles and responsibilities for leaders. When describing the United Methodist Church, Long states, "A managerial episcopacy is concerned primarily with making the church function effectively. It views the office of bishop in functional terms, as involving managerial skills, rather than giving it theological dimensions or sacerdotal significance."[18]

Long argues that the governance pattern of the United Methodist Church was heavily developed "in an era in which efficiency was becoming a desired goal in the culture as a whole, when the business world was developing complex logistical systems, and when decisions, more than heritage, were seen as influential in human affairs."[19] He argues that the defining role of denominational leadership is managerial, as symbolized by the location of episcopal offices in office centers rather than in congregations or cathedrals and by the episcopal attire, which is more commonly of the same order as secular organizational leaders than defined by symbols of the office.

Mystery has been downplayed in the past but is increasingly becoming a part of the substance of leadership in organizations and a culture in which people search for meaning. A number of years ago I was somewhat surprised by an Episcopal bishop who fulfilled his role as supervisor and overseer of clergy in his diocese by leading Bible studies with them. It took me some time to realize that he was very aware of attending to the skill levels and the competencies of his clergy so that he could care for the functional aspects of his oversight. However, he was reclaiming a sacerdotal role and was willing to keep the clergy in his system connected to the biblical text, keep them connected to the purpose of their congregations, but provide the space necessary for the mystery of God to be at work as well. He did not allow the functional aspects of his organizational role to reduce the space that God used to alter the story of his clergy and congregations.

As will be explored in the next chapter, seeking to control things in the wilderness is a flawed strategy that can bring institutions to ruin. The hubris of organizational leaders who fall to the trap of functional atheism, assuming that the future is to be shaped by their own hands rather than God's, will humble even the most skilled. A significant portion of the substantive work of quietly courageous leaders is to provide for the space and learning found in the mystery of the hand of God that will not only form the world differently in the future but will also surprise us in the process.

11

LESSONS IN STYLE

The previous chapter offered some early learning about the substance of quietly courageous leadership. In this early stage of a new form of leadership there is a similarity to the early expeditions in which navigators were first probing the shores of the new land of America, aware only of the most basic shape of the unfamiliar land mass and not at all sure of what lay beyond the coast. Much more was ahead to be discovered. Chapter 10 named some of the most promising and productive levers for leadership in a nonlinear liquid culture. Much more is to be discovered.

At the beginning of that chapter a distinction was made between the substance (*what* leaders pay attention to) and the style of leadership (*how* leaders think about their task). As noted, it is somewhat of an arbitrary distinction. However, substance points to what leaders can effectively put their hands to. In a discussion of style I turn more to a description of how quietly courageous leaders think about what differences in strategy and organization are necessary in their institutions in order to thrive and be effective in a reshaping mission field. Different from the work that leaders do, this discussion about style is more closely related to what new principles or modes of operation are proving to be most effective for the leaders, researchers, and consultants who are moving ahead.

The new leadership is about more than identifying best practices, because seeking even our best practices is tied to improving what we already know. Beyond best practices are *new practices*. Quietly courageous leaders remain tightly tethered to their mission and purpose but willingly range widely beyond what is familiar in order to explore what is appropriately effective. Among the new, less familiar principles or modes of operation are the following four:

- The critical role of conversation: For important reasons intentional conversation must accompany (perhaps be given primacy over) committee meetings, problem solving, decision making, or executive direction.
- Working slowly in a fast time: It is counterintuitive, but in a liquid culture in which constantly shifting change creates a sense of immediacy, quietly courageous leaders must learn to work slowly and methodically in short periods of time.
- Getting loose from a tight past: Most of the constraints on our institutions are the product of the controls installed in order to "run a tight ship" through rules, policies, and practices that were developed to organize and optimize the institutions we were so familiar with. This was, in its appropriate time, good and worthy work. In the postaberrant time the pendulum must swing away from tightly run organizations lest they break apart in the turbulence of the present time.
- Working from the edge, not the center: Wisdom and experience are no longer housed at the center of our institutions where control remains with the top leaders and administrators. Institutions now do their learning at their organizational edges where they engage their clients and their mission field. The shift from center to edge precipitates a significant and necessary organizational change in style. I will explore each of these "styles" of quietly courageous leadership in an effort to describe what can be seen so far.

THE CRITICAL ROLE OF CONVERSATION

Margaret Wheatley wrote, "We remember that conversation is the natural way humans think together. In conversation we are remembering perhaps as much as we are learning."[1] The important possibility of conversation is that it is able to bring together that which we already know (what we remember) with what we are able to teach each other because we do not know. This is another expression of the vertical learning that was explored in chapter 6 concerning the formation of leadership in which leaders in learning groups dig down into their own experience and context in order to see something new together. Wisdom no longer comes from the expert entering the room with answer in hand, and in fact we are at a moment when as soon as the expert appears, learning ceases.

In order to understand what is meant by conversation it will be helpful to parse a few necessary distinctions between other forms of talk, such as meetings, discussion, or debate. Meetings are perhaps the more formal of the organizational ways in which people speak to one another. As such they are fraught with learned behavior in which the authority leading the meeting follows an agenda that is designed to address specific issues that will lead to action. The organizational learned behavior of the protocols of meetings undergirds the propensity of meetings to lead to Red Queen activities—exhausting in their increased effort to work harder at what is already familiar but not helpful. While there is much talking at meetings, it is talking that is positional and oriented to action with little space for new learning. Little time and space is given to intentional conversation in a meeting.

Distinct from meetings, discussion or debate may be free from formal protocols and may be more freely flowing but may also begin with positions or conclusions. Discussion or debate is often an effort in persuading others to move to the conclusions of the speaker. Often such discussion and debate do not seek new insights but seek to strengthen already established conclusions or convictions. Little is learned because there is little intentional listening practiced. It has been said that in discussion and debate, people listen only long enough to decide what to say next.

In contrast intentional conversation with a purpose of learning begins with listening and connecting, which is very different work from the task of persuading. Conversation will also be described shortly as "dialogue" because of the work that has been done to understand the impact of conversation/dialogue on change. Note, however, that conversation/dialogue is a different order of work for leaders that requires giving time and space to connecting the dots between what we already know (Wheatley's "what we remember") and what we are yet to learn.

Connecting the dots that provide new insights is the real power of conversation for quietly courageous leaders.

Let's begin with the discipline of knowledge management. As the global culture moved from agrarian based to industry based to information based over the past one hundred years, more and more attention was given to understanding what information is and how it is developed. In one of the earlier studies of "working knowledge," Thomas Davenport and Laurence Prusak made the following progressive distinctions between the different orders of information, beginning with *data*, moving to *information*, and then to *knowledge*.[2]

They define *data* as a set of discrete, objective facts about events—as structured records of transactions. Data are the baseline of what we know or the details of our experience. Distinct from data and more helpful, *information* is a message (commonly in the form of a document or verbal communication). Information is data formed in a way to have an impact on the receiver. Davenport and Prusak describe information as *data that make a difference*. Information is produced from data, but work must be applied to the data in order to make the transition—work that they identify in a series of methods, all beginning with C:

- Contextualized: we know for what purpose the data were gathered.
- Categorized: we know the units of analysis or key components of the data.
- Calculated: the data may have been analyzed mathematically or statistically.
- Corrected: errors have been removed from the data.
- Condensed: the data may have been summarized in a more concise form.

While the work as defined in this list of Cs may be more descriptive of the disciplines of the information/knowledge industries for which Davenport and Prusak were writing, the Cs are still operative in less formal and often intuitive ways in all efforts to move from discrete data to information.

Making a further distinction from information, Davenport and Prusak then go on to describe *knowledge* as a fluid mix of experience, values, context, and insight. Knowledge allows leaders to evaluate and incorporate the new things that they must face. Again, however, to move from information to knowledge, work must be applied, this time involving a second set of Cs:

- Comparisons: how does the information about this situation compare to other situations we have known?
- Consequences: what implications does the information have for decisions and actions?
- Connections: how does this bit of knowledge relate to others?
- Conversation: what do other people think about this information?

Note that movement from information to knowledge involves engaging a set of questions—it is a path of inquiry. By seeking to address the C questions, new thoughts, new insights, and new knowledge are produced. The significant point is that it takes actual and intentional work to move from data through information to knowledge. People have to put themselves to this work as a discipline in order to have new insights, shape new information, and develop a sense of knowledge that allows movement ahead into uncharted waters. This is the work of the inquiry necessary for quietly courageous leadership. It is the shift of the leader's attention from problem solving to exploration, a central argument of this book.

Davidson and Prusak were specifically writing to information-based organizations concerned about and intent on producing new knowledge that would be their "value-added" product offered to clients. Interestingly, along the way in their discussion they make the argument that at the heart of developing new knowledge is the bringing together of people.[3] Their argument might be paraphrased by saying that the way to develop new information and knowledge is to hire the smartest people you can find (smartest in both understanding and experience) and make them talk to one another. The work of discovery is not a solitary pursuit. It requires conversation. Conversation is the messiness of "let me tell you what I see so that you can tell me what you see."

The late David Bohm, one of the greatest physicists and foremost thinkers of this century, was a fellow of the Loyal Society and emeritus professor of physics at Birbeck College at the University of London. Late in his career he turned his attention to dialogue because of his need to understand from where new knowledge comes. He saw dialogue as a process in which people would work together to "make something in common."[4] Again, note the messiness of the process. Bohm described the process of dialogue as something like this: I say something. Then, in your response to what I said, I now know that you did not understand what I was trying to say, so I clarify. In my clarification, you now understand that I didn't understand what you were trying to say, so you clarify. . . . The critical aspect of this dialogue is that it is based on careful listening to the response of the other, not on advancing what the speaker is saying on his or her own part. The point of dialogue (or conversation) is that if people stay in this exchange of speaking and critical listening long enough, they will teach each other what neither of them would be able to see for themselves. They will make something in common.

Bohm is clear that "thought," the product of the individual, is a limited medium because people think in fragments.[5] Dialogue is necessary to connect the fragments. It is the work of connecting the dots—the work of the Cs identified earlier by Davenport and Prusak. William Isaacs, a follower of Bohm's work, notes that such thinking together has not become the natural contemporary way for people.[6] People more naturally bring their own fragmentary truths to the table as answers for others to accept. Answers, however, are "old" knowledge at a time when new insight is needed because of the changed conditions of the culture. The new knowledge is only accessible by *listening for what is behind* what is already known or concluded.

In this sense, the learning that allows movement ahead is much like the classic distinction in conflict management between working with positions and interests. *Positions* are conclusions that people put forward in any contest as a truth that they want others to accept. The *interests* are the additional pieces of information that lie behind, are the reasons (the logic) for a person to take a position, and are the only workable part of the conflicted engagement. Positions are clearly stated and understood by the speaker. Interests can only be discovered by inquiry and listening. However, it is only by uncovering the interests that people can negotiate ways to move ahead.

Positions are not negotiated, but interests can be—a critical distinction made in the report on the Harvard Negotiation Project by authors Roger Fisher and William Ury.[7] Consider the simple story of a librarian quietly watching two men working at the same table in a library. As the librarian watches, one man gets up and opens the large window at the end of the table. After a few minutes the other man gets up, moves to the window, and closes it. The two men have established their *positions*. One man's position is that the window should be open, the other man's position is that the window should be closed.

After a few minutes the first man moves back to the window and opens it again, but only half as wide as the first time. Shortly, the second man gets up again and closes the window—all the way. (When I tell this story to groups I commonly ask people to predict what the second man will do with a half-opened window. The most common answer is that he will close the window a quarter of the way, anticipating compromise as a solution to the situation. But a quarter-open window is still an open window. The second man's position is closed, not open. Positions—conclusions—are not negotiable, which is why discussion and debate commonly do not lead to new learning. A partially open window is still open, and that is not acceptable to the second man who wants the window closed.)

At this point in the story, intrigued, the librarian moves to the two men at the table and begins to explore their *interests* underlying their positional contest about the window. When she asks the first man why he wants the window open, he explains that he is working on a project with a looming deadline and that he feels sleepy from the warm, stuffy library air. He wants fresh air. By listening, the librarian now has a better idea of the interests this man is trying to satisfy. Turning to the second man, she asks why he closes the window. He reports that he is also working on a project and each time the window is open his papers blow about and he is distracted. Behind both positions lie interests that justify the contested positions.

Positions are not negotiable, but interests are because they have more information allowing the work of the connecting Cs. After careful listening for the interests, the librarian can now connect ideas and suggest multiple ways forward for the two men. She can suggest that one man move to another table. She can offer to turn on the air conditioning. She can open the window from the top rather than from the bottom. She can tell the drowsy man where to get coffee. In fact, the alternatives for moving ahead multiply when anchored by the interests of the two men rather than by their positions. In such conversations, note the critical importance of staying engaged with questions and the necessity of listening.

After more than several decades of working as a consultant with congregations in conflict, I have encountered many positions and I am fully aware of how difficult and laborious it is to uncover the interests beneath those positions. In fact, the interests are often hidden from the very people who hold a position because it is their positions and their preferred outcomes that capture most of their attention. Conversation is work on everyone's part. It is the work of inquiry, the critical activity of exploration necessary in changed conditions.

We are learning more about conversation.

In order to move beyond committee meetings, discussion, and debate in organizations, leaders must overcome learned behavior—the well-established norms about how people will talk with each other and about what. One of the first issues is space. Familiar space triggers familiar behavior. Whatever the announced purpose of a gathering, if you put people in a room with a table and chairs commonly used for a committee meeting, they will have a committee meeting. Learned behavior provides well-established norms for how people in such a setting will engage one another, how they will defer to the leader, and how they will advance their conclusions.

"Leadership is both active and reflective. One has to alternate between participating and observing," notes Ron Heifetz.[8] The metaphor that Heifetz uses for these two different functions is the dance floor and the balcony. The dance floor is where the action happens. It is the active place where any group must engage in order to move their work ahead. However, the dance floor (including the committee room) is the least thoughtful space for leaders and workers because it is driven by immediacy that prompts a dependence on what people already know. It is reactive space. In contrast, balcony space is where the leader takes people to withdraw from the dance floor of activity in order to become reflective—a place where the dots and the Cs can be connected reflectively through conversation.

If leadership is both active and reflective, leadership must also have both active and reflective space and do the appropriate work in each space. Adult (less institutional) space, with adult seating (not committee tables and chairs), large enough to accommodate expanded thinking but not too large to make the group (and its thinking) feel small, with windows and refreshments to help people feel comfortable and at home, all helps to set balcony space apart from the normative institutional work space that will pull most people back into their learned active/reactive committee mode. Balcony space is supported by the important use of circles, where people sit in a configuration of equality without an authority figure at the "head of the conversation" inviting deferral of the conversation to the opinions or the agenda of the leader. Balcony space requires balcony time—the more relaxed, less pressured time that is not driven by an agenda that must produce action. I will return to the issue of time in the next section.

If conversation that can produce learning needs its own intentional space, it also needs thoughtful, open-ended, non-problem-solving questions as a prompt. The questions that leaders ask are critically important because the way that people respond is so often shaped by the question that is asked. I have long loved the story of a young priest in training who went to his supervising priest with a question: "Father, may I smoke while I pray?" to which the answer was a definitive "No! Prayer should be given your full attention." A bit later in the day the young priest's friend, also in training, went to the same supervisor asking, "Father, may I pray while I smoke?" This time the answer was "Yes, pray at every opportunity!"

A bit of humor, yes. However, the question a leader asks does shape the answer received. Problem-oriented questions prompt responses seeking action. Open-ended questions that don't demand action prompt responses that are more thoughtful and investigative. It is critical for leaders to know whether the issue before their people is technical work for which there are clear and known solutions. If so, problem-oriented questions seeking conclusions are appropriate and lead directly to next steps. However, if the issue before the people is a condition such as adapting to the postaberrant time, so central to the argument of this book, then problem-oriented questions will lead people astray and into exhaustion when what is needed instead is inquiry and insight. Leaders need to know if the purpose of the talk people are invited to be part of is the solution of next steps and action or whether the purpose is exploration and inquiry. It matters what leaders ask of people, because the questions used will determine the work to which people will give their attention.

For example, it is common for groups in the midst of discussion to suddenly go silent. Perhaps the group has reached a point of disagreement, discomfort, or simple uncertainty. Whatever the reason, everyone who has led groups recognizes that moment when people who feel fully free to have a spirited conversation with the one or two people seated next to them suddenly go silent when prompted to share their ideas with the full group. What felt like a room full of conversational energy suddenly is quiet and without any energy at all.

It matters what question the leader asks at such a moment because the next steps will be directed by the question. If the leader asks a problem-solving question that has an appearance of expecting a response to "solve" the puzzle of the quick silence—that is, "Why did our group go silent?" it is most likely that the silence will continue. There might not be a clear reason why the group went silent. If there is a reason for the public silence, and if it is based on a discomfort or a disagreement the group is having within itself, no one will want to bring the answer forward, so silence is the more judicious response. Whatever the reason or reasons, problem-solving questions call for a clarity that might not exist, for airing a discomfort that the group might not want to admit, or for action that is uncertain—all reasons that shut down the learning that might come from conversation because the question seeks a conclusion or a conviction that people in the group may not want to admit or be accountable for.

Consider what might happen if the leader asks the group not to "solve" their silence but to explore it. One of the questions that I have come to trust with groups has to do with their hypotheses. When a group goes suddenly silent I commonly point out the change in the behavior of the group and then ask for ideas, not answers. I might say, "Our group was loud and animated in our smaller table conversations, but when I asked for people to share their thinking in the full group, we all went silent. What are your hypotheses about our group right now that would explain that change?" Such a question is open ended and does not assume that there is a right answer. People are simply asked for their own ideas without needing to be correct and without feeling evaluation. I am always surprised by the number of ideas a group will produce at such a moment and further surprised by how gathering the group's hypotheses prompts a new round of energy for the conversation to continue.

In the metrics work done at the Texas Methodist Foundation it became increasingly clear that whatever counting and measuring there was to be done about the changes sought by an institution, the metrics needed to be in service to the questions asked. Through that metrics work I developed a series of "cascading" questions—a series of open-ended questions of inquiry meant to invite people into balcony conversations of listening and learning about their own work. The nine questions are as follows:

Descriptive Work:
1. Who are we, now? *(The identity question)*
2. Who is our neighbor, now? *(The context question)*
Discernment Work:
3. What does God call us to do, now? *(The purpose question)*
The Work of Boldness and Courage:
4. In order to address God's call, what difference do we believe God has called us to make in the next three to five years? *(The outcome question)*
5. What would it look like in three to five years if we are faithful and fruitful with our call? *(The possibility question)*
Implementation Work:
6. How will we do it? *(The strategy question)*
7. How will we measure our progress toward fulfilling our call? *(The metrics question)*
Learning Work:
8. What have we learned from our experience? *(The learning/evaluation question)*
9. What reshaping or changing do we need to work on because of what we have learned? *(The ready-aim-fire question)*

"Cascading" implies only that the questions are arranged in a sequence. Working with such a list of questions is not a linear process of starting with number 1 and working through to number 9. Such controlled conversation would be an exercise in problem solving—of completing an assigned task. The work of quietly courageous leaders would be to use such a list of cascading questions to determine which is the critical conversation of inquiry the people most need to address at a given moment in order to move ahead. What part of their story do they need to revisit to remind themselves to be bold and faithful? What part of their story do they need to question, examine, challenge, or rewrite in order to gain more clarity about their purpose? What part of their work do they need to invent and build experiments to learn how to move ahead? What part of the work do they need to examine in order to learn more?

Conversation is how people can learn what no one can teach them. It is creating something new together. The work of quietly courageous leaders is to learn how to shape and ask open-ended questions of learning and then hold the people in balcony space long enough to avert the temptation of action and activity so that something new can appear.

A final learning about conversation concerns the importance of facilitation. The art of facilitating a conversation is the process of making a group's work transparent to itself. Facilitators ask, re-ask, and reshape a question for a group so the conversation can continue and learning can occur. More importantly, a good facilitator will track the significant insights in the conversation and then report and rehearse what the group has uncovered for itself so that the group can claim its hard work of learning. Consider again that conversation is a messy process of speaking and critical listening. In such a messy process multiple paths might be explored, diversions encountered, and unhelpful trails followed. Yet in the "telling what I see so that you can tell what you see," there will be insights and discoveries that resonate with the group. A good facilitator captures the resonating insights to be saved and shared, as conversation is reframed in order to move ahead. Wandering is the important nature of conversation because it is in the wandering that discoveries are made. Yet because of the wandering it is common for groups to find it difficult to make their own discoveries transparent to themselves. A good facilitator is one who fully understands the purpose of conversation, understands the process of groups, and willingly uses his or her leadership to serve the work of the group rather than the need for an answer. Because the learned behavior of institutional talk invites people to defer to authority, it is often helpful that it is not the organization's authority (pastor, bishop, executive, team leader) who is doing the work of facilitation.

"I believe we can change the world if we start listening to one another again," writes Margaret Wheatley. "Not mediation, negotiation, problem solving, debate or public meetings. Simple, truthful conversation where we each have a chance to speak, we each feel heard, and we each listen well."[9] A critical style of quietly courageous leadership is in fact as simple as honest talk and careful listening. Yet to do this simple but critical new work of learning, leaders must recalculate their mindset—challenge old assumptions, avoid diverting temptations, resist easy (but unhelpful) solutions, and be satisfied with just the next step.

WORKING SLOW IN A FAST TIME

Festina lente is a Latin expression meaning "make haste slowly." Balcony space where transparent speaking and critical listening can produce new learning has its own pace, and it is slower rather than faster. Learning has a pace and rhythm that must be respected or learning will be lost. Curiously, the pace and rhythm needed for new inquiry and discovery are counterintuitive.

Zygmunt Bauman's metaphor of a liquid culture suggests speed. If the notion of this highly technological and rapidly changing cultural moment is such that conditions will continuously morph even before one has the opportunity to structure a response to the first changes encountered, it would seem logical that leaders must up their game— speed up their responses. However, simply speeding up our known responses to the new changes encountered is very much like the Red Queen's running faster and faster just to remain in the same place. It is activity that will exhaust, or worse, lead us astray because it is directed by old assumptions and practices. It may seem counterintuitive, but in a liquid time leaders must become intentional rather than quick.

The difference is captured well in the story a colleague tells about his son who was training to be a brain surgeon. In the moment when his son was about to begin his first solo brain surgery, the son's mentor was standing beside him to observe and support. Just before the surgery began, the mentor stopped the young surgeon and said, "Don't forget, from the time you remove the skull and begin your first procedure you only have three minutes before the patient will experience distress. So work slowly." Working slowly, judiciously, and intentionally may seem like the wrong recipe for the stress of an environment changing so rapidly that it challenges people to keep up. But like a brain surgeon in a hurry, leaders flailing about trying whatever might come to mind will surely make the situation worse, not better.

Henry Joyner is a retired vice president for planning with American Airlines and well versed in both the strategies for planning and how those strategies have adapted as the cultural context for organizations has changed. In working with a client, he divided the planning work into three categories: do, discern, and walking around. The "do" work was easily understood. This was the technical work of Ron Heifetz, described several times earlier in this book—the application of known solutions to known problems. From a planning perspective, such "do" work needs only to be identified and assigned to competent staff, while the executives and board move on to deeper questions. The "discern" work takes a bit more homework, some discovery. It is still familiar territory, but more information needs to be gathered and additional variables considered before a response can be certain. Executives and the board need to track this work to be sure that its purpose is being followed so that unintended consequences are not encountered.

And then there is "walking around" work, the work of conversation. Liquid culture is, by definition, uncertain and shifting. Impulsive and quick responses are as easily wrong as they might be helpful, and simply stirring up important things like institutional purpose (or brain matter by an impulsive surgeon) can be very costly and damaging. Deeper learning work of moving from data to information to knowledge by connecting the dots requires time and space.

Understanding the various forms of intuition helps to explain the need for time and space when instant responses seem most necessary. William Duggan, in his book *Strategic Intuition*, points to three types of intuition.[10] The first is "ordinary intuition," which is a feeling, a gut reaction in which a person "just knows." Something in the stomach, or elsewhere, seems to simply tell a person, often with considerable accuracy. And with ordinary intuition the action is quick. There is little time and space used in ordinary intuition and, importantly, such intuition needs to be understood as a feeling response. Feelings do not require the time and space of thinking.

The second is "expert intuition." It is intuition informed by experience. A person has faced a situation enough times to "just know." Additional thought is not needed, and the person moves to action as if by impulse. It is always fast and only operates in familiar situations. This expert intuition is similar to the stage of proficiency described in chapter 6 in the discussion of how a person learns their profession. The situation the person faces is sufficiently familiar that he or she seems to act "without thinking." Nonetheless, expert intuition is anything but feeling; it is the earned response from previous thought and learning that can simply be put to action without further reflection. Like ordinary intuition, expert intuition is also quick.

The third, which Duggan calls "strategic intuition," is more thinking than feeling. This form of intuition may be familiar to the church under the name of *discernment*. The end result feels quick—an inspiration, an insight, a flash "knowing" that moves us to something new. But Duggan shows how such insight is a flash of recognition that comes only as a result of a slow, deliberate listening and connecting—the kind of thing that happens in prolonged, thoughtful conversation. This strategic intuition is the product of connecting the Cs described by Davenport and Prusak. As "intuition" suggests, we may not be aware of the connecting that is being done, but strategic intuition requires a period of daydreaming, a series of nighttime dreams, or a period of prayer in which new connections are quietly being made—only to be experienced as a sudden flash of insight or a clarity of purpose. For groups, this strategic intuition comes through intentional balcony conversations. People speak to one another, listen, and in the process challenge, correct, confirm, influence, and inform one another until a flash of insight, something that they didn't know before, moves them to something new. It comes from people knowing themselves deeply but not rigidly. It comes from opening themselves up to and understanding others in vulnerable ways. It comes from allowing God to weave new commitments from older thoughts, ideas, and passions into something previously unknown that demands courage.

When we were working on our Holy Conversations project at the Alban Institute, my colleague Alice Mann talked of discernment as the intersection of God's will, our passion, and the community's need.[11] It was conversation with God through the disciplines of prayer and scripture. It was conversation with ourselves through pondering, mulling (perhaps stewing), and living with our own questions of purpose and passion. It was talking with the community by paying attention, standing with, and getting involved. To stay in such a rich conversation over time is to see new things, connect old thoughts and experiences, and be led into new commitments. We are moved to discern something new that drives us into acts of faithfulness that are new.

In the many conversations I have facilitated with leaders, I've para-phrased Margaret Wheatley often, saying "conversation is the currency of change." Not every conversation produces insight. Some perhaps not even light. But continued, thoughtful conversation among leaders, like ongoing prayer, leads us to understand what no one can explain. And both we and our actions are changed. Yet it happens slowly and inten-tionally. The pace of discernment and learning does not match the more frenetic anxiety of people faced with a new situation. Quietly courageous leaders simply hold the people in conversation with their question, content that next steps will be found.

GETTING LOOSE FROM A TIGHT PAST

Continuing to explore the new principles or modes of operation that are developing as the promising styles of quietly courageous leaders, next to be described is the shift to help institutions get loose from their tight organizational pasts. Conversations that lead to new learning have al-ready been described as messy, wandering, and intentional but not controllable. That messiness matches the very nature of change in a liquid culture. Wheatley describes that nature of change as having the logic of play. She writes, "Life's process of creating is quite different from what we had thought. There are enough underlying principles to this process that we could call it a logic, a logical play."[12] Consider just four of the key elements she identifies and note how fluid and unstruc-tured they are:

- Everything is in a constant process of discovery and creating. Everything is changing all the time: individuals, systems, environ-ments, the rules, the processes of evolution. Even change changes. Every organism reinterprets the rules, creates exceptions for itself, creates new rules.
- Life uses messes to get to well-ordered solutions. Life doesn't seem to share our desires for efficiency or neatness. It uses redun-dancy, fuzziness, dense webs of relationships, and unending trials and errors to find what works.
- Life is intent on finding what works, not what's "right." It is the ability to keep finding solutions that is important; any one solution

is temporary. There are no permanently right answers. The capacity to keep changing, to find what works now, is what keeps any organism alive.

- Life creates more possibilities as it engages with opportunities. There are no "windows of opportunity," narrow openings in the fabric of space-time that soon disappear forever. Possibilities beget more possibilities; they are infinite.

Such a logic of play in the world is not the product of planning and control but of engagement and discovery. Engagement and discovery require flexibility, responsiveness, and agility to adapt to constantly changing circumstances. Engagement and discovery also require the willingness of leaders to release control to allow for the buffeting and bruising that come with riding the waves of a liquid culture but that are also the source of learning, change, and vitality.

Nassim Taleb, professor of risk engineering at New York University's Polytechnic Institute, makes his case for the necessity of organizations to be "antifragile"—of being able to benefit from shocks, and of thriving and growing when exposed to volatility, randomness, disorder, and stress.[13] Because we are in a time of cultural unpredictability, rigidly structured and tightly controlled institutions do not thrive on such volatility but are stressed by the opacity of constant change. Because of their tight structures and the efforts of leaders to control them, the familiar, well-established institutions of the aberrant time become fragile. It is looser, less connected systems that thrive.

Consider the comparison between banks and airplanes that Taleb uses in his work on antifragile systems.[14] The U.S. banking system is a very large, fully connected, highly regulated, structured, and controlled system of interdependent parts. Every bank is tied into and interconnected with every other bank through rules, regulations, standard practices, and procedures. As such, the institution of banking deeply reflects the culture and the organizational structures of the earlier aberrant time in the first half of the twentieth century. In comparison, the airline industry is also a very large and highly regulated industry, but its activities are decentralized and unconnected—every airline flight is not connected to all of the other flights, and each flight is a discreet event. In the case of banks, when one bank crashes it makes the crash of other banks more likely. Because the system is highly centralized, all activities are linked, and the actions of one part of the system are interdependent with the actions of all other parts of the system; it is a tight structure susceptible to threat, it is rigid, and it is unable to adapt. Conversely, the airline industry is antifragile. Each flight is a separate activity within the regulated system and is not dependent on other flights. If one plane crashes it does not threaten other planes. In fact, if one plane crashes it makes the next one less likely to crash because each crash immediately prompts a very deep investigation and learning cycle that actually makes the rest of the system more responsive, more agile, and more proficient.

Although not laudable, consider the resilience and adaptability of systems such as drug traffickers and terrorist groups, examples of some of the most flexible and decentralized systems in operation. Michael Kenney provides a remarkable contrast between the fluidity of these illegal systems and the rigidity of the government systems that seek to defeat them. These illegal systems thrive in chaos:

> In contrast to centralized hierarchies that feature tight coupling be-tween units and formal decision-making hierarchies, . . . criminal entrepreneurs use networks to segment workers into loosely orga-nized, functionally specific compartments, minimizing potentially destabilizing contact between participants. Entrepreneurs also ex-ploit network forms of organization to decentralize their decision-making authority and rely on brokers and intermediaries to buffer themselves from direct complicity in criminal activity.[15]

In these criminal organizations each decision impacts only those direct-ly involved. Each failure is a learning experience that prompts a more resilient response. When drug traffickers lost a shipment of cocaine at sea as a boat was intercepted by law enforcement, some noticed that units of cocaine that spilled overboard floated. That discrete failure of one smuggling attempt directly led to experiments of airdropping ship-ments into the ocean where they would float and be picked up later in less trackable boats.[16] The lack of rigidly established and enforced prac-tices allowed the criminals to remain one step ahead of the chaos that they confronted.

Uniformity, standards and standardization, regulation, and control all seem to have the feeling of security and vitality. Nonetheless, resil-ience, robustness, and the capacity to adapt to a fast-changing environment belong to loose systems that actually thrive under stress, because when exposed to volatility they learn with the freedom to adapt. Institutional response to change does not need to be controlled, regulated, and systematized as if there is one right way to move ahead. Healthy institutional response in a liquid culture does, however, need to be tolerant of messiness and diversity, which stand in contrast to the assumptions named in earlier chapters.

Institutional tightness is the product of previous decisions, policies, and practices, each of which made sense at the time they were established but over time came to create an impenetrable "hairball" of organizational constraints. Gordon MacKenzie tells the story of the beginning of the Hallmark Card Company in 1910, when Joyce Clyde Hall left Norfolk, Nebraska, for Kansas City, Missouri, to establish a mail-order postcard business, an industry that did not exist at that time. Without guides to follow, Hall began with very basic, intuitive, and instinctive decisions. As MacKenzie tells it,

> He may very well have said to himself something like: *"My gut tells me it would be more effective if I did this this way. And it would make sense to do that that way."*
> *This and that,* Hall's first two business decisions, were also the first two hairs of the hairball that was to become Hallmark. For decades, J. C. Hall and the thousands of Hallmarkers who have followed him have—quite appropriately—been making business decision after business decision, creating procedures and generating policies. And in so doing, they have been adding countless hairs to the Hairball.[17]

Consider the hairball of constraining decisions, rules, policies, and practices that have developed over the years in institutional religion. The dependence on democratic practices of representative groups that meet with ongoing regular schedules to pass legislation, make rules, and set standards has developed extensive books of polity that constrain and commonly defeat any adaptation to the mission field that is not approved and standardized—the opposite of what is needed to be agile and antifragile in a missional liquid culture. All of that work, appropriate to an earlier time, provides clarity and organizational alignment, provides channels of clear communication and decision making, provides standards and accountability, but constrains the movement of

God's Spirit in a changed day and a different time. It is also what our institutional leaders know how to do. However, more of what ails us will certainly not cure us, and in a time that requires agility and resilience our institutions have become rigid and fragile.

Quietly courageous leaders are moving in the opposite direction, seeking to make their systems looser rather than tighter. Obviously this flies in the face of the assumptions of change, resources, democracy, structure, egalitarianism, and codified standards of leadership that were named earlier in the book. Becoming looser means fitting with the culture and learning to "speak to" the culture—it is not capitulating to the culture. Almost seventy years ago H. Richard Niebuhr wrote his classic book *Christ and Culture*, in which he explored the nature of Christ *against* culture, Christ *of* culture, Christ *above* culture, or Christ the *transformer* of culture.[18] The relationship between Christ and the surrounding culture was not then, and is not now, a problem to be solved and an answer to be given for all time. It is a constant conversation that must go on between the church and the mission field and must be resolved again and again because of the fluidity of the culture and the mission of the church.

To continue to be tightly structured and bound together as institutional religion has been in the past means that the people of the church must agree on and share the same definitions and expressions of the faith and share, and be limited to, the same practices. Yet increasingly, people today are formed in faith in a wider and wider array of pathways, even to the point of the growing number of persons going to seminary without ever having been actively related to a congregation or having experienced a formal expression of faith. Yet the mission field is also exceedingly diverse, having gone through the cultural transition from a convergent to a divergent time. In the face of such changes tightly bound, standardized institutions of religion cannot speak to the culture or the people of the culture if participation in the faith depends on sharing the same definitions and the same practices universally.

To be loosely bound means to be unified not by *definition and practice* but by *identity and purpose*. In the case of my own denomination, the mission of the United Methodist Church is to make disciples of Jesus Christ for the transformation of the world. In a loose church living in a liquid culture that is agile and seeks to be responsive and antifragile, being part of the United Methodist Church is to share its purpose of making disciples, to share its outcomes of intentional change, and to function with a clear sense of God's grace, which is a central mark of Methodism. But the ways in which the mission is accomplished (the strategies, structures, practices, audiences) must be free to vary appropriately with the divergences of the mission field. Other denominations would have their own expressions of an appropriately "loose unity."

"Ideology is the glue that holds decentralized organizations together," wrote Ori Brafman and Rod Beckstrom in their study of decentralized ("leaderless") organizations.[19] People in loose organizations do not need to be regulated; they need to be informed—to be part of the conversation. As part of his steep learning curve in the Iraq War, General Stanley McChrystal learned to restructure his force on transparent information sharing ("shared consciousness") and decentralized decision making ("empowered execution").[20] Older, tight forms of the organizational chain of command in which people only knew and did their part were insufficient. Conversely, people did not need to know everything about everything (which is not possible). But people did need to know about the full story; they needed to know the purpose and the intended outcomes, and they needed to know that they were free to contribute in the best way they could. In loose organizations decision making needs to migrate from the people at the top/center of the organization to the outer edges, where the work actually engages the field. The dictionary defines "subsidiarity" as the principle that the central authority in a system should perform only those tasks and make only those decisions that cannot be made at the more local level. It is a further form of decentralization, of moving authority out of the center. Moving decision making to the local level is an act of agility, of connection to the mission field. Practicing subsidiarity and moving decision making and action to the edge of the institution will be the subject of the next section.

For the moment it is important to recognize the quiet courage it takes for a leader to cede control at the very time that the changes confronting institutions increase the anxiety and stress that people feel. The natural response of many people in a time of stress is to reward leaders for taking more control. Instead of increasing control and regulation, the appropriate response to a fast-changing mission field is to share information, extend conversations to include more people, give permission to modified practices, downsize structures, and invite people to build learning into their actions. Yes, of course, a looser form of leadership will produce a messiness (for which leaders will not be rewarded) and will lead to other issues down the road.

Getting loose from a tight past will both address some critical issues and create others. In the earlier chapter about structure and process I referred to the Chinese principle of yin and yang—how strength overused leads to weakness. When an institution is clearly structured with a centralized authority system, it functions smoothly with all of its people and parts in alignment and everyone knowing their role. Being overstructured for too long, however, leads to rigidity, disconnected silos, and impermeable boundaries that no longer allow the institution to appropriately engage the mission field that is changing all about it. The strength of structure, regulation, and control becomes the institution's weakness. To address the weakness stemming from overtightness, quietly courageous leaders need to steer their institutions toward the looseness that is described here so that learning can occur and agility can be developed to function in a liquid culture. Note, however, that moving in the direction of looseness will create its own eventual issues. Giving permission for variations in practice, opening up the framework of theology to permit people to experience and explore their formation in the Spirit with new languages and new ideas, and planning experiments of community that don't look like congregations will all unleash a creativity deeply needed at this time. However, looseness practiced too deeply and for too long will itself eventually become a strength turned to weakness as leaders will later need to face the loss of theological boundaries and the chaos of less disciplined practices that will result. Looseness is not the "solution" to debilitating tightness; it is merely a necessary choice at this moment, which eventually will produce a situation that will need tightening. Quietly courageous leaders simply recognize that chaos and messiness are not our current challenges. The current debilitating challenge is the tightness of established rules and practices that now threaten our institutions. And so quietly courageous leaders proceed to address the rigidity that now separates religious institutions from their own intended mission.

WORKING FROM THE EDGE, NOT THE CENTER

We now address one of the most critical but, to date, least understood of the new principles or modes of operation that marked the style of quietly courageous leaders: the shift of attention from the center of the institution to the edge. The image here is of the institution as a circle with an interior (that which is inside the circle) and an exterior (that which is outside the circle). One of the helpful ways that the difference between center and edge is currently being explored is in the need for institutional religion to shift from being exclusively attractional (internally focused) to starting to be missional (externally focused). In his revised and updated book of the five practices of fruitful congregations Robert Schnase differentiates between those practices of congregations that are attractional (aimed at getting those outside the church to come inside the church) and those practices that are missional (aimed at getting the church to go to the places, communities, and networks that people already inhabit).[21] Importantly, he offers ideas for congregations to learn how to do both/and—a necessary strategy for religious institutions that live within the punctuated equilibrium discussed in chapter 9, in which current institutions now "cohabitate" in an environment along with newly forming initiatives in the meaning making that was once the sole province of the church.

We are now at a moment in which it is important for leaders to know when it is appropriate to focus their attention internally toward the center of their institutional circle and when attention must focus beyond the edge to the mission field outside of their circle. Facing the interior of an institution requires a different mindset and a radically different strategy than facing outward. One stance requires the use of carefully guarded power and a stance of protectionism. The other requires shared power and a stance of collaboration.

In order to thrive, the edge (the "circle" that differentiates what is inside from what is outside of the institution) must be porous. Porous boundaries that provide connection to the surrounding environment were described earlier as a prerequisite for life. Without porous boundaries the nutrients that sustain life are cut off. For religious institutions a porous boundary is more than a threshold allowing new members entry so that they may become the next cohort of people to continue institutional practices as they have familiarly been done in the past. A sufficiently porous boundary also allows the changing culture in, allows reshaped generational preferences in, allows the fresh questions of meaning in, allows reformatted lifestyles in, allows the changing issues of the day in, etc. Christianity over the past half century has found much more fertile soil for growth in the southern hemisphere and in developing countries where the gospel directly engages the actual concerns and questions that people are living. The circle that defines the institutions of religion in such settings is much more porous where the sacred is not kept wholly within the institution and the secular without.

A first step for quietly courageous leaders is to recognize that the primary task of their leadership is not about *protecting* and *preserving* the institution of the church but about *using* the institution of the church. Yet authority is commonly given to religious leaders on the assumption that it will be used to protect and preserve that which already is. For example, when a person is elected to be a bishop in the United Methodist Church, he or she is invested into the office by taking a vow of three parts: to guard the faith of the church, to exercise the discipline of the church, and to seek the unity of the church. All three parts of the vow ask the person elected to this central and critical role of leadership to focus attention and resources on the interior life of the institution. There is no accompanying vow to keep the church connected to its purpose or to keep the church engaged with a changing culture and a shifting mission field. Pastors, laity, and local congregations are similarly expected to conform to the rules and practices of polity and to the expectations of satisfying the established preferences of the people already inside the institution—all internal expectations. The religious institutions developed during and still remembering the aberrant mid-century time want the flow of people and money to come in across their boundaries but are much less intentional in developing ways in which the surrounding culture and the purpose of the church flow back and forth across that same boundary.

Vows, polity, and job descriptions that are so highly institutional protect and preserve an interior agenda that has become a hairball of rules and constraints. Quietly courageous leaders are intuiting that they must continue to be credentialed and highly experienced in the central hairball of their institution. However, they must also move much closer to the edge of the institution, where they can engage purpose, culture, and change. Leadership is no longer only about gathering and protecting the power of the institution.

In his discussion of how power has changed around the globe, Moisés Naím begins by recognizing that in the past, organizations and institutions developed and maintained their power by becoming large and by establishing barriers that would fend off rivals.[22] By becoming large, by establishing a presence in the marketplace or public place, by formalizing the standards for performance and credibility, and by monopolizing resources, organizations and institutions established their position and fended off rivals who could not compete against the barriers represented by such strength. Under such conditions mainline Protestants and their institutions could once both thrive and dominate. However, by continued attention to its own strength, such forms of institutional religion also became increasingly internalized, captured by the need to care for their own hairballs. The place in which they engage the mission field became a hardened boundary over which it became increasingly difficult for people, energy, and ideas to flow.

Naím then goes on to describe how over the past three decades a host of variables have shifted power away from the large and now favor the "small players" instead. He describes a new kind of power that he calls "micropower."[23] The shift is related to a weaving of influences from demographics, economic transformations, information technologies, political shifts, and generational expectations. Importantly, he describes this as a global change. These are not changes that present specific problems only to religious organizations. These are changed conditions that everyone must learn to attend to—businesses, governments, military, corporations, families, and individuals.

This change will not do away with large, established institutions that will continue to have a role. Naím notes, "Big government, big armies, big business, and big universities will be constrained and confined as never before, but they will certainly stay relevant and their actions and decisions will carry great weight."[24] However, it will no longer be safe only to look internally to manage themselves and be able to assume that the culture around them will align and comply with their needs. What the younger generation and the newer culture cannot find for themselves within the big institutions will simply be invented and constructed by the micropowers that have discovered new freedom to create their own. The continual birthing of small, free-form faith communities, the formation of intimate and short-lived communities of meaning making, and the entry of marketing and merchandising to capture people's pursuit of values all attest to the brave new world in which institutional religion will find former strengths to be their current weaknesses.

Congregations and denominations are not to be abandoned. People will continue to turn to them. Despite the current anxiety about falling memberships and attendance, America is still the most religious developed nation on the globe and there is little evidence that this will shift immediately. Congregations and denominations are, however, no longer the only game in town. Leaders can no longer attend only to their own structure, resources, polity, and practices and hope to remain vital. Protectionism hardens the boundary at the edge by increasing the rules by which people can participate in the institution. Purpose makes the boundary more porous—for purpose requires learning more about the questions that people now face, learning the language and practices that if used by religious institutions can be understood by the people who are seeking. Curiously, this turn of events at the edge of institutions now requires leaders to know more about their own purpose and their intentional outcomes than it requires them to know about their own history, polity, and established practices.

The metaphor used to describe this shift is learning to be "of but not in the institution." Leaders must learn to be "of" their institution. Edge organizations, edge initiatives, and edge leaders all directly serve the mission of their institution—in other words, all of their efforts are "of" the institution. However, they are not "in" the institution—they are not captured and constrained by the established rules, regulations, and practices protected by a nonporous boundary. Being on the edge, being of but not in the institution, is a very tricky position in an anxious time for leaders who are, on the one hand, expected to uphold and enforce the rules and regulations at the center but, on the other hand, must direct attention and resources to the edge, where the rules and regulations are less constraining (and may even need to be disregarded).

From Player to Platform

A part of what is yet to be learned is how to help institutions shift from being a player to becoming a platform. Being a "player" means to be firm in understanding one's position or place in the environment and influencing others to one's own benefit. Becoming a "platform" requires a shift from understanding oneself as central to understanding that one is part of a much larger, more organic, and constantly shifting ecosystem. As a player, the question is how to establish and protect one's own presence. As a platform, the question is how to participate in the larger ecosystem by shaping a role (a platform) that serves the needs of others. As a player, one dominates. As a platform, one participates.

Marco Iansiti and Roy Levien write about developing a keystone strategy as a way to thrive at the edge.[25] They use the examples of Walmart and Microsoft, both of which deliberately chose strategies that formed relationships with the other organizations and competitors they needed for their own success. Both Walmart and Microsoft built a business platform in which they would be the keystone link that would support and enhance the whole network (ecology) of firms that would use the technological and business model they provided. Walmart and Microsoft became successful in part through their strategy of investing in the other firms on whom they depended by providing the technology and relationships to help those other firms, which, in turn, created a dependence on Walmart and Microsoft, supporting their own success.

What is essential about being a platform is recognizing that it requires two major elements: both the platform and the users.[26] Institutions and organizations can no longer focus on and understand only themselves. An easily understood platform is Apple's iOS operating software system, which is their organizational platform through which they serve their ecology by connecting their users. Note that their own vitality and sustainability is not defined simply by selling their phones, iPads, and computers to owners. In one sense no one actually "owns" their phone, tablet, or computer because people don't go their own way with their instrument disconnected from the shared iOS system or take a screwdriver to open their appliance up and customize it for their own use. The iOS system in each of those appliances is the connection to the shared platform that brings everyone together. On the one side are the 300 million users who utilize their phones, tablets, and computers. On the other side are the one million apps that are the tools people use to get information, organize activities, develop communities, and play games. In the middle is the critically necessary software platform that provides the space and context to help everyone on each side thrive in their own way. Apple thrives by providing a shared and hospitable platform that enables others to meet their own needs.

A platform is where others are invited to come to do their own work. The success of the platform depends on supporting the success of the users of the platform. As such, platforms are more about the users than the platform itself. Such a new world requires a reversal of assumptions and actions by the religious institutions that were established and thrived in the past century. Religious leaders can no longer see their role as protecting and strengthening their institution (to make their institution a player) but now seek ways to use their institution to become a platform to serve others who pursue their needs and their questions of meaning in their own way (the institution as a participant).

Religious denominations were players in that earlier culture and in the communities of the past. They controlled resources, exerted authority, required membership, established standards, and required compliance. All of these values no longer do well in the changed liquid culture in which micropowers are easily breaching such institutional barriers. To change the institutional role from player to platform shifts the work of leadership from attending to the requirements of the institution to attending to providing space, attention, and support to any and all "users" who share their identity and purpose—without requiring conformity. Faith communities that share identity and purpose with a denomination but do not conform to the structure, economic model, or practice of a traditional congregation need to be offered a relationship with hospitable space on the denominational platform. Instead of requiring the newly forming and curiously shaped new faith communities to conform to denominational standards, a platform denomination will help these new forms of faith communities to be more authentically themselves, thereby advancing the identity and purpose of both the denomination and the new faith communities. Instead of requiring standardized, regulated preparation and certification of leaders/pastors of all new experiments of mission, a platform denomination will provide hospitable space to all who share their denominational purpose and help them in their own formation and practice to be agents of the faith and the mission.

Similarly, local congregations were players in the earlier culture at the local level as membership organizations. People who wanted a place in the institution and in the community had to join and conform to basic standards. As a player, congregations expected people to bend to the needs and requirements of the institution. As membership organizations lost their cultural prominence and the stream of new members dwindled, congregations shifted from being membership organizations to being program providers, giving people a different reason to align with their institution. All of these efforts had an intent to meet the needs of the institution.

To become platform organizations, congregations will need to shift the focus from meeting the needs of the institution to providing hospitable space to help people in their own search to address life questions, issues of meaning, and concerns of community and safety. Along with providing programs of daycare, congregations will need to provide a platform for the wider community to organize around issues of the family, education, drugs, and social media addiction. Along with providing gun-free public space, congregations will need to provide a platform for the wider community to organize around issues of violence and mental health. Along with providing public space for worship, congregations will need to provide a platform for the people in the wider community who want to learn more about their individual and corporate lives through conversation with one another.

Moving from player to platform has deep institutional repercussions. Much is yet to be learned. Approached as an idea, it is possible to begin a picture of the necessary shift. However, it is still so early in the discoveries of the changed culture that it is yet quite unclear how leaders will bring about the actual shift of their institutions from players to platforms. Quietly courageous leaders will need to shift their attention from the center, where there are innumerable institutional constraints, to the edge, where there are more possibilities, more freedom, and more risk. It will require discovery that comes from conversation. It will require the patience of a slow process of connecting the dots while being buffeted by a quick culture. It will mean getting loose from a tight past.

This brings us back to the spiritual anchors that will hold us steady and give us balance in such turbulence. Returning to Bill Coffin's prayer, quietly courageous leaders will need

- a hope that is made wise by experience and is undaunted by disappointment;

- an anxiety about the future that shows them new ways to look at new things but does not unnerve them;
- to remember that their influence is greatest when their power is weakest; and
- to know that they have simple blessings that will see them through—health, food, sleep, one another, and the seasons of God's creative hand.

However, beyond the simple blessings, quietly courageous leaders are now offered the more difficult blessings of being purposeful in a changed time and culture, blessings that are complicated indeed.

NOTES

I. NASHON'S QUIET COURAGE

1. Lawrence Kushner, *God Was in This Place and I, I Did Not Know* (Woodstock, VT: Jewish Lights, 1994), 15.

2. Reuven Hammer, trans., *The Classic Midrash: Tannaitic Commentaries on the Bible* (New York: Paulist Press, 1995), 92.

3. Ronald Heifetz, *Leadership without Easy Answers* (Cambridge, MA: The Belknap Press of Harvard University Press, 1994), 99.

4. Robert Quinn, *Deep Change: Discovering the Leader Within* (San Francisco: Jossey-Bass, 1996), 91

5. Ibid., 3; emphasis added.

6. Heifetz, *Leadership without Easy Answers*, 87; emphasis added.

7. Leo S. Thorne, ed., *Prayers from Riverside* (New York: Pilgrim Press, 1983), 49–50.

8. Angie Thurston and Casper ter Kuile, "Faithful," *How We Gather*, 2017, https://www.howwegather.org/reports.

9. Angie Thurston and Casper ter Kuile, "How We Gather," *How We Gather*, 2015, https://www.howwegather.org/reports.

10. Sid Schwarz, *Jewish Megatrends: Charting the Course of the American Jewish Future* (Woodstock, VT: Jewish Lights, 2013).

11. Gil Rendle, *Journey in the Wilderness: New Life for Mainline Churches* (Nashville: Abingdon Press, 2010), 3.

2. THE CHANGE THAT DEMANDS
QUIET COURAGE

1. Lovett Weems, "A Lewis Center Report on Clergy Age Trends in the United Methodist Church; 2015 Report" (Washington, DC: The Lewis Center for Church Leadership, 2015). Referencing the UMC, the report states, "Elders between ages 55 and 72 comprise 55 percent of all active elders, the highest percentage in history. This group reached 50 percent for the first time ever in 2010. . . . The median age of elders remained at 56 in 2015, the highest in history. The median age was 50 in 2000 and 45 in 1973. The average age remains at 53, a historic high, though unchanged for six years. The mode age (the single age most represented) is 60, down from 61 last year." While focused on the United Methodist Church, the report also notes similar averages for six other American denominations.

2. Ross Douthat, *Bad Religion: How We Became a Nation of Heretics* (New York: Free Press, 2012), 21.

3. Ibid., 22.

4. Hampton Sides, *Blood and Thunder: An Epic of the American West* (New York: Anchor Books, 2006), 256; emphasis added.

5. Yuval Levin, *The Fractured Republic: Renewing America's Social Contract in the Age of Individualism* (New York: Basic Books, 2016).

6. Ibid., 32.

7. Moisés Naím, *The End of Power: From Boardrooms to Battlefields and Churches, to States, Why Being in Charge Isn't What It Used to Be* (New York: Basic Books, 2013).

8. Gil Rendle and Alice Mann, *Holy Conversations: Strategic Planning as a Spiritual Practice for Congregations* (Bethesda, MD: The Alban Institute, 2003).

9. Ronald A. Heifetz, *Leadership without Easy Answers* (Cambridge, MA: The Belknap Press of Harvard University Press, 1994).

10. Ibid., 2.

11. Ibid., 84.

12. Ronald A. Heifetz and Marty Linsky, *Leadership on the Line: Staying Alive through the Dangers of Leading* (Boston: Harvard Business Review Press, 2002).

13. Yuval Noah Harari, *Sapiens: A Brief History of Humankind* (New York: HarperCollins, 2015), 250.

14. Gil Rendle, *Journey in the Wilderness: New Life for Mainline Churches* (Nashville: Abingdon Press, 2010), 17–32.

15. Paul Taylor, *The Next America: Boomers, Millennials, and the Looming Generational Showdown* (New York: Public Affairs, 2014), 30.

16. Gil Rendle, "Waiting for God's New Thing: Spiritual and Organizational Leadership in the In-Between Time," Texas Methodist Foundation, 2015, https://www.tmf-fdn.org/leadership-ministry/learning-resources/congregational-resources.

17. Charles Handy, *Beyond Certainty: The Changing Worlds of Organizations* (Boston: Harvard Business Review Press, 1996), 154.

18. Charles Murray, *Coming Apart: The State of White America, 1960–2000* (New York: Crown Forum, 2012), 6.

19. Joseph Turow, *Breaking Up America: Advertisers and the New Media World* (Chicago: University of Chicago Press, 1997), 3.

20. Rex Miller, *The Millennial Matrix: Reclaiming the Past, Reframing the Future of the Church* (San Francisco: Jossey-Bass, 2004), 59–69.

21. Turow, *Breaking Up America*, 7.

22. Ibid., 2.

23. Harari, *Sapiens*, 392.

24. Hugh Heclo, *On Thinking Institutionally* (Boulder, CO: Paradigm Publications, 2008), 11–12.

25. Ibid., 11.

26. Ibid., 33.

27. Ibid., 35.

28. Daniel Yankelovich, *New Rules: Searching for Self-Fulfillment in a World Turned Upside Down* (New York: Bantam Books, 1982), 7.

29. Robert Jones, *The End of White Christian America* (New York: Simon and Schuster, 2016), 31.

30. Ibid., 8.

31. Ibid., 14.

32. Ibid., 228.

33. Robert Putnam, *Bowling Alone: The Collapse and Revival of American Community* (New York: Simon and Schuster, 2000), 19.

34. Robert Putnam, *Our Kids: The American Dream in Crisis* (New York: Simon and Schuster, 2015), 34.

35. Murray, *Coming Apart*, 2012.

36. David Brooks, "The Great Divorce," *New York Times*, January 30, 2012.

37. Murray, *Coming Apart*, 69–80.

38. J. D. Vance, *Hillbilly Elegy: A Memoir of a Family and Culture in Crisis* (New York: Harper and Row, 2016).

39. Angie Thurston and Casper ter Kuile, "How We Gather" and "Something More," *How We Gather*, 2015, https://www.howwegather.org/reports.

3. A WORD ABOUT HOW

1. Zygmunt Bauman, *Liquid Times: Living in an Age of Uncertainty* (Cambridge: Polity Press, 2007), 1.

2. Gil Rendle and Alice Mann, *Holy Conversations: Strategic Planning as a Spiritual Practice for Congregations* (Bethesda, MD: The Alban Institute, 2003), 209.

3. Bryce Hoffman, *American Icon: Alan Mulally and the Fight to Save Ford Motor Company* (New York: Crown Business, 2012).

4. Stanley McChrystal, with Tantum Collins, David Silberman, and Chris Fussell, *Team of Teams: New Rules of Engagement for a Complex World* (New York: Penguin, 2015), 57.

5. Ibid., 19.

6. Ibid., 57.

7. Ronald A. Heifetz, *Leadership without Easy Answers* (Cambridge, MA: The Belknap Press of Harvard University Press, 1994), 76.

8. Michael Fullan, *Leading in a Culture of Change* (San Francisco: Wiley, 2001), 45–46; 108–9.

9. Ken Wilber, *Trump and a Post-Truth World* (Boulder: Shambhala Press, 2017), 144.

10. Rendle and Mann, *Holy Conversations*, 210.

11. John Scherer, "The Role of Chaos in the Creation of Change," *Creative Change* 12, no. 2 (Spring 1991): 19.

12. Ibid., 19.

13. Ibid., 20.

14. Michael Crichton, *The Lost World* (New York: Ballantine Books, 1995), 192.

15. Fritjof Capra, *The Turning Point: Science, Society, and the Rising Culture* (New York: Bantam Books, 1982), 269–71.

16. Alan Roxburgh, *Structured for Mission: Renewing the Culture of the Church* (Downers Grove, IL: IVP Books, 2015), 100–102.

17. Ibid., 101.

4. A WORD ABOUT ENOUGH

1. Anat Shenker-Osorio, "Why Americans All Believe They Are 'Middle Class,'" *The Atlantic*, August 1, 2013, https://www.theatlantic.com/politics/archive/2013/08/why-americans-all-believe-they-are-middle-class/278240.

2. Thomas Friedman and Michael Mandelbaum, *That Used to Be Us: How America Fell Behind in the World It Invented and How We Can Come Back* (New York: Farrar, Straus and Giroux, 2011), 160.

3. Lynne Twist, *The Soul of Money: Reclaiming the Wealth of Our Inner Resources* (New York: Norton, 2003), 3.

4. Ibid., 43.

5. Ibid., 51.

6. Ibid., 74.

7. Suresh Srivastva and David Cooperrider, *Appreciative Management and Leadership: The Power of Positive Thought and Action in Organizations* (San Francisco: Jossey-Bass, 1990).

8. Sue Annis Hammond, *The Thin Book of Appreciative Inquiry* (Plano, TX: Thin Book Publishing, 1998), 6.

9. W. Edwards Deming, *Out of the Crisis* (Cambridge, MA: Massachusetts Institute of Technology, Center for Advanced Engineering Study, 1986).

10. For a fuller discussion of Deming's model and its application to the changed paradigm we now face in the United Methodist Church, please see Gil Rendle, *Back to Zero: The Search to Rediscover the Methodist Movement* (Nashville: Abingdon, 2011), 37–46.

11. Reggie McNeil, *Missional Renaissance: Changing the Scorecard for the Church* (San Francisco: Jossey-Bass, 2009).

12. Jim Collins, *Good to Great in the Social Sector* (Boulder, CO: Jim Collins, 2005).

13. Stephen R. Covey, *The 7 Habits of Highly Effective People* (New York: Simon and Schuster, 1989), 96.

14. Let me encourage readers to hear stories directly from Mike that can be found on YouTube at https://www.youtube.com/watch?v=WOET3FReOfM and https://www.youtube.com/watch?v=CVSnkrCAhUQ.

15. Kenneth Carter and Audrey Warren, *Fresh Expressions: A New Kind of Methodist Church for People Not in Church* (Nashville: Abingdon Press, 2017).

16. Angie Thurston and Casper ter Kuile, "How We Gather," *How We Gather*, https://www.howwegather.org/reports.

17. Moisés Naím, *The End of Power: From Boardrooms to Battlefields and Churches, to States, Why Being in Charge Isn't What It Used to Be* (New York: Basic Books, 2013), 9.

18. Eric Liu, *You're More Powerful Than You Think: A Citizen's Guide to Making Change Happen* (New York: PublicAffairs, 2017), 4.

19. Ibid., 26.

20. Walter Brueggemann, *The Word That Redescribes to World: The Bible and Discipleship* (Minneapolis: Fortress Press, 2011), 20.

5. A WORD ABOUT STRUCTURE
AND PROCESS

1. Joseph Ellis, *Founding Brothers: The Revolutionary Generation* (New York: Vintage Books, 2002), 120–62.

2. John R. Silber, *Seeking the North Star* (Boston: David R. Godine, 2014), 68.

3. Richard Lischer, *Open Secrets: A Spiritual Journey through a Country Church* (New York: Doubleday, 2001), 67.

4. William Willimon, *Bishop: The Art of Questioning Authority by an Authority in Question* (Nashville: Abingdon Press, 2012), 67.

5. Brooks Holifield, *God's Ambassadors: A History of the Christian Clergy in America* (Grand Rapids, MI: Eerdmans, 2007), 60–61.

6. David Roozen and James Nieman, eds., *Church, Identity, and Change: Theology and Denominational Structures in Unsettled Times* (Grand Rapids, MI: Eerdmans, 2005), 596.

7. Ronald A. Heifetz and Marty Linsky, *Leadership on the Line: Staying Alive through the Dangers of Leading* (Boston: Harvard Business Review Press, 2002).

8. Craig Dykstra and James Hudnut-Beumler, "The National Organizational Structures of Protestant Denominations: An Invitation to a Conversation," in *The Organizational Revolution: Presbyterians and American Denominationalism*, edited by Milton Coalter, John Mulder, and Louis Weeks (Louisville, KY: Westminster John Knox Press, 1992), 307–31.

9. Robert Schnase, "Multiplying Our Witness: *Missio Dei* and the United States Toward a Faithful United Methodist Witness," unpublished paper (October 2017).

10. Donald House, "A National Projection Model for the Denomination in the US," unpublished paper (February 2012).

11. Lovett Weems, "Reset and Focus: Reset Financially in Order to Focus on Reaching More People—Reflections on Call to Action Projects—Operational Assessment and Vital Congregations," unpublished paper (September 2010).

12. Gordon MacKenzie, *Orbiting the Giant Hairball: A Corporate Fool's Guide to Surviving with Grace* (New York: Viking Penguin, 1996).

13. Russell Richey, "From Christmas Conference to General Conference— Today's Untied Methodism: Living with/into Its Two Centuries of Regular Division," unpublished paper (April 2017).

14. Stanley McChrystal, with Tantum Collins, David Silberman, and Chris Fussell, *Team of Teams: New Rules of Engagement for a Complex World* (New York: Penguin, 2015), viii.

15. Ibid., 76.

16. Ori Brafman and Rob Beckstrom, *The Starfish and the Spider: The Unstoppable Power of Leaderless Organizations* (New York: Penguin, 2006), 95.

17. Michael Kenney, *From Pablo to Osama: Trafficking and Terrorist Networks, Government Bureaucracies, and Competitive Advantage* (University Park: Pennsylvania State University Press, 2007), 51.

18. John Wigger, *American Saint: Francis Asbury and the Methodists* (Oxford: Oxford University Press, 2009), 13.

19. Holifield, *God's Ambassadors*.

20. Steven Saint and James Lawson, *Rules for Reaching Consensus: A Modern Approach to Decision Making* (San Francisco: Jossey-Bass, 1994), xii.

21. Peter Block, *Community: The Structure of Belonging* (San Francisco: Berrett-Koehler, 2008), 94.

22. Wally Armbruster, *A Bag of Noodles* (St. Louis: Concordia Publishing House, 1972), 5.

23. General Board of Higher Education and Ministry, "Minutes of Several Conversations Between the Study of Ministry Commission, Chairs of Orders and Boards of Ordained Ministry of Annual Conferences, Various Laity and Clergy across the Connection, and the General Conference of the United Methodist Church" (unpublished document of the General Board of Higher Education and Ministry, 2008), 8.

24. Ibid., 33.

25. Marcus Buckingham and Curt Coffman, *First, Break All the Rules: What the World's Greatest Managers Do Differently* (New York: Simon and Schuster, 1999), 153.

26. Ibid., 57.

27. Everett Rogers, *Diffusion of Innovations* (New York: Free Press, 1995).

6. A WORD ABOUT LEARNING

1. Janice Riggle Huie, "A New Paradigm for Clergy Leadership: Cultivating an Ecosystem of Excellence," Texas Methodist Foundation, 2013, https://www.tmf-fdn.org/leadership-ministry/learning-resources/congregational-resources, 2–3.

2. David Gortner, "Clergy Leadership for the 21st Century: Are We Up to the Task?" (a white paper submitted to the Board of Trustees at Virginia Theological Seminary, January 2014), 3.

3. Ibid., 3.

4. Robert Quinn, *Deep Change: Discovering the Leader Within* (San Francisco: Jossey-Bass, 1996).

5. Gortner, "Clergy Leadership for the 21st Century," 5.

6. Ibid., 6.

7. Andrew Abbott, *The System of Professions: An Essay on the Division of Expert Labor* (Chicago: University of Chicago Press, 1988), 8.

8. Patricia Benner, *From Novice to Expert: Excellence and Power in Clinical Nursing Practice* (Upper Saddle River, NJ: Prentice Hall Health, 2001), ix.

9. Christian Scharen, "Learning Ministry Over Time: Embodying Practical Wisdom," in *For Life Abundant: Theology, Theological Education and Christian Ministry*, edited by Dorothy Bass and Craig Dykstra (Grand Rapids, MI: Eerdmans, 2008), 268–86.

10. William Willimon, *Bishop: The Art of Questioning Authority by an Authority in Question* (Nashville: Abingdon Press, 2012), 29.

11. Tony Wagner, *The Global Achievement Gap: Why Even Our Best Schools Don't Teach the New Survival Skills Our Children Need—And What We Can Do about It* (New York: Perseus Books Group, 2010).

12. Tony Wagner, *Creating Innovators: The Making of Young People Who Will Change the World* (New York: Scribner, 2012), 25.

13. Huie, "A New Paradigm for Clergy Leadership," 7.

14. Edwin Friedman, *A Failure of Nerve: Leadership in the Age of the Quick Fix* (New York: Seabury Books, 2007), ix.

15. Peter Block, *Community: The Structure of Belonging* (San Francisco: Berrett-Koehler, 2008), 63–64.

16. William Duggan, *Strategic Intuition: The Creative Spark in Human Achievement* (New York: Columbia University Press, 2007), 2.

17. Malcolm Gladwell, *Outliers: The Story of Success* (New York: Little, Brown, 2008), 39–40.

18. Nick Petrie, "Future Trends in Leadership Development" (white paper, Center for Creative Leadership, 2014).

19. Ibid., 15.

20. Robert Reber and Bruce Roberts, eds., *A Lifelong Call to Learn* (Nashville: Abingdon Press, 2000).

21. Mike Schmoker, *Results Now: How We Can Achieve Unprecedented Improvements in Teaching and Learning* (Alexandria, VA: ASCD, 2006), 23.

22. Ibid., 24.

23. Etienne Wenger, *Communities of Practice: Learning, Meaning, and Identity* (Cambridge: Cambridge University Press, 1998).

24. Penny Long Marler and Janet Maykus, "Is the Treatment the Cure? A Study of Participation in Pastoral Leader Peer Groups" (unpublished report, 2010).

25. Jagdish Sheth and Andrew Sobel, *Clients for Life* (New York: Simon and Schuster, 2000).

26. Ibid., 89.

27. Shunryu Suzuki, *Zen Mind, Beginner's Mind* (New York: Weatherill, 1994), 21.

28. Huie, "A New Paradigm for Clergy Leadership," 4.

29. Angie Thurston and Casper ter Kuile, "Thresholds," *How We Gather*, 2018, https://www.howwegather.org/reports, 6.

30. Ibid., 9.

7. THE TEMPTATION OF PLAYING IT SAFE

1. Mark Lilla, *The Shipwrecked Mind: On Political Reaction* (New York: New York Review Books, 2016).

2. Ibid., xii–xiii.

3. Ibid., xiii.

4. Alan Roxburgh, *Structured for Mission: Renewing the Culture of the Church* (Downers Grove, IL: IVP Books, 2015), 26.

5. Lilla, *The Shipwrecked Mind*, xiii.

6. Yuval Levin, *The Fractured Republic: Renewing America's Social Contract in the Age of Individualism* (New York: Basic Books, 2016), 32.

7. Levin, *The Fractured Republic*, 2.

8. Ibid., 15.

9. Ibid., 18.

10. C. Kirk Hadaway, *FACTS on Growth: 2010* (Hartford, CT: Hartford Institute for Religion Research, 2010).

11. Chris Argyris, *Overcoming Organizational Defenses: Facilitating Organizational Learning* (Needham Heights, MA: Allyn and Bacon, 1990), 25.

12. Ibid., 43.

13. Gil Rendle and Alice Mann, *Holy Conversations: Strategic Planning as a Spiritual Practice for Congregations* (Bethesda, MD: The Alban Institute, 2003).

8. THE TEMPTATION OF
CHRISTIAN EMPATHY

1. Daniel Goleman, Richard Boyatzis, and Annie McKee, *Primal Leadership: Realizing the Power of Emotional Intelligence* (Boston: Harvard Business Review Press, 2002), 66.

2. Christopher Beeley, *Leading God's People: Wisdom from the Early Church for Today* (Grand Rapids, MI: Eerdmans, 2012), 8.

3. Hugh Heclo, *On Thinking Institutionally* (Boulder, CO: Paradigm Publications, 2008), 33.

4. Beeley, *Leading God's People*, 41.

5. Ibid., 65.

6. Mark Chavez, *American Religion: Contemporary Trends* (Princeton, NJ: Princeton University Press, 2011), 56.

7. Donald House, "A National Projection Model for the Denomination in the US," unpublished paper (February 2012).

8. Thomas Friedman and Michael Mandelbaum, *That Used to Be Us: How America Fell Behind in the World It Invented and How We Can Come Back* (New York: Farrar, Straus and Giroux, 2011), 160.

9. David Roozen and James Nieman, eds., *Church, Identity, and Change* (Grand Rapids, MI: Eerdmans, 2005), 596.

10. Edwin Friedman, *A Failure of Nerve: Leadership in the Age of the Quick Fix* (New York: Seabury Books, 2007), 24.

11. Ibid., 133.

12. Ibid., 69.

13. Daniel Goleman, *Working with Emotional Intelligence* (New York: Bantam Books, 2000), 144.

14. Barry Schwartz and Kenneth Sharpe, *Practical Wisdom: The Right Way to Do the Right Thing* (New York: Riverhead Books, 2010), 75.

15. Friedman, *A Failure of Nerve*, 24.

16. Goleman, Boyatzis, and McKee, *Primal Leadership*, 6.

17. Chip Heath and Dan Heath, *Switch: How to Change Things When Change Is Hard* (New York: Broadway Books, 2010), 6.

18. Ibid., 7–10.

9. THE TEMPTATION OF TIREDNESS

1. Lewis Carroll, *Through the Looking Glass* (New York: Bantam Classic Books, 2006), 67.

2. Ken Wilber, *The Marriage of Sense and Soul: Integrating Science and Religion* (New York: Random House, 1998), 3.

3. Jim Collins, *Good to Great in the Social Sector* (Boulder, CO: Jim Collins, 2005).

4. Michael Lerner, *Surplus Powerlessness: The Psychodynamics of Everyday Life and the Psychology of Individual and Social Transformation* (Oakland, CA: Institute for Labor and Mental Health, 1986), i.

5. Ibid., ii.

6. Ibid., 15, 54–55.

7. Gil Rendle, *Journey in the Wilderness: New Life for Mainline Churches* (Nashville: Abingdon Press, 2010).

8. Gil Rendle, *Doing the Math of Mission: Fruits, Faithfulness, and Mission* (New York: Rowman & Littlefield, 2014), 17–32.

9. Ibid., 13–18.

10. Ibid., 23.

11. Edwin Friedman, *A Failure of Nerve: Leadership in the Age of the Quick Fix* (New York: Seabury Books, 2007), 32.

12. Alpesh Bhatt, *The Triple-Soy Decaf-Latte Era: How Businesses and Organizations Are Fundamentally Transforming* (San Bernardino, CA: The Center for Leadership Studies, 2012), 5.

13. Thomas Kuhn, *The Structure of Scientific Revolutions* (Chicago: University of Chicago Press, 1970).

14. Robert Schnase, *Five Practices of Fruitful Congregations* (Nashville: Abingdon Press, 2007).

10. TELLING THE STORY THAT WILL GET US THROUGH THE WILDERNESS

1. Chris Argyris, "Double Loop Learning in Organizations," *Harvard Business Review* (September 1997): 2.

2. Ronald A. Heifetz, *Leadership without Easy Answers* (Cambridge, MA: The Belknap Press of Harvard University Press, 1994), 69.

3. Walter Brueggemann, *The Word That Redescribes the World: The Bible and Discipleship* (Minneapolis: Fortress Press, 2011), xiii.

4. Ken Wilber, *The Marriage of Sense and Soul: Integrating Science and Religion* (New York: Random House, 1998), xi.

5. Moisés Naím, *The End of Power: From Boardrooms to Battlefields and Churches, to States, Why Being in Charge Isn't What It Used to Be* (New York: Basic Books, 2013).

6. Although his writings are over fifty years old, Buckminster Fuller was at the beginning of a modern redescription of the world that looked at the globe as a living system that was sustainable. See, in particular, *Operating Manual for Spaceship Earth* (Carbondale, IL: Southern Illinois University Press, 1968) and *Critical Path* (New York: St. Martin's Press, 1981).

7. William Willimon, *Bishop: The Art of Questioning Authority by an Authority in Question* (Nashville: Abingdon Press, 2012), 113.

8. Howard Gardner, *Leading Minds: An Anatomy of Leadership* (New York: Basic Books, 1995), ix.

9. Ibid., 10.

10. Ibid., 11.

11. Phyllis Tickle, *The Great Emergence: How Christianity Is Changing and Why* (Grand Rapids, MI: Baker Books, 2008), 16.

12. William Isaacs, *Dialogue and the Art of Thinking Together* (New York: Doubleday, 1999), 252–87.

13. Wilfred Drath and Charles Palus, *Making Common Sense: Leadership and Meaning Making in a Community of Practice* (Greensboro, NC: The Center for Creative Leadership, 1994), 2.

14. Gardner, *Leading Minds*, ix.

15. Howard Gardner, *Changing Minds: The Art and Science of Changing Our Own and Other People's Minds* (Boston: Harvard Business Review Press 2004), 69.

16. William Bridges, *Making Sense of Life's Transitions* (Reading, MA: Addison-Wesley, 1980).

17. Frederick Buechner, *Wishful Thinking: A Theological ABC* (New York: Harper and Row, 1973), 64.

18. Edward Leroy Long Jr., *Patterns of Polity* (Cleveland, OH: Pilgrim Press, 2001), 29.

19. Ibid., 31.

I I. LESSONS IN STYLE

1. Margaret Wheatley, *Turning to One Another: Simple Conversations to Restore Hope to the Future* (San Francisco: Berrett-Koehler, 2002), 32.

2. Thomas Davenport and Laurence Prusak, *Working Knowledge: How Organizations Manage What They Know* (Boston: Harvard Business Review Press, 1998), 2–6.

3. Ibid., 60.

4. David Bohm, *On Dialogue* (New York: Routledge, 1996), 2.

5. Ibid., vii.

6. William Isaacs, *Dialogue and the Art of Thinking Together* (New York: Doubleday, 1999), 28.

7. Roger Fisher and William Ury, *Getting to Yes: Negotiating Agreement without Giving In* (New York: Penguin Books, 1981).

8. Ronald A. Heifetz, *Leadership without Easy Answers* (Cambridge, MA: The Belknap Press of Harvard University Press, 1994), 252.

9. Wheatley, *Turning to One Another*, 3.

10. William Duggan, *Strategic Intuition: The Creative Spark in Human Achievement* (New York: Columbia University Press, 2007), 2.

11. Gil Rendle and Alice Mann, *Holy Conversations: Strategic Planning as a Spiritual Practice for Congregations* (Bethesda: The Alban Institute, 2003), 139–52.

12. Margaret Wheatley and Myron Kellner-Rogers, *A Simpler Way* (San Francisco: Berrett-Koehler, 1996), 13.

13. Nassim Taleb, *Antifragile: Things That Gain from Disorder* (New York: Random House, 2012), 3.

14. Ibid., 73.

15. Michael Kenney, *From Pablo to Osama: Trafficking and Terrorist Networks, Government Bureaucracies, and Competitive Adaptation* (University Park: Pennsylvania State University Press, 2007), 27.

16. Ibid., 49.

17. Gordon MacKenzie, *Orbiting the Giant Hairball: A Corporate Fool's Guide to Surviving with Grace* (New York: Viking Press, 1996), 30.

18. H. Richard Niebuhr, *Christ and Culture* (New York: Harper and Row, 1951).

19. Ori Brafman and Rod Beckstrom, *The Starfish and the Spider: The Unstoppable Power of Leaderless Organizations* (New York: Penguin, 2006), 95.

20. Stanley McChrystal, with Tantum Collins, David Silberman, and Chris Fussell, *Team of Teams: New Rules of Engagement for a Complex World* (New York: Penguin, 2015), 20.

21. Robert Schnase, *Five Practices of Fruitful Congregations: Revised and Updated* (Nashville: Abingdon Press, 2018).

22. Moisés Naím, *The End of Power: From Boardrooms to Battlefields and Churches, to States, Why Being in Charge Isn't What It Used to Be* (New York: Basic Books, 2013), 10–15.

23. Ibid., 13.

24. Ibid.

25. Marco Iansiti and Roy Levien, *The Keystone Advantage: What the New Dynamics of Business Ecosystems Mean for Strategy, Innovation, and Sustainability* (Boston: Harvard Business Review Press, 2004).

26. Tiwana Amnit, *Platform Ecosystems: Aligning Architecture, Governance and Strategy* (Burlington, MA: Morgan Kaufmann, 2014), 5–12.

BIBLIOGRAPHY

Abbott, Andrew. *The System of Professions: An Essay on the Division of Expert Labor.* Chicago: University of Chicago Press, 1988.

Amnit, Tiwana. *Platform Ecosystems: Aligning Architecture, Governance and Strategy.* Burlington, MA: Morgan Kaufmann, 2014.

Argyris, Chris. "Double Loop Learning in Organizations." *Harvard Business Review* (September 1997), https://hbr.org/1977/09/double-loop-learning-in-organizations.

———. *Overcoming Organizational Defenses: Facilitating Organizational Learning.* Needham Heights, MA: Allyn and Bacon, 1990.

Armbruster, Wally. *A Bag of Noodles.* St. Louis: Concordia Publishing House, 1972.

Bauman, Zygmunt. *Liquid Times: Living in an Age of Uncertainty.* Cambridge: Polity Press, 2007.

Beeley, Christopher. *Leading God's People: Wisdom from the Early Church for Today.* Grand Rapids, MI: Eerdmans, 2012.

Benner, Patricia. *From Novice to Expert: Excellence and Power in Clinical Nursing Practice.* Upper Saddle River, NJ: Prentice Hall Health, 2001.

Bhatt, Alpesh. *The Triple-Soy Decaf-Latte Era: How Businesses and Organizations Are Fundamentally Transforming.* San Bernardino, CA: The Center for Leadership Studies, 2012.

Block, Peter. *Community: The Structure of Belonging.* San Francisco: Berrett-Koehler, 2008.

Bohm, David. *On Dialogue.* New York: Routledge, 1996.

Brafman, Ori, and Rob Beckstrom. *The Starfish and the Spider: The Unstoppable Power of Leaderless Organizations.* New York: Penguin, 2006.

Bridges, William. *Making Sense of Life's Transitions.* Reading, MA: Addison-Wesley, 1980.

Brooks, David. "The Great Divorce." *New York Times,* January 30, 2012.

Brueggemann, Walter. *The Word That Redescribes to World: The Bible and Discipleship.* Minneapolis: Fortress Press, 2011.

Buckingham, Marcus, and Curt Coffman. *First, Break All the Rules: What the World's Greatest Managers Do Differently.* New York: Simon and Schuster, 1999.

Buechner, Frederick. *Wishful Thinking: A Theological ABC.* New York: Harper and Row, 1973.

Capra, Fritjof. *The Turning Point: Science, Society, and the Rising Culture.* New York: Bantam Books, 1982.

Carroll, Lewis. *Through the Looking Glass.* New York: Bantam Classic Books, 2006.

Carter, Kenneth, and Audrey Warren. *Fresh Expressions: A New Kind of Methodist Church for People Not in Church.* Nashville: Abingdon Press, 2017.

Chavez, Mark. *American Religion: Contemporary Trends.* Princeton, NJ: Princeton University Press, 2011.

Collins, Jim. *Good to Great in the Social Sector.* Boulder, CO: Jim Collins, 2005.

Covey, Stephen. *The 7 Habits of Highly Effective People.* New York: Simon and Schuster, 1989.

Crichton, Michael. *The Lost World.* New York: Ballantine Books, 1995.

Davenport, Thomas, and Laurence Prusak. *Working Knowledge: How Organizations Manage What They Know.* Boston: Harvard Business Review Press, 1998.

Deming, Edwards. *Out of Crisis.* Cambridge, MA: Massachusetts Institute of Technology, Center for Advanced Engineering Study, 1986.

Douthat, Ross. *Bad Religion: How We Became a Nation of Heretics.* New York: Free Press, 2012.

Drath, Wilfred, and Charles Palus. *Making Common Sense: Leadership and Meaning Making in a Community of Practice.* Greensboro, NC: The Center for Creative Leadership, 1994.

Duggan, William. *Strategic Intuition: The Creative Spark in Human Achievement.* New York: Columbia University Press, 2007.

Dykstra, Craig, and James Hudnut-Beumler. "The National Organizational Structures of Protestant Denominations: An Invitation to a Conversation." In *The Organizational Revolution: Presbyterians and American Denominationalism*, edited by Milton Coalter, John Mulder, and Louis Weeks, 307–31. Louisville, KY: Westminster John Knox Press, 1992.

Ellis, Joseph. *Founding Brothers: The Revolutionary Generation.* New York: Vintage Books, 2002.

Fisher, Roger, and William Ury. *Getting to Yes: Negotiating Agreement without Giving In.* New York: Penguin Books, 1981.

Friedman, Edwin. *A Failure of Nerve: Leadership in the Age of the Quick Fix.* New York: Seabury Books, 2007.

Friedman, Thomas, and Michael Mandelbaum. *That Used to Be Us: How America Fell Behind in the World It Invented and How We Can Come Back.* New York: Farrar, Straus and Giroux, 2011.

Fullan, Michael. *Leading in a Culture of Change.* San Francisco: Wiley, 2001.

Fuller, Buckminster. *Critical Path.* New York: St. Martin's Press, 1981.

———. *Operating Manual for Spaceship Earth.* Carbondale, IL: Southern Illinois University Press, 1970.

Gardner, Howard. *Changing Minds: The Art and Science of Changing Our Own and Other People's Minds.* Boston: Harvard Business Review Press, 2004.

———. *Leading Minds: An Anatomy of Leadership.* New York: Basic Books, 1995.

General Board of Higher Education and Ministry. "Minutes of Several Conversations Between the Study of Ministry Commission, Chairs of Orders and Boards of Ordained Ministry of Annual Conferences, Various Laity and Clergy across the Connection, and the General Conference of the United Methodist Church." Unpublished document of the General Board of Higher Education and Ministry, 2008.

Gladwell, Malcolm. *Outliers: The Story of Success.* New York: Little, Brown, 2008.

Goleman, Daniel. *Working with Emotional Intelligence.* New York: Bantam Books, 2000.

Goleman, Daniel, Richard Boyatzis, and Annie McKee. *Primal Leadership: Realizing the Power of Emotional Intelligence.* Boston: Harvard Business Review Press, 2002.

Gortner, David. "Clergy Leadership for the 21st Century: Are We Up to the Task?" A white paper submitted to the Board of Trustees at Virginia Theological Seminary, January 2014.

Hadaway, C. Kirk. *FACTS on Growth: 2010.* Hartford, CT: Hartford Institute for Religion Research, 2010.

Hammer, Reuven, trans. *The Classic Midrash: Tannaitic Commentaries on the Bible.* New York: Paulist Press, 1995.

Hammond, Sue Annis. *The Thin Book of Appreciative Inquiry.* Plano, TX: Thin Book Publishing, 1998.

Handy, Charles. *Beyond Certainty: The Changing Worlds of Organizations.* Boston: Harvard Business Review Press, 1996.

Harari, Yuval Noah. *Sapiens: A Brief History of Humankind.* New York: HarperCollins, 2015.

Heath, Chip, and Dan Heath. *Switch: How to Change Things When Change Is Hard.* New York: Broadway Books, 2010.

Heclo, Hugh. *On Thinking Institutionally.* Boulder, CO: Paradigm Publications, 2008.

Heifetz, Ronald A. *Leadership without Easy Answers.* Cambridge, MA: The Belknap Press of Harvard University Press, 1994.

Heifetz, Ronald A., and Marty Linsky. *Leadership on the Line: Staying Alive through the Dangers of Leading.* Boston: Harvard Business Review Press, 2002.

Hoffman, Bryce. *American Icon: Alan Mulally and the Fight to Save Ford Motor Company.* New York: Crown Business, 2012.

Holifield, Brooks. *God's Ambassadors: A History of the Christian Clergy in America.* Grand Rapids, MI: Eerdmans, 2007.

House, Donald. "A National Projection Model for the Denomination in the US." Unpublished paper (February 2012).

Huie, Janice Riggle. "A New Paradigm for Clergy Leadership: Cultivating an Ecosystem of Excellence." Texas Methodist Foundation, 2013, https://www.tmf-fdn.org/leadership-ministry/learning-resources/congregational-resources, 2–3.

Iansiti, Marco, and Roy Levien. *The Keystone Advantage: What the New Dynamics of Business Ecosystems Mean for Strategy, Innovation, and Sustainability.* Boston: Harvard Business Review Press, 2004.

Isaacs, William. *Dialogue and the Art of Thinking Together.* New York: Doubleday, 1999.

Jones, Robert. *The End of White Christian America.* New York: Simon and Schuster, 2016.

Kenney, Michael. *From Pablo to Osama: Trafficking and Terrorist Networks, Government Bureaucracies, and Competitive Adaptation.* University Park: Pennsylvania State University Press, 2007.

Kuhn, Thomas. *The Structure of Scientific Revolutions.* Chicago: University of Chicago Press, 1970.

Kushner, Lawrence. *God Was in This Place and I, I Did Not Know.* Woodstock, VT: Jewish Lights, 1994.

Lerner, Michael. *Surplus Powerlessness: The Psychodynamics of Everyday Life and the Psychology of Individual and Social Transformation.* Oakland, CA: Institute for Labor and Mental Health, 1986.

Levin, Yuval. *The Fractured Republic: Renewing America's Social Contract in the Age of Individualism.* New York: Basic Books, 2016.

Lilla, Mark. *The Shipwrecked Mind: On Political Reaction.* New York: New York Review Books, 2016.

Lischer, Richard. *Open Secrets: A Spiritual Journey through a Country Church.* New York: Doubleday, 2001.

Liu, Eric. *You're More Powerful Than You Think: A Citizen's Guide to Making Change Happen.* New York: PublicAffairs, 2017.

Long, Edward Leroy, Jr. *Patterns of Polity.* Cleveland, OH: Pilgrim Press, 2001.

MacKenzie, Gordon. *Orbiting the Giant Hairball: A Corporate Fool's Guide to Surviving with Grace.* New York: Viking Penguin, 1996.

Marler, Penny Long, and Janet Maykus. "Is the Treatment the Cure? A Study of Participation in Pastoral Leader Peer Groups." Unpublished report (2010).

McChrystal, Stanley, with Tantum Collins, David Silberman, and Chris Fussell. *Team of Teams: New Rules of Engagement for a Complex World.* New York: Penguin, 2015.

McNeil, Reggie. *Missional Renaissance: Changing the Scorecard for the Church.* San Francisco: Jossey-Bass, 2009.

Miller, Rex. *The Millennial Matrix: Reclaiming the Past, Reframing the Future of the Church.* San Francisco: Jossey-Bass, 2004.

Murray, Charles. *Coming Apart: The State of White America, 1960–2000.* New York: Crown Forum, 2012.

Naím, Moisés. *The End of Power: From Boardrooms to Battlefields and Churches, to States, Why Being in Charge Isn't What It Used to Be.* New York: Basic Books, 2013.

Niebuhr, H. Richard. *Christ and Culture.* New York: Harper and Row, 1951.

Petrie, Nick. "Future Trends in Leadership Development." White paper, Center for Creative Leadership, 2014.

Putnam, Robert. *Bowling Alone: The Collapse and Revival of American Community.* New York: Simon and Schuster, 2000.

———. *Our Kids: The American Dream in Crisis.* New York: Simon and Schuster, 2015.

Quinn, Robert. *Deep Change: Discovering the Leader Within.* San Francisco: Jossey-Bass, 1996.

Reber, Robert, and Bruce Roberts, eds. *A Lifelong Call to Learn.* Nashville: Abingdon Press, 2000.

Rendle, Gil. *Back to Zero: The Search to Rediscover the Methodist Movement.* Nashville: Abingdon, 2011.

———. *Doing the Math of Mission: Fruits, Faithfulness, and Mission.* New York: Rowman & Littlefield, 2014.

———. *Journey in the Wilderness: New Life for Mainline Churches.* Nashville: Abingdon Press, 2010.

———. "Waiting for God's New Thing: Spiritual and Organizational Leadership in the In-Between Time." Texas Methodist Foundation, 2015, https://www.tmf-fdn.org/leadership-ministry/learning-resources/congregational-resources.

Rendle, Gil, and Alice Mann. *Holy Conversations: Strategic Planning as a Spiritual Practice for Congregations.* Bethesda, MD: The Alban Institute, 2003.

Richey, Russell. "From Christmas Conference to General Conference—Today's Untied Methodism: Living with/into Its Two Centuries of Regular Division." Unpublished paper (April 2017).

Rogers, Everett. *Diffusion of Innovations.* New York: Free Press, 1995.

Roozen, David, and James Nieman, eds. *Church, Identity, and Change: Theology and Denominational Structures in Unsettled Times.* Grand Rapids, MI: Eerdmans, 2005.

Roxburgh, Alan. *Structured for Mission: Renewing the Culture of the Church.* Downers Grove, IL: IVP Books, 2015.

Saint, Steven, and James Lawson. *Rules for Reaching Consensus: A Modern Approach to Decision Making.* San Francisco: Jossey-Bass, 1994.

Scharen, Christian. "Learning Ministry Over Time: Embodying Practical Wisdom." In *For Life Abundant: Theology, Theological Education and Christian Ministry*, edited by Dorothy Bass and Craig Dykstra, 265–88. Grand Rapids, MI: Eerdmans, 2008.

Scherer, John. "The Role of Chaos in the Creation of Change." *Creative Change* 12, no. 2 (Spring 1991): 17–24.

Schmoker, Mike. *Results Now: How We Can Achieve Unprecedented Improvements in Teaching and Learning.* Alexandria, VA: ASCD, 2006.

Schnase, Robert. *Five Practices of Fruitful Congregations.* Nashville: Abingdon Press, 2007.

———. *Five Practices of Fruitful Congregations: Revised and Updated.* Nashville: Abingdon Press, 2018.

———. "Multiplying Our Witness: *Missio Dei* and the United States Toward a Faithful United Methodist Witness." Unpublished paper (October 2017).

Schwartz, Barry, and Kenneth Sharpe. *Practical Wisdom: The Right Way to Do the Right Thing.* New York: Riverhead Books, 2010.

Schwarz, Sid. *Jewish Megatrends: Charting the Course of the American Jewish Future.* Woodstock, VT: Jewish Lights, 2013.

Shenker-Osario, Anat. "Why Americans All Believe They Are 'Middle Class.'" *The Atlantic*, August 1, 2013. https://www.theatlantic.com/politics/archive/2013/08/why-americans-all-believe-they-are-middle-class/278240.

Sheth, Jagdish, and Andrew Sobel. *Clients for Life.* New York: Simon and Schuster, 2000.

Sides, Hampton. *Blood and Thunder: An Epic of the American West.* New York: Anchor Books, 2006.

Silber, John R. *Seeking the North Star.* Boston: David R. Godine, 2014.

Srivastva, Suresh, and David Cooperrider. *Appreciative Management and Leadership: The Power of Positive Thought and Action in Organizations.* San Francisco: Jossey-Bass, 1990.

Suzuki, Shunryu. *Zen Mind, Beginner's Mind*. New York: Weatherill, 1994.

Taleb, Nassim. *Antifragile: Things That Gain from Disorder*. New York: Random House, 2012.

Taylor, Paul. *The Next America: Boomers, Millennials, and the Looming Generational Showdown*. New York: Public Affairs, 2014.

Thorne, Leo S., ed. *Prayers from Riverside*. New York: Pilgrim Press, 1983.

Thurston, Angie, and Casper ter Kuile. "Faithful." *How We Gather*, 2017. https://www.howwegather.org/reports.

———. "How We Gather." *How We Gather*, 2015. https://www.howwegather.org/reports.

———. "Something More." *How We Gather*, 2017. https://www.howwegather.org/reports.

———. "Thresholds." *How We Gather*, 2018. https://www.howwegather.org/reports.

Tickle, Phyllis. *The Great Emergence: How Christianity Is Changing and Why*. Grand Rapids, MI: Baker Books, 2008.

Turow, Joseph. *Breaking Up America: Advertisers and the New Media World*. Chicago: University of Chicago Press, 1997.

Twist, Lynne. *The Soul of Money: Reclaiming the Wealth of Our Inner Resources*. New York: Norton, 2003.

Vance, J. D. *Hillbilly Elegy: A Memoir of a Family and Culture in Crisis*. New York: Harper and Row, 2016.

Wagner, Tony. *Creating Innovators: The Making of Young People Who Will Change the World*. New York: Scribner, 2012.

———. *The Global Achievement Gap: Why Even Our Best Schools Don't Teach the New Survival Skills Our Children Need—And What We Can Do about It*. New York: Perseus Books Group, 2010.

Weems, Lovett. "A Lewis Center Report on Clergy Age Trends in the United Methodist Church; 2015 Report." Washington, DC: The Lewis Center for Church Leadership, 2015.

———. "Reset and Focus: Reset Financially in Order to Focus on Reaching More People—Reflections on Call to Action Projects—Operational Assessment and Vital Congregations." Unpublished paper (September 2010).

Wenger, Etienne. *Communities of Practice: Learning, Meaning, and Identity*. Cambridge: Cambridge University Press, 1998.

Wheatley, Margaret. *Turning to One Another: Simple Conversations to Restore Hope to the Future*. San Francisco: Berrett-Koehler, 2002.

Wheatley, Margaret, and Myron Kellner-Rogers. *A Simpler Way*. San Francisco: Berrett-Koehler, 1996.

Wigger, John. *American Saint: Francis Asbury and the Methodists*. Oxford: Oxford University Press, 2009.

Wilber, Ken. *The Marriage of Sense and Soul: Integrating Science and Religion*. New York: Random House, 1998.

———. *Trump and a Post-Truth World*. Boulder, CO: Shambhala Press, 2017.

Willimon, William. *Bishop: The Art of Questioning Authority by an Authority in Question*. Nashville: Abingdon Press, 2012.

Yankelovich, Daniel. *New Rules: Searching for Self-Fulfillment in a World Turned Upside Down*. New York: Bantam Books, 1982.

INDEX

Abbott, Andrew, 132
abundance, 80–81
action research, 13
activities, institutional, 194, 196–197, 202, 230
additive decision making, 76–77, 78–79
advertising, 24, 37–39
al Qaeda in Iraq (AQI), 63, 66
Anasazi Indians, 22–23, 221
antifragile, 255–256
antilearning, 165, 196
apartheid, 25
appreciative inquiry, 81, 82
Argyris, Chris, 165, 167, 196, 217
Asbury, Bishop Francis, 112
aspirations, 83, 84, 194, 196–199, 201–202, 203, 206, 230

balcony space, 246–247, 251, 253
Bauman, Zygmunt, 59. *See also* liquid culture/liquid modernity
Beeley, Christopher, 173, 176–177
best practices, 239
Bhatt, Alpesh, 207
Block, Peter, 114, 140, 176
Blue Thunder, 189–190
Bohm, David, 243
Brafman, Ori, and Rob Beckstrom, 110
Bridges, William, 232
Brueggemann, Walter, 26, 91, 213, 220, 221, 223

Buechner, Frederick, 236

call stories, 228–229
Carol, Lewis, 195
cascading questions, 249 •
centralized/decentralized organizations, 110, 255–256, 259
change: asked for/rewarded for, 12; linear change, 58, 60–61, 62, 66, 207, 210; models of change, 15, 26, 66, 68–69; nonlinear change, 58, 60–61, 66, 67–72
chaos, 71–72, 72, 256, 260. *See also* wilderness
clergy professional peer groups, 145, 228–229
closed systems, 126, 130, 149
coalition of coalitions, as an organization, 6
Coffin, Bill, 10–11, 21, 32, 77, 193, 222, 267
Collins, Jim, 84, 199
communities of meaning and purpose, 12
communities of practice, 143–146. *See also* Texas Methodist Foundation (clergy development groups); clergy professional peer groups
community, 114, 140, 176
competency-based education, 133, 142
competing organizational mission. *See* public/private missions
complicated/complex, 63–64, 67

congregations: countercultural, 4, 31, 39,
    46, 221; massive growth, 19; renewal,
    transformation, 22, 29–30; size of staff,
    36–37; three questions of
    congregational formation, 26–27;
    visioning in congregations, 25; vital
    congregations, 22, 125, 164–165, 211.
    See also lifecycle of a congregation
consensus, 114
convergent to divergent culture, 33–34,
    62, 78, 109, 113–114, 116
conversation, 240–241, 246–248,
    250–251, 252. *See also* dialogue
counting, in organizational systems, 84,
    205
Covey, Stephen, 85
critical thinking, 137–138, 142

data, 242–243
Davenport, Thomas, and Laurence
    Prusak, 242, 244, 253
death tsunami, 106, 128
deconstruction of narrative, 226–227
deep generalist, 147
Deming, W. Edwards, 82, 203
democracy, 111
dependency, clergy, 130, 131, 140
developmental planning, 60–61
diagnosis, 161–162, 163–164, 170–171,
    177
dialogue, 243. *See also* conversation
diffusion of innovations, 122
distrust, institutional, 41, 42
disturbing the system, 66–67, 69, 98
Doctor of Ministry programs, 128, 138
Dreyfus model of skill acquisition,
    133–135, 147
drug cartels, 110, 256
Duggan, William, 140, 252
Dutch Reformed Church, 25
Dykstra, Craig, and James Hudnut-
    Beumler, 103

early church fathers, 173, 177
egalitarianism, 49, 115, 119–122
Eisenhower, President Dwight D., 36
empathy, 174, 175, 176–180, 188
empathy distress, 185
enough, 79–80, 82, 88

evolution, 207–209
expert, expertise, 16, 71, 109, 134–135,
    141, 142, 146–147, 148, 241

failure, 10, 11, 92, 163, 193, 200–201, 221,
    231, 256
fear, 95
Ford Motor Company, 62–63
frame-bending planning, 67
free-floating anxiety, 182
Fresh Expressions movement, 88
Friedman, Ed, 139–140, 182, 184, 188,
    206
Friedman, Thomas, and Michael
    Mandelbaum, 78, 178
Fullan, Michael, 66
Fuller, R. Buckminster, 222
functional atheism, 16, 77, 86, 238

Gardner, Howard, 224–225, 227
giant hairball, organizational, 107–108,
    109, 257, 262
giving/getting compact. *See* social contract
Gladwell, Malcolm, 141
Goleman, Daniel, 173, 185, 189
Gortner, David, 128, 136
gridlock, organizational, 106, 112, 116,
    162–163

Handy, Charles, 33, 62, 65
happiness, 39, 45, 46, 49, 79, 97
harmony, 116–117
Hartford Institute for Religion Research,
    164
Harvard Negotiating Project, 244
Haverford College, 118
Heath, Chip and Dan, 190
Heclo, Hugh, 40, 175
Heifetz, Ronald, 5, 8, 27–28, 65, 103,
    215–216, 219, 230, 246
Heller, Joseph, 79
Holifield, Brooks, 99
homosexuality, 35, 64–65
hope, 10, 11–12, 20, 229
House, Donald, 106
Huie, Bishop Janice, 125, 129, 139, 149

Iansiti, Marco, and Roy Levien, 265
identity, organizational, 47–48, 224

ideology, organizational, 110, 259
ignorance (not knowing), 29, 232
individualism, 4, 23–24, 39, 175–176. *See also* social contract
information, 242–243
intuition, 134–135, 140–141, 252
Isaacs, William, 226, 244
Isaacson, Walter, 109

Japanese manufacturing, 82
Jones, Robert, 47

Kenney, Michael, 110, 256
keystone strategy, 265
knowledge, 242–243
knowledge management, 242
Kuhn, Thomas, 209

leading in community, 98–100, 101, 115, 131, 174
learning, 9, 13, 16, 28–32, 60, 63, 65–66, 69, 72, 78, 108–110, 122, 131–141, 193; horizontal and vertical, 142, 144–145, 228, 241; at organizational edge, 240–264; pace of learning, 251–252, 254; and planning, 166–167; single loop/double loop, 217; through conversation, 240–244; unmotivated to, 184
Lerner, Michael, 200
Levin, Yuval, 23–24, 162
liberalism, 39
lifecycle of a congregation, 168–170
Lilla, Mark, 158
limited human resource, 194
liquid culture/liquid modernity, 59, 65, 66, 72, 74, 90, 105, 109, 126, 148, 152, 215, 240, 251. *See also* Bauman, Zygmunt
Lischer, Richard, 97
Liu, Eric, 90
Long, Edward Leroy, 237

MacKenzie, Gordon, 107, 257
Mather, Mike, 87
McChrystal, General Stanley, 63, 66, 259
meaning making, 197, 199, 220, 227
meaning making communities, 12, 51–52
measuring, in organizational systems, 205

media, society-making/segment making, 37
membership based organizations, 22, 23
mētis, 111
metrics, 96, 97–98, 204, 205–206, 249
micropowers, 24, 89, 182, 263, 266
middle class, 49, 75
Midrash, 3
mirroring in leadership, 189–190, 191
moral polestar. *See* social contract
Murray, Charles, 35–49
mystery, 72, 77, 236–237, 238

Naím, Moisés, 89, 263
narrative (story), 115, 219, 220–228
Nashon, son of Amminidab, 3
Niebuhr, H. Richard, 258
noble savage, 201
nostalgia, 156, 157–158, 160, 167–168, 169–170, 181, 215–216

open system, 149, 152
organizational defensive routines, 165, 167, 196
organizational structure, 103–111
outcomes, 83–84, 85, 199, 204, 205–207, 227

pain, 69, 70, 134, 139, 156, 176, 177–180, 183, 185, 186, 187–191, 234
paradigm shift, 208, 209
Pareto Principle, 121, 183
placeholder clergy, 128, 131, 140, 149, 176, 224
plan to grow/to shrink, 78, 106, 178
platform, 264–267
Plato, 95
player, 264, 266
polarity (purpose and relationship), 96–98, 101, 173, 180, 190
porous boundary, systems, 236, 261
positions and interests, 244–245
postmodernism, 59, 210
potential, 91, 92
Prigogine, Ilya, 73
problem solving, 9, 16, 27, 60, 61, 62, 65, 81, 132, 166, 168, 215, 223, 224
progressivism, 61

proximate goals/outcomes, 201, 219, 230, 231
public/private missions, 6–8, 106, 108, 112
Public Religion Research Institute, 47
punctuated equilibrium, 207–209, 261
Putnam, Robert, 48–49

Quinn, Robert, 6, 8, 128

Red Queen effect, 195, 208, 211, 230, 241, 251
representation, 115–119
resilience, 110. See also antifragile
reversing the field, 86, 87
rewards, 8, 9, 13, 97, 98, 100–103, 123, 131, 157, 161, 174, 180–181, 188, 193–194, 199, 200, 201, 203
Richey, Russell, 107
Robert's Rules of Order, 113

sabotage, 28, 103, 182, 183, 184
Saint Augustine, 9
scarcity, 80, 81, 86, 88, 90, 92
Scherer, John, 68, 261
Schnase, Bishop Robert, 104, 211
Scylla and Charybdis, 196–197, 203
seminary, 125, 126, 127, 129, 130, 131–132, 135, 137, 138–139, 140
Silber, John, 95
single/double loop learning, 217
social capital, 48
social contract, 42, 45, 175; defined, 45; giving /getting compact, 45; moral polestar, 42, 46
stewardship, 91–92
strategic planning, 26–27, 59–60, 227, 230
Study of Ministry Commission, UMC, 120
subsidiarity, 259
suffering, localized, 185–186
sufficiency, 78, 81
surplus powerlessness, 200–202
Sustaining Pastoral Excellence, Lilly Foundation, 145
Suzuki, Shunryu, 148
SWOT analysis, 230
systems, fully aligned, 189–190
systems model, simple, 83, 203
systems, self organizing, 73

T-shaped expertise, 147
tacit information, 9, 55, 70, 156, 216
Takayama, Peter, 101, 173, 180
Taleb, Nassim, 255
talented but tenuous clergy, 128, 131, 140, 146, 149, 224
technical and adaptive work, 27–28
technology, 24, 37–39, 57, 63, 89
ter Kuile, Casper, and Angie Thurston, 51, 52, 88, 150–151
terrorist groups, 110, 256
Texas Methodist Foundation, 17; clergy development groups, 145, 228–229; gathering of senior denominational leaders, 11; leadership monographs, 14; metrics project, 205, 249; stewarding potential, 91–92; Wesleyan Potential Forum, 223
Third law of Power, 88, 90
Tickle, Phyllis, 225
transition, stages of, 232–234
Turow, Joseph, 37
Twist, Lynne, 80
tyranny of the all, 120

unbundling, 90, 151
United Methodist Church, 7, 15, 87, 104–105, 106, 107, 120, 178, 237–238, 258–259, 262, 270n1, 273n10

Vance, J. D., 50
voluntary association organizations, 97, 125, 174
Vonnegut, Kurt, 76

Wagner, Tony, 137–138
Wenger, Etienne, 144
Wheatley, Margaret, 240, 250, 254
Wigger, John, 112
Wilber, Ken, 67, 197, 220
wilderness, as a place of change, 14, 26, 32, 73–74, 218
Willimon, Bishop Will, 98, 136, 139, 224
work avoidance, 70, 196, 227
worthy work, 72

Yankelovich, Daniel, 45–46
yin and yang, 93, 260

ABOUT THE AUTHOR

Gil Rendle is an internationally respected consultant, author, and teacher in the world of religious institutions. Following sixteen years as pastor of two urban congregations, he has been a practicing consultant for more than three decades, working with Protestant, Catholic, and Jewish systems across North America, Europe, and Africa. He is trained in action research with a PhD in organizational development and systems theory. Now retired, Gil served as a denominational executive, senior consultant with the Alban Institute, and senior vice president with the Texas Methodist Foundation. With an early emphasis on issues of conflict and planning, Gil has most recently focused on issues of change in tradition-based institutions and on leadership. He is the author of nine previous books, multiple articles, and a series of United Methodist monographs on leadership. He lives in Haverford, Pennsylvania, with his wife, Lynne.